# The
# Reference Shelf®

# Artificial Intelligence

The Reference Shelf
Volume 90 • Number 4
H.W. Wilson
A Division of EBSCO Information Services, Inc.

Published by
**GREY HOUSE PUBLISHING**
Amenia, New York
2018

# The Reference Shelf

The books in this series contain reprints of articles, excerpts from books, addresses on current issues, and studies of social trends in the United States and other countries. There are six separately bound numbers in each volume, all of which are usually published in the same calendar year. Numbers one through five are each devoted to a single subject, providing background information and discussion from various points of view and concluding with an index and comprehensive bibliography that lists books, pamphlets, and articles on the subject. The final number of each volume is a collection of recent speeches. Books in the series may be purchased individually or on subscription.

Publisher's Cataloging-In-Publication Data
(Prepared by The Donohue Group, Inc.)

Names: Grey House Publishing, Inc., compiler.

Title: Artificial intelligence / [compiled by] Grey House Publishing.

Other Titles: Reference shelf ; v. 90, no. 4.

Description: [First edition]. | Amenia, New York : Grey House Publishing, 2018. | Includes bibliographical references and index.

Identifiers: ISBN 9781682178676 (v. 90, no. 4) | ISBN 9781682177471 (volume set)

Subjects: LCSH: Artificial intelligence--Social aspects.

Classification: LCC Q334.7 .A78 2018 | DDC 006.31--dc23

Printed in Canada

# Contents

# 3

## War Games: AI in the Military

# 4

## Robot Overlords: Robots and AI in Fiction and American Fears

# 5

## Engineering Evolution: AI and Humanity's Future

# Preface

## The Intelligence Machine

Artificial intelligence, or "AI," has become one of the great debates of the 2010s as the acceleration of technology has brought the world closer to true artificial intelligence than ever before. In a decade that saw a machine beat the famed "Turing test," an increasing focus on AI development in military weapons, and a robot becoming the first artificial being to be granted citizenship to one of the world's countries, the AI field seems to be developing at an exponential rate even as governments and societies are struggling to determine how to adjust to these new technological frontiers.

## What Is Artificial Intelligence?

Put simply, "artificial intelligence," "AI," or "machine intelligence" is a field of scientific exploration that involves creating machines capable of completing tasks that typically require human intelligence. To understand what this means, it is important to differentiate between intelligence, awareness, and sentience.

Intelligence can be broadly defined as the ability to learn information and then to use that knowledge to complete tasks. Humans are intelligent organisms, as are many other types of animals capable of learning and applying learned information to various situations or tasks. Humanity has created a variety of machines that are also intelligent, meaning that the machines can learn and apply information.

In science fiction, artificial intelligences, which often appear in the form of "robots" (mechanical devices designed to complete certain tasks), are often depicted as not only intelligent, but also as being aware. Awareness means to have knowledge or perception of a thing or phenomenon, and humans have a special type of awareness known as "self-awareness," which can be defined as knowledge of oneself and one's own feelings, desires, and actions. Self-awareness is so integral to what it means to be human that many people rarely consider the nature of awareness as a phenomenon. A being that is self-aware has knowledge of itself, meaning that it understands that it exists and that it is an entity separate from, but embedded within, its environment.

The concept of self-awareness has fascinated humanity for millennia and, over the years, scientists, philosophers, and other intellectuals have worked hard to try and quantify and measure this aspect of human existence. People have thus wondered whether or not any other type of organism on earth, or perhaps elsewhere in the universe, is also self-aware and this had led to methods designed to measure whether or not a being can be called self-aware. Induction puzzles, for instance, are logical puzzles that are solved by "inductive reasoning" or "induction" in which premises given at the outset can be used as evidence to support a certain conclusion.[1] Such puzzles can be used to test self-awareness.

For instance, the "wise men puzzle," poses a hypothetical situation in which a king calls three wise men forward and puts either a white or blue hat on their heads. They can see each other's hats, but not their own. The king tells them that at least one of them is wearing a blue hat and that the test is fair in that none of the three possesses information that the other two do not. Thus, the wise men must figure out, by observing the hats on the other two men and from the premises given by the king, what color hat is on their own head. While this seems a simple puzzle, determining the answer requires that one can view him or herself in the context of the information provided.

In 2015, for the first time in history, a Nao robot at Rensselaer Polytechnic Institute was able to pass a version of the "wise man test," demonstrating the ability to recognize itself in relation to the information given.[2] While this achievement represents an impressive leap forward in programming and machine learning, the "self-awareness" demonstrated by the Nao robot is only superficially similar to human self-awareness. The machine in question had to be programmed specifically to handle the type of information (premises) given to pass the test and so had been programmed to have awareness only within a narrow context. By contrast, self-awareness is part of the basic substrate of the human mind and humans unconsciously and consciously apply their sense of self to each and every situation they encounter.

A related concept is sentience, which is defined in the 2010 Elsevier *Encyclopedia of Animal Behavior* as a "multidimensional subjective phenomenon that refers to the depth of awareness an individual possesses about himself or herself and others."[3] Sentience is the capability of sensing and responding to the world and it is a matter of degree. Most animals are capable of responding to stimuli from their environment but when the term "sentience" is used in common parlance, it is not typically used to refer to this basic level of sensory reactiveness but rather to a conscious reaction to stimuli that involves intelligence *and* self-awareness.[4]

Sentience, self-awareness, and intelligence filter into the concept of "consciousness," which is a nebulously defined phenomenon that strikes at the very philosophical nature of what it means to be human. On one level, consciousness refers to what might be called "wakefulness," the state of a mind operating in a fully conscious, as opposed to unconscious, manner. When the term "consciousness" is generally used to describe the human mind, what is typically meant is the characteristic form of intelligence, self-awareness, and sentience associated with the human mind. Whether or not humans are the only creatures with this type of consciousness is a matter of debate and disagreement. This is because it is difficult to quantitatively measure or define consciousness as an element of existence separate from other types of thought and emotional, intellectual behavior. Consider how a person knows that he or she is conscious. Is it possible to determine if another person is actually conscious or just a machine emulating consciousness, while experiencing an entirely different type of reality? The subjective nature of experience makes the mind a philosophical "black box," where scientists can view the behavior of the mind from the outside but can never experience through another mind and so cannot determine the clear line between self-aware consciousness and any other types of mental existence that appear similar, but might, in actuality, relate to entirely different types of awareness.

Artificial intelligence does not necessarily mean artificial emotion, consciousness, self-awareness, or sentience, but one of the long-term goals for many AI researchers is to achieve just that—an artificial mind that is fully aware and intelligent. As of 2018, humans have not created a truly conscious machine. However, the advancement of engineering, neuroscience, and programming means that machines of this type may someday be scientific reality.

## AI, Robots, and Automatons

Robots are machines that are designed specifically to complete certain jobs or tasks. In fiction, many robots are depicted as "automatons," which are machines designed to imitate humans or, at least, to imitate some type of human action. Androids are machines that are designed not only to function like humans, but also to look like humans. In reality, most robots look nothing like humans and are not really designed to imitate humanity. Many robots, like the Curiosity Mars Rover that is currently exploring the Martian landscape, are designed to handle tasks and to work in ways that would be impossible for humans. The Curiosity rover, for instance, utilizes senses unavailable to humans to explore its environment and is capable of surviving in environments that would be fatal for a human explorer.[5]

While robots are physical machines, an artificial intelligence does not need to have a physical body. Given the potential for virtual connectivity and wireless functionality, the AIs of today and of the future could exist as distributed unities whose logic processes are created through a gestalt mix of processing that actually takes place over great distances. However, many of the specialists currently working in AI, and perhaps inspired by fiction, are working on blending the lines between robotics and artificial intelligence, creating robots, whether automatons or not, that are also intelligent and capable of learning and developing.

Robots have been a factor in long-standing debate over automation, which is the process in which human workers are replaced by automated systems, robots, or other types of machines. Automation began during the Industrial Revolution, which is the period in history in which much of humanity transitioned from agrarian to urban lifestyles. The transition from human labor to automated labor occurred over a long-period and affected the lives and livelihoods of millions around the world. The introduction of the tractor, for instance, resulted in job losses for millions in the farming industry with the percentage of Americans employed in the field plummeting from 70 percent at the beginning of the twentieth century, to less than 3 percent in the 2010s. The generations of Americans who left the farms for the factories of the cities faced the threat of automation again as more and more factory jobs were automated, eventually resulting in the robot-dominated factories of the modern world where a relatively small staff handles work that would once have required (and supported) a much larger human workforce.[6] As robotic automation gradually gives way to digital automation and AI, many are concerned that the workforce will face disruption again, with AI rapidly supplanting humans in fields once seen as the exclusive purvey of humanity.

## The Problem(s) with AI

For many years, machines were only able to handle physical work that did not require decision making. This has changed with the advance of computing technology and the invention of thinking machines capable of evaluation and adaptive task management. What this represents, for some critics of the AI field, is that machines of the future will increasingly take "thinking" and managerial jobs, in addition to jobs that primarily involve manual labor. For instance, since the mid-2010s, it has been becoming apparent that computer coding can be handled by automated programs more efficiently and with fewer errors than when completed by human coders. In fact, a study released by Gallup in 2017 indicated that as many as 37 percent of millennials could find themselves replaced by AI automation in their lifetime, with automation affecting at least some jobs in nearly every field of human endeavor.[7]

The integration of humanity and technology is not just about AI, but is an issue affecting nearly every aspect of human life. Internet use is changing the way that people learn and mobile phones are changing the nature of communities and social interaction. In many ways, these advancements have made life more convenient for many people and artificial intelligence, as it advances, promises to do the same. Critics, however, have raised many different ethical issues surrounding the increasing integration of intelligent machines into daily life. Some critics are concerned about the ways in which the integration of AI might shape human behavior and so change human society in unforeseen ways. For instance, one of the major criticisms of the current wave of AI research concerns the ways in which companies might use AI to manipulate consumers, adding to the privacy rights debate that has already arisen from the emergence of the big data market of the Digital Age.

On a more philosophical side, others have expressed concern that the development of intelligent beings raises ethical issues that will force humanity to confront the morality of creating beings that may essentially constitute a slave workforce. Concerns like these may become more pointed if and when AI technology evolves to reproduce artificial emotion and self-awareness in addition to artificial intelligence. Still others are concerned that the new generation of intelligent machines might, like the villainous AIs of fiction, pose a new danger to humanity itself, whether because dangerous AI technology might fall into the wrong human hands or be used by criminals and rogue states to create frightening new weapons, or because the mechanical beings of the future will themselves rise up to take over humanity.

The life and death stakes of the AI question is nowhere more apparent than in the controversy surrounding the use of AI in the military. Drones—unmanned flying machines that are used for reconnaissance, information gathering, and to attack targets—have been a key feature of US warfare in the 2010s. The United States has launched hundreds of drone attacks intended to weaken radical groups operating in the Middle East, with thousands of casualties, both of enemy combatants and of civilians. As of 2018, the US military is investing heavily in automated military technology, including the use of AI in evaluating and addressing threats and this raises a number of ethical and moral issues. Critics have argued that the decision to kill, potentially killing noncombatants as well, is one that should not be allowed to be made by an automated system without the emotional cognizance to evaluate the ethical dimensions of the decision. The debate over the ethics of military AI is the cutting edge of the moral debate over the use of AI in society and many feel that now is the time to establish moral and ethical guidelines for both the development and use of AI so as to forestall future disasters. A number of prominent scientists and figures in the field have supported this effort but, so far, in the United States, there have been few efforts at substantive regulation.

Though there are many concerns about how AI will impact the world, the field also promises a whole range of potential benefits. Supporters of AI research argue that artificial intelligence, if ethically implemented, will create jobs, free humans from dangerous or undesirable tasks, and will open up new vistas of exploration and development. Research indicates that AI may be useful in education, in managing complex scientific research, and even in modifying the human body to be more powerful, capable, and efficient. In the 2010s, AI research is helping to create intuitive artificial limbs and intelligent computer aides to help people with disabilities and AI programs have helped researchers to make major breakthroughs in studying the human mind and body, research that may lead to major medical breakthroughs in the future. The promises of AI are many and varied, but the true driver of development is economic and the speed with which AI is currently being explored is a direct consequence of the fact that corporations see financial benefits from the implementation of AI tools in the future. Some of these tools, fueled by corporate development, may provide new and unforeseen boons to humanity, much as the Digital Age has provided conveniences and opportunities for social connectivity that may have seemed impossible in the 1980s.

## The Option of Artificial Intelligence

Artificial intelligence is not a necessity for humanity but the development of more and more advanced AI will almost certainly continue unabated. This is, in part, because corporations have a financial interest in AI technology and so actively fund development. However, the drive towards more advanced AI is part of an even deeper curiosity characteristic of humanity, the need and desire to push forward and to explore the unknown. Humans have been fantasizing about creating intelligent automata for at least two thousand years and the possibility to make this ancient fantasy a reality is also a driving factor behind development in the field. It is impossible to know, in 2018, how artificial intelligence may change human culture in the future though it is likely that the spread of AI will, like the Industrial Revolution, bring about changes that benefit some, while deepening inequality for others. Because the development of AI technology is an option, and not a requirement for humanity's present or immediate future, it is possible for humanity to approach the coming AI age in a different way than societies approached and prepared for (or failed to prepare for) the Industrial Revolution or the Digital Age.

Micah L. Issitt

## Works Used

"Animal Consciousness." *Plato. Stanford.* Stanford Encyclopedia of Philosophy. Oct 24, 2016. Web. Retrieved from https://plato.stanford.edu/entries/consciousness-animal/.

Autor, David H. "Why Are There Still So Many Jobs? The History and Future of Workplace Automation." *MIT.* Journal of Economic Perspectives. 2015. Pdf. Retrieved from https://economics.mit.edu/files/11563.

Graham-Rowe, Duncan. "Introduction: Robots." *New Scientist.* New Scientist Ltd. Sep 4, 2006. Web. Retrieved from https://www.newscientist.com/article/dn9973-introduction-robots/.

"Inductive Logic." *Plato.Stanford.* Stanford Encyclopedia of Philosophy. Mar 19, 2018. Retrieved from https://plato.stanford.edu/entries/logic-inductive/.

MacDonald, Fiona. "A Robot Has Just Passed a Classic Self-Awareness Test for the First Time." *Science Alert.* Jul 17, 2015. Web. Retrieved from https://www.sciencealert.com/a-robot-has-just-passed-a-classic-self-awareness-test-for-the-first-time.

Marino, L. "Sentience," in *Encyclopedia of Animal Behavior.* Academic Press: 2010, 132–38.

McGrady, Vanessa. "New Study: Artificial Intelligence Is Coming for Your Job, Millennials." *Forbes.* Forbes, Inc. Jun 9, 2017. Retrieved from https://www.forbes.com/sites/vanessamcgrady/2017/06/09/millennial-jobs/#339f902530c8.

## Notes

1.  "Inductive Logic," *Plato.Stanford.*
2.  MacDonald, "A Robot Has Just Passed a Classic Self-Awareness Test for the First Time."
3.  Marino, "Sentience."
4.  "Animal Consciousness," *Plato.Stanford.*
5.  Graham-Rowe, "Introduction: Robots."
6.  Autor, "Why Are There Still So Many Jobs? The History and Future of Workplace Automation."
7.  McGrady, "New Study: Artificial Intelligence Is Coming for Your Job, Millennials."

# 1

# From Myth to Reality: Artificial Intelligence in History

Photo by Gregory Bugni, via Wikimedia Commons

In 1988, Robin Burgener invented the key software components of the handheld game 20Q, based on the spoken parlor game in which a player is asked to think of an object and is then asked a series of yes or no questions in order for the questioner to guess what they're thinking. The 20Q AI uses an artificial neural network to pick the questions and to guess. After the player has answered the twenty questions posed (sometimes fewer), 20Q makes a guess. If it is incorrect, it asks more questions, and then guesses again. It makes guesses based on what it has learned; it is not programmed with information or what the inventor thinks.

# Creating Life: The Dream of Artificial Intelligence

In ancient Greek myth, the supernatural blacksmith Hephaestus was said to have created mechanical automatons—machines built to emulate humans—to act as servants to the gods of Olympus. These mythical beings ranged from metal hand-maidens to a building-sized bronze guardian, Talos, built to defend a city from ravaging hordes. In the ancient epic poem the *Iliad*, the mythical author Homer wrote of Hephaestus's creations, describing two mechanical servant women built of gold: "There is intelligence in their hearts, and there is speech in them and strength, and from the immortal gods they have learned how to do things."[1]

An automaton is a machine designed to perform a function typically associated with humans. This could be a mechanical action, like holding a comb and brushing one's hair, or an intellectual process. Robots, by contrast, are self-governed, programmable machines built for a specific function and are not necessarily designed to mimic human actions or abilities. In myth, Hephaestus created robots that were also automatons, having human shape and function and so, capable of handling many of the same tasks as a human, but independent and mechanical. The concept of robotics and artificial intelligence was thus born out of myth in antiquity, but the allure of this idea, of creating mechanical servants and guardians, became an enduring fantasy throughout history. Over the ensuing centuries, a whole host of brilliant mathematicians, engineers, and scientists from a variety of fields worked to turn Homer's fantasies into reality.

## From Logic to Programming

The number of steps between the earliest dream of thinking machines and the modern field of artificial intelligence is also the history of science itself. This is a path that saw the introduction of syllogistic logic by the famed intellectual Aristotle in the fourth century BCE and many other key developments in mathematics and logic that ultimately resulted in the ability to encode information in mathematical form. On the mechanical side of the equation, the invention of clockwork systems in the fifteenth and sixteenth centuries was one of the key steps towards the field of robotics. From there, inventors used clockwork gears, levers, and springs to create moving statues and figures, including a now famous "walking lion" built of metal by the inventor Leonardo DaVinci for the King of France.[2]

In 1801, French weaver, merchant, and inventor Joseph Marie Jacquard debuted an automated weaving loom that could be "programmed" to create different designs. The machine, typically called the "Jacquard Loom," was able to read a punch card containing a formula for a certain pattern and could then automatically weave the pattern. Essentially, each punch card functioned like a modern computer program, furnishing the machine with encoded instructions that informed a set of mechanical processes. This machine, though simple by modern standards, was arguably the inspiration for all modern programming and inspired an eccentric mathematical genius named Charles Babbage who, along with his friend and fellow mathematical prodigy Ada Lovelace, designed the world's first computational machine.

Babbage and Lovelace's device, called a "Babbage Engine" or an "Analytical Engine," wasn't finished during their lifetime and was, essentially, a giant and staggeringly complex calculator.

The second of two engines that Babbage and Lovelace designed was 11 feet long, had 8,000 parts, and weighed several thousand pounds. In Lovelace's writings, it is clear that the machine was the direct descendant of Jacquard's loom, "We may say most aptly that the Analytical Engine weaves algebraic patterns just as the Jacquard-loom weaves flowers and leaves."[3]

## From the World Wars to the Digital Age

It was in the twentieth century that the idea of thinking machines and robotic automata became familiar and it was during this time that scientists began to wonder if the human mind itself was really just a type of machine. Young British polymath Alan Turing's 1950 paper *Computing Machinery and Intelligence* discussed the possibility of building a thinking machine and, further, detailed methods that might be used to test such a machine's intelligence.[4] Turing didn't just imagine thinking machines, but also imagined that machines would one day be able to achieve consciousness, free-will, and self-awareness. Turing developed a test, now known as the "Turing test," but called "The Imitation Game" by Turing, involving a conversation in which a judge would try to determine whether the "person" that he or she was conversing with was a machine or a human.[5]

Six years after Turing's seminal paper on machine intelligence was published, a group of similarly minded academics and researchers held the world's first conference on machine learning. Pioneering theorists Allen Newell, Cliff Shaw, Herbert Simon, John McCarthy, and Marvin Minsky, who took part in the 1956 conference, became the pioneers of artificial intelligence over the next half century, with much of their research funded and supported by the Defense Advanced Research Projects Agency (DARPA), one of the world's largest military research organizations. From the beginning, therefore, the development of computational technology that would give way to artificial intelligence was funded and supported, in part, by the military with the goal of using robotics and thinking machines to aid in defense and warfare. It was pioneer John McCarthy who has been credited with creating the term "artificial intelligence" (AI) at the conference.

From the late 1950s to the early 1970s, military and government grants pushed AI development, with massive advances in computer technology coming as a result. Among the most notable milestones was the creation of ELIZA, created by Joseph Weizenbaum between 1964 and 1965 at the Massachusetts Institute of Technology (MIT) Artificial Intelligence Laboratory. ELIZA was a language-processing machine that simulated conversation and could "listen" to a person and choose from a set list of responses based on a pattern-matching algorithm. ELIZA was thus one of the first of what are now called "chatbots," machines designed to engage in conversation, and it was this branch of AI research, the creation of chatbots or "chatterbots," that emerged from the effort to create a machine that could pass the Turing test.[6]

Despite the many successes of the early wave of AI research, there were problems that prevented the development of AI from moving past a certain threshold. One problem was that the technology for computational power was limited, and so even the most complex machine built in the 1960s or 70s was far too weak to imitate the human mind. Further, researchers learned that even simple decisions made by humans required handling a huge number of variables and that it was nearly impossible, given the state of technology, to create a machine that could handle this level of complexity. Problems like these stalled progress and many of the governments and military organizations that had been funding AI programs began withdrawing support.

AI researchers call the period from 1974 to 1980 the "First AI Winter," during which there was little in the way of either advancement or funding available for anyone hoping to study artificial intelligence. The winter ended in 1980 because Japanese research teams who were making major advancements in the field caused US agencies to start funding research again out of fear of falling behind. This burst of research not only furthered AI, but also saw the advent of the technology behind the internet. In the late 1980s, however, a second "AI Winter" coincided with a downturn in the consumer electronics market. This ended in 1993, as the consumer electronics market grew and the companies building computers began providing private funding for AI research in the hopes of using the technology for consumer applications. One of these companies, IBM, funded the construction of the famed computer Deep Blue, which became the first computer to beat chess champion Garry Kasparov in a 1997 chess game.[7]

In the 2000s, the AI field diversified, giving rise to a variety of subfields focused on different aspects of AI research. Among the most prolific were "machine learning," which focuses on creating machines that can incorporate new information into their programming, "machine translation," which focuses on creating machines that can translate data from one form to another, and "machine reading," which focuses on creating machines that can read textual information and follow instructions given in written form.[8]

## The Coming Prometheus

Weak or "narrow" AI involves using machine intelligence that is narrowly tailored to solve a specific problem. By the 2000s, this level of AI had been achieved with a variety of robots and intelligent programs able to complete certain tasks better than human counterparts. However, some theorists in the field see this as only a small step towards the bigger problem, sometimes called "full" or "strong" AI, which means building a machine that can engage in the entire range of human intellectual activities. The strong form of AI remains an elusive goal and there is little agreement in the field about when or how such an achievement would be possible. Over time, and thanks in part to the foreboding visions of science fiction writers—the idea of full AI became a frightening concept to many people. Some believe that intelligent machines will replace humans in the workforce (which they have and will), while others believe that such machines might eventually "want" to take over the world. Still others have expressed concern that the creation of intelligent machines might constitute a form of slavery, with the resulting mechanical servants being deprived of the rights that should be afforded any intelligent being. Although these concerns are, at present, speculative, with each leap forward in AI capability, journalists, scientists, and other public figures renew their concern for the possible consequences of the world's march towards machine intelligence.

In 2011, a computer known as Watson competed on the television program *Jeopardy!*, defeating two former champions from previous seasons of the series. Watson's victory was significant, as the machine needed not only encyclopedic recall, but also the ability to understand the rules of the game and to interpret at times purposefully vague questions. Former champion Ken Jennings, who won 74 games in a row before being called back to play against Watson, joked, after his loss, "I, for one, welcome our new computer overlords."[9]

While many journalists and science experts reacted to Watson's victory with skepticism and concern for humanity's future, an even more controversial development was on the horizon. In 2015, Hanson Robotics, in collaboration with Alphabet Inc. (Google's parent company) activated Sophia, a robot built to resemble Audrey Hepburn. Sophia, in some ways, represents the peak of AI technology as it developed through the 2000s and 2010s, utilizing visual facial recognition and speech recognition to interpret and respond to humans. Sophia can emulate facial expressions, can make conversation on a limited number of topics, and is designed to learn, becoming smarter and better at tasks over time. In 2017, Saudi Arabia granted Sophia citizenship, making her the first robotic citizen in history. Though Sophia's "citizenship" is more publicity stunt than a meaningful political statement, the announcement brought criticism from many who saw the robot's achievement as an insult to all the humans still struggling to achieve parity and rights around the world.

Sophia is not a conscious or self-aware machine. Despite having the capability to learn and to interact with individuals, on many levels the sophistication of Sophia's programming is not altogether different from personal assistant programs like Siri or Alexa that are currently installed on consumer electronics systems. It is, in many ways, the fact that Sophia looks vaguely human and can emulate expressions that has placed her, perceptively, in another category. As of 2018, the dream of "full AI" is still elusive and scientists are uncertain how to design a machine that could function like a living being, much less to grasp the emotional complexity that defines human existence.[10] The science of AI, however, is advancing at a rapid pace and there are many critics who argue that human culture is not equipped to cope with the challenges of creating what might essentially be a form of artificial life. Fears about AI range from rational to irrational and fanciful, but the field has raised many legitimate questions about the future of humanity in a rapidly changing world and, perhaps more importantly, has shone an interesting light on the state of human rights and well-being made more potent by the possibility of a new type of existence.

Micah L. Issitt

## Works Used

Anyoha, Rockwell. "The History of Artificial Intelligence." *SITN*. Science in the News. Harvard University. Aug 28, 2017. Web. Retrieved from http://sitn.hms.harvard.edu/flash/2017/history-artificial-intelligence/.

Bramer, Max. *Artificial Intelligence: An International Perspective*. New York: Springer, 1998.

Etzioni, Oren, Michele Banko, and Michael J. Cafarella. "Machine Reading." *AAAI*. American Association for Artificial Intelligence. 2006. Pdf. Retrieved from http://www.aaai.org/Papers/Symposia/Spring/2007/SS-07-06/SS07-06-001.pdf.

Kleinman, Zoe. "CES 2018: A Clunky Chat with Sophia the Robot." *BBC News*. BBC. Jan 9, 2018. Web. Retrieved from http://www.bbc.com/news/technology-42616687.

Lewis, Tanya. "A Brief History of Artificial Intelligence." *Life Science*. Live Science. Dec 4, 2014. Retrieved from https://www.livescience.com/49007-history-of-artificial-intelligence.html.

Markoff, John. "Computer Wins on 'Jeopardy!': Trivial, It's Not." *The New York Times*. The New York Times Co. Feb 16, 2011. Web. Retrieved from https://www.nytimes.com/2011/02/17/science/17jeopardy-watson.html.

Moon, Francis C. *The Machines of Leonardo Da Vinci and Franz Reuleaux: Kinematics of Machines*. New York: Springer Press, 2007.

Park, Edwards. "What a Difference the Difference Engine Made: From Charles Babbage's Calculator Emerged Today's Computer." *Smithsonian*. Smithsonian Institution. Feb 1996. Web. Retrieved from https://www.smithsonianmag.com/history/what-a-difference-the-difference-engine-made-from-charles-babbages-calculator-emerged-todays-computer-109389254/.

"The Turing Test." *University of Toronto*. Psychology Department. 2017. Web. Retrieved from http://www.psych.utoronto.ca/users/reingold/courses/ai/turing.html.

Turing, Alan M. "Computing Machinery and Intelligence." *Mind*. 49 (1950): 433–60. Web. Retrieved from https://www.csee.umbc.edu/courses/471/papers/turing.pdf.

## Notes

1. Bramer, *Artificial Intelligence*, 1.
2. Moon, *The Machines of Leonardo Da Vinci and Franz Reuleaux: Kinematics of Machines*, 276.
3. Park, "What a Difference the Difference Engine Made: From Charles Babbage's Calculator Emerged Today's Computer."

4.  Turing, "Computing Machinery and Intelligence."
5.  "The Turing Test," *University of Toronto*.
6.  Anyoha, "The History of Artificial Intelligence."
7.  Lewis, "A Brief History of Artificial Intelligence."
8.  Etzioni, Banko, and Cafarella, "Machine Reading."
9.  Markoff, "Computer Wins on 'Jeopardy!': Trivial, It's Not."
10. Kleinman, "CES 2018: A Clunky Chat with Sophia the Robot."

# The Great A.I. Awakening

By Gideon Lewis-Kraus

*The New York Times Magazine*, December 14, 2016

## Prologue: You Are What You Have Read

Late one Friday night in early November, Jun Rekimoto, a distinguished professor of human-computer interaction at the University of Tokyo, was online preparing for a lecture when he began to notice some peculiar posts rolling in on social media. Apparently Google Translate, the company's popular machine-translation service, had suddenly and almost immeasurably improved. Rekimoto visited Translate himself and began to experiment with it. He was astonished. He had to go to sleep, but Translate refused to relax its grip on his imagination.

Rekimoto wrote up his initial findings in a blog post. First, he compared a few sentences from two published versions of *The Great Gatsby*, Takashi Nozaki's 1957 translation and Haruki Murakami's more recent iteration, with what this new Google Translate was able to produce. Murakami's translation is written "in very polished Japanese," Rekimoto explained to me later via email, but the prose is distinctively "Murakami-style." By contrast, Google's translation—despite some "small unnaturalness" —reads to him as "more transparent."

The second half of Rekimoto's post examined the service in the other direction, from Japanese to English. He dashed off his own Japanese interpretation of the opening to Hemingway's *The Snows of Kilimanjaro*, then ran that passage back through Google into English. He published this version alongside Hemingway's original, and proceeded to invite his readers to guess which was the work of a machine.

NO. 1: Kilimanjaro is a snow-covered mountain 19,710 feet high, and is said to be the highest mountain in Africa. Its western summit is called the Masai "Ngaje Ngai," the House of God. Close to the western summit there is the dried and frozen carcass of a leopard. No one has explained what the leopard was seeking at that altitude.

NO. 2: Kilimanjaro is a mountain of 19,710 feet covered with snow and is said to be the highest mountain in Africa. The summit of the west is called "Ngaje Ngai" in Masai, the house of God. Near the top of the west there is a dry and frozen dead body of leopard. No one has ever explained what leopard wanted at that altitude.

Even to a native English speaker, the missing article on the leopard is the only real giveaway that No. 2 was the output of an automaton. Their closeness was a source of wonder to Rekimoto, who was well acquainted with the capabilities of the previous service. Only 24 hours earlier, Google would have translated the same Japanese passage as follows:

> Kilimanjaro is 19,710 feet of the mountain covered with snow, and it is said that the highest mountain in Africa. Top of the west, "Ngaje Ngai" in the Maasai language, has been referred to as the house of God. The top close to the west, there is a dry, frozen carcass of a leopard. Whether the leopard had what the demand at that altitude, there is no that nobody explained.

Rekimoto promoted his discovery to his hundred thousand or so followers on Twitter, and over the next few hours thousands of people broadcast their own experiments with the machine-translation service. Some were successful, others meant mostly for comic effect. As dawn broke over Tokyo, Google Translate was the No. 1 trend on Japanese Twitter, just above some cult anime series and the long-awaited new single from a girl-idol supergroup. Everybody wondered: How had Google Translate become so uncannily artful?

Four days later, a couple of hundred journalists, entrepreneurs and advertisers from all over the world gathered in Google's London engineering office for a special announcement. Guests were greeted with Translate-branded fortune cookies. Their paper slips had a foreign phrase on one side—mine was in Norwegian—and on the other, an invitation to download the Translate app. Tables were set with trays of doughnuts and smoothies, each labeled with a placard that advertised its flavor in German (zitrone), Portuguese (baunilha) or Spanish (manzana). After a while, everyone was ushered into a plush, dark theater.

Sadiq Khan, the mayor of London, stood to make a few opening remarks. A friend, he began, had recently told him he reminded him of Google. "Why, because I know all the answers?" the mayor asked. "No," the friend replied, "because you're always trying to finish my sentences." The crowd tittered politely. Khan concluded by introducing Google's chief executive, Sundar Pichai, who took the stage.

Pichai was in London in part to inaugurate Google's new building there, the cornerstone of a new "knowledge quarter" under construction at King's Cross, and in part to unveil the completion of the initial phase of a company transformation he announced last year. The Google of the future, Pichai had said on several occasions, was going to be "A.I. first." What that meant in theory was complicated and had welcomed much speculation. What it meant in practice, with any luck, was that soon the company's products would no longer represent the fruits of traditional computer programming, exactly, but "machine learning."

A rarefied department within the company, Google Brain, was founded five years ago on this very principle: that artificial "neural networks" that acquaint themselves with the world via trial and error, as toddlers do, might in turn develop something like human flexibility. This notion is not new—a version of it dates to the earliest stages of modern computing, in the 1940s—but for much of its history most computer scientists saw it as vaguely disreputable, even mystical. Since 2011, though, Google Brain has demonstrated that this approach to artificial intelligence could solve many problems that confounded decades of conventional efforts. Speech recognition didn't work very well until Brain undertook an effort to revamp it; the application of machine learning made its performance on Google's mobile platform, Android, almost as good as human transcription. The same was true of image recognition. Less than a year ago, Brain for the first time commenced with the gut renovation of an entire consumer product, and its momentous results were being celebrated tonight.

Translate made its debut in 2006 and since then has become one of Google's most reliable and popular assets; it serves more than 500 million monthly users in need of 140 billion words per day in a different language. It exists not only as its own stand-alone app but also as an integrated feature within Gmail, Chrome and many other Google offerings, where we take it as a push-button given—a frictionless, natural part of our digital commerce. It was only with the refugee crisis, Pichai explained from the lectern, that the company came to reckon with Translate's geopolitical importance: On the screen behind him appeared a graph whose steep curve indicated a recent fivefold increase in translations between Arabic and German. (It was also close to Pichai's own heart. He grew up in India, a land divided by dozens of languages.) The team had been steadily adding new languages and features, but gains in quality over the last four years had slowed considerably.

Until today. As of the previous weekend, Translate had been converted to an A.I.-based system for much of its traffic, not just in the United States but in Europe and Asia as well: The rollout included translations between English and Spanish, French, Portuguese, German, Chinese, Japanese, Korean and Turkish. The rest of Translate's hundred-odd languages were to come, with the aim of eight per month, by the end of next year. The new incarnation, to the pleasant surprise of Google's own engineers, had been completed in only nine months. The A.I. system had demonstrated overnight improvements roughly equal to the total gains the old one had accrued over its entire lifetime.

Pichai has an affection for the obscure literary reference; he told me a month earlier, in his office in Mountain View, Calif., that Translate in part exists because not everyone can be like the physicist Robert Oppenheimer, who learned Sanskrit to read the Bhagavad Gita in the original. In London, the slide on the monitors behind him flicked to a Borges quote: *"Uno no es lo que es por lo que escribe, sino por lo que ha leído."*

Grinning, Pichai read aloud an awkward English version of the sentence that had been rendered by the old Translate system: "One is not what is for what he writes, but for what he has read."

To the right of that was a new A.I.-rendered version: "You are not what you write, but what you have read."

It was a fitting remark: The new Google Translate was run on the first machines that had, in a sense, ever learned to read anything at all.

Google's decision to reorganize itself around A.I. was the first major manifestation of what has become an industrywide machine-learning delirium. Over the past four years, six companies in particular—Google, Facebook, Apple, Amazon, Microsoft and the Chinese firm Baidu—have touched off an arms race for A.I. talent, particularly within universities. Corporate promises of resources and freedom have thinned out top academic departments. It has become widely known in Silicon Valley that Mark Zuckerberg, chief executive of Facebook, personally oversees, with phone calls and video-chat blandishments, his company's overtures to the most desirable graduate students. Starting salaries of seven figures are not unheard-of. Attendance at the field's most important academic conference has nearly quadrupled. What is at stake is not just one more piecemeal innovation but control over what very well could represent an entirely new computational platform: pervasive, ambient artificial intelligence.

The phrase "artificial intelligence" is invoked as if its meaning were self-evident, but it has always been a source of confusion and controversy. Imagine if you went back to the 1970s, stopped someone on the street, pulled out a smartphone and showed her Google Maps. Once you managed to convince her you weren't some oddly dressed wizard, and that what you withdrew from your pocket wasn't a black-arts amulet but merely a tiny computer more powerful than the one that guided Apollo missions, Google Maps would almost certainly seem to her a persuasive example of "artificial intelligence." In a very real sense, it is. It can do things any map-literate human can manage, like get you from your hotel to the airport—though it can do so much more quickly and reliably. It can also do things that humans simply and obviously cannot: It can evaluate the traffic, plan the best route and reorient itself when you take the wrong exit.

Practically nobody today, however, would bestow upon Google Maps the honorific "A.I.," so sentimental and sparing are we in our use of the word "intelligence." Artificial intelligence, we believe, must be something that distinguishes HAL from whatever it is a loom or wheelbarrow can do. The minute we can automate a task, we downgrade the relevant skill involved to one of mere mechanism. Today Google Maps seems, in the pejorative sense of the term, robotic: It simply accepts an explicit demand (the need to get from one place to another) and tries to satisfy that demand as efficiently as possible. The goal posts for "artificial intelligence" are thus constantly receding.

When he has an opportunity to make careful distinctions, Pichai differentiates between the current applications of A.I. and the ultimate goal of "artificial general intelligence." Artificial general intelligence will not involve dutiful adherence to explicit instructions, but instead will demonstrate a facility with the implicit, the interpretive. It will be a general tool, designed for general purposes in a general context. Pichai believes his company's future depends on something like this. Imagine if you could tell Google Maps, "I'd like to go to the airport, but I need to stop off on the way to buy a present for my nephew." A more generally intelligent version of that service—a ubiquitous assistant, of the sort that Scarlett Johansson memorably disembodied three years ago in the Spike Jonze film *Her*—would know all sorts of things that, say, a close friend or an earnest intern might know: your nephew's age, and how much you ordinarily like to spend on gifts for children, and where to find an open store. But a truly intelligent Maps could also conceivably know all sorts of things a close friend wouldn't, like what has only recently come into fashion among preschoolers in your nephew's school—or more important, what its users actually want. If an intelligent machine were able to discern some intricate if murky regularity in data about what we have done in the past, it might be able to extrapolate about our subsequent desires, even if we don't entirely know them ourselves.

The new wave of A.I.-enhanced assistants—Apple's Siri, Facebook's M, Amazon's Echo—are all creatures of machine learning, built with similar intentions. The corporate dreams for machine learning, however, aren't exhausted by the goal of consumer clairvoyance. A medical-imaging subsidiary of Samsung announced this year that its new ultrasound devices could detect breast cancer. Management consultants are falling all over themselves to prep executives for the widening industrial applications of computers that program themselves. DeepMind, a 2014 Google acquisition, defeated the reigning human grandmaster of the ancient board game Go, despite predictions that such an achievement would take another 10 years.

In a famous 1950 essay, Alan Turing proposed a test for an artificial general intelligence: a computer that could, over the course of five minutes of text exchange, successfully deceive a real human interlocutor. Once a machine can translate fluently between two natural languages, the foundation has been laid for a machine that might one day "understand" human language well enough to engage in plausible conversation. Google Brain's members, who pushed and helped oversee the Translate project, believe that such a machine would be on its way to serving as a generally intelligent all-encompassing personal digital assistant.

What follows here is the story of how a team of Google researchers and engineers—at first one or two, then three or four, and finally more than a hundred—made considerable progress in that direction. It's an uncommon story in many ways, not least of all because it defies many of the Silicon Valley stereotypes we've grown accustomed to. It does not feature people who think that everything will be unrecognizably different tomorrow or the next day because of some restless tinkerer in his garage. It is neither a story about people who think technology will solve all our problems nor one about people who think technology is ineluctably bound to create apocalyptic new ones. It is not about disruption, at least not in the way that word tends to be used.

It is, in fact, three overlapping stories that converge in Google Translate's successful metamorphosis to A.I. —a technical story, an institutional story and a story about the evolution of ideas. The technical story is about one team on one product at one company, and the process by which they refined, tested and introduced a brand-new version of an old product in only about a quarter of the time anyone, themselves included, might reasonably have expected. The institutional story is about the employees of a small but influential artificial-intelligence group within that company, and the process by which their intuitive faith in some old, unproven and broadly unpalatable notions about computing upended every other company within a large radius. The story of ideas is about the cognitive scientists, psychologists and wayward engineers who long toiled in obscurity, and the process by which their ostensibly irrational convictions ultimately inspired a paradigm shift in our understanding not only of technology but also, in theory, of consciousness itself.

The first story, the story of Google Translate, takes place in Mountain View over nine months, and it explains the transformation of machine translation. The second story, the story of Google Brain and its many competitors, takes place in Silicon Valley over five years, and it explains the transformation of that entire community. The third story, the story of deep learning, takes place in a variety of far-flung laboratories—in Scotland, Switzerland, Japan and most of all Canada—over seven decades, and it might very well contribute to the revision of our self-image as first and foremost beings who think.

All three are stories about artificial intelligence. The seven-decade story is about what we might conceivably expect or want from it. The five-year story is about what it might do in the near future. The nine-month story is about what it can do right this minute. These three stories are themselves just proof of concept. All of this is only the beginning.

## Part I: Learning Machine

### 1. The Birth of Brain

Jeff Dean, though his title is senior fellow, is the de facto head of Google Brain. Dean is a sinewy, energy-efficient man with a long, narrow face, deep-set eyes and an earnest, soapbox-derby sort of enthusiasm. The son of a medical anthropologist and a public-health epidemiologist, Dean grew up all over the world—Minnesota, Hawaii, Boston, Arkansas, Geneva, Uganda, Somalia, Atlanta—and, while in high school and college, wrote software used by the World Health Organization. He has been with Google since 1999, as employee 25ish, and has had a hand in the core software systems beneath nearly every significant undertaking since then. A beloved artifact of company culture is Jeff Dean Facts, written in the style of the Chuck Norris Facts meme: "Jeff Dean's PIN is the last four digits of pi." "When Alexander Graham Bell invented the telephone, he saw a missed call from Jeff Dean." "Jeff Dean got promoted to Level 11 in a system where the maximum level is 10." (This last one is, in fact, true.)

One day in early 2011, Dean walked into one of the Google campus's "microkitchens"—the "Googley" word for the shared break spaces on most floors of the Mountain View complex's buildings—and ran into Andrew Ng, a young Stanford computer-science professor who was working for the company as a consultant. Ng told him about Project Marvin, an internal effort (named after the celebrated A.I. pioneer Marvin Minsky) he had recently helped establish to experiment with "neural networks," pliant digital lattices based loosely on the architecture of the brain. Dean himself had worked on a primitive version of the technology as an undergraduate at the University of Minnesota in 1990, during one of the method's brief windows of mainstream acceptability. Now, over the previous five years, the number of academics working on neural networks had begun to grow again, from a handful to a few dozen. Ng told Dean that Project Marvin, which was being underwritten by Google's secretive X lab, had already achieved some promising results.

Dean was intrigued enough to lend his "20 percent" —the portion of work hours every Google employee is expected to contribute to programs outside his or her core job—to the project. Pretty soon, he suggested to Ng that they bring in another colleague with a neuroscience background, Greg Corrado. (In graduate school, Corrado was taught briefly about the technology, but strictly as a historical curiosity. "It was good I was paying attention in class that day," he joked to me.) In late spring they brought in one of Ng's best graduate students, Quoc Le, as the project's first intern. By then, a number of the Google engineers had taken to referring to Project Marvin by another name: Google Brain.

Since the term "artificial intelligence" was first coined, at a kind of constitutional convention of the mind at Dartmouth in the summer of 1956, a majority of researchers have long thought the best approach to creating A.I. would be to write a very big, comprehensive program that laid out both the rules of logical reasoning and sufficient knowledge of the world. If you wanted to translate from English to Japanese, for example, you would program into the computer all of the grammatical rules of English, and then

> **Even enormous institutions like Google will be subject to this wave of automation; once machines can learn from human speech, even the comfortable job of the programmer is threatened.**

the entirety of definitions contained in the Oxford English Dictionary, and then all of the grammatical rules of Japanese, as well as all of the words in the Japanese dictionary, and *only after all of that* feed it a sentence in a source language and ask it to tabulate a corresponding sentence in the target language. You would give the machine a language map that was, as Borges would have had it, the size of the territory. This perspective is usually called "symbolic A.I." —because its definition of cognition is based on symbolic logic—or, disparagingly, "good old-fashioned A.I." There are two main problems with the old-fashioned approach. The first is that it's awfully time-consuming on the human end. The second is that it only really works in domains where rules and definitions are very clear: in mathematics, for example, or chess. Translation, however, is an example of a field where this approach fails horribly, because words cannot be reduced to their dictionary definitions, and because languages tend to have as many exceptions as they have rules. More often than not, a system like this is liable to translate "minister of agriculture" as "priest of farming." Still, for math and chess it worked great, and the proponents of symbolic A.I. took it for granted that no activities signaled "general intelligence" better than math and chess.

There were, however, limits to what this system could do. In the 1980s, a robotics researcher at Carnegie Mellon pointed out that it was easy to get computers to do adult things but nearly impossible to get them to do things a 1-year-old could do, like hold a ball or identify a cat. By the 1990s, despite punishing advancements in computer chess, we still weren't remotely close to artificial general intelligence.

There has always been another vision for A.I. —a dissenting view—in which the computers would learn from the ground up (from data) rather than from the top down (from rules). This notion dates to the early 1940s, when it occurred to researchers that the best model for flexible automated intelligence was the brain itself. A brain, after all, is just a bunch of widgets, called neurons, that either pass along an electrical charge to their neighbors or don't. What's important are less the individual neurons themselves than the manifold connections among them. This structure, in its simplicity, has afforded the brain a wealth of adaptive advantages. The brain can operate in circumstances in which information is poor or missing; it can withstand significant damage without total loss of control; it can store a huge amount of knowledge in a very efficient way; it can isolate distinct patterns but retain the messiness necessary to handle ambiguity.

There was no reason you couldn't try to mimic this structure in electronic form, and in 1943 it was shown that arrangements of simple artificial neurons could carry out basic logical functions. They could also, at least in theory, learn the way we do. With life experience, depending on a particular person's trials and errors, the synaptic connections among pairs of neurons get stronger or weaker. An artificial neural network could do something similar, by gradually altering, on a guided trial-and-error basis, the numerical relationships among artificial neurons. It wouldn't need to be preprogrammed with fixed rules. It would, instead, rewire itself to reflect patterns in the data it absorbed.

This attitude toward artificial intelligence was evolutionary rather than creationist. If you wanted a flexible mechanism, you wanted one that could adapt to its environment. If you wanted something that could adapt, you didn't want to begin with the indoctrination of the rules of chess. You wanted to begin with very basic abilities—sensory perception and motor control—in the hope that advanced skills would emerge organically. Humans don't learn to understand language by memorizing dictionaries and grammar books, so why should we possibly expect our computers to do so?

Google Brain was the first major commercial institution to invest in the possibilities embodied by this way of thinking about A.I. Dean, Corrado and Ng began their work as a part-time, collaborative experiment, but they made immediate progress. They took architectural inspiration for their models from recent theoretical outlines—as well as ideas that had been on the shelf since the 1980s and 1990s—and drew upon both the company's peerless reserves of data and its massive computing infrastructure. They instructed the networks on enormous banks of "labeled" data—speech files with correct transcriptions, for example—and the computers improved their responses to better match reality.

"The portion of evolution in which animals developed eyes was a big development," Dean told me one day, with customary understatement. We were sitting, as usual, in a whiteboarded meeting room, on which he had drawn a crowded, snaking timeline of Google Brain and its relation to inflection points in the recent history of

neural networks. "Now computers have eyes. We can build them around the capabilities that now exist to understand photos. Robots will be drastically transformed.
They'll be able to operate in an unknown environment, on much different problems." These capacities they were building may have seemed primitive, but their
implications were profound.

### 2. The Unlikely Intern

In its first year or so of existence, Brain's experiments in the development of a machine with the talents of a 1-year-old had, as Dean said, worked to great effect. Its
speech-recognition team swapped out part of their old system for a neural network
and encountered, in pretty much one fell swoop, the best quality improvements
anyone had seen in 20 years. Their system's object-recognition abilities improved
by an order of magnitude. This was not because Brain's personnel had generated a
sheaf of outrageous new ideas in just a year. It was because Google had finally devoted the resources—in computers and, increasingly, personnel—to fill in outlines
that had been around for a long time.

A great preponderance of these extant and neglected notions had been proposed
or refined by a peripatetic English polymath named Geoffrey Hinton. In the second
year of Brain's existence, Hinton was recruited to Brain as Andrew Ng left. (Ng
now leads the 1,300-person A.I. team at Baidu.) Hinton wanted to leave his post at
the University of Toronto for only three months, so for arcane contractual reasons
he had to be hired as an intern. At intern training, the orientation leader would say
something like, "Type in your LDAP" —a user login—and he would flag a helper to
ask, "What's an LDAP?" All the smart 25-year-olds in attendance, who had only ever
known deep learning as the sine qua non of artificial intelligence, snickered: "Who
is that old guy? Why doesn't he get it?"

"At lunchtime," Hinton said, "someone in the queue yelled: 'Professor Hinton! I
took your course! What are you doing here?' After that, it was all right."

A few months later, Hinton and two of his students demonstrated truly astonish-
ing gains in a big image-recognition contest, run by an open-source collective called
ImageNet, that asks computers not only to identify a monkey but also to distinguish
between spider monkeys and howler monkeys, and among God knows how many
different breeds of cat. Google soon approached Hinton and his students with an
offer. They accepted. "I thought they were interested in our I.P.," he said. "Turns out
they were interested in us."

Hinton comes from one of those old British families emblazoned like the Dar-
wins at eccentric angles across the intellectual landscape, where regardless of tit-
ular preoccupation a person is expected to make sideline contributions to minor
problems in astronomy or fluid dynamics. His great-great-grandfather was George
Boole, whose foundational work in symbolic logic underpins the computer; another
great-great-grandfather was a celebrated surgeon, his father a venturesome ento-
mologist, his father's cousin a Los Alamos researcher; the list goes on. He trained
at Cambridge and Edinburgh, then taught at Carnegie Mellon before he ended up
at Toronto, where he still spends half his time. (His work has long been supported

by the largess of the Canadian government.) I visited him in his office at Google there. He has tousled yellowed-pewter hair combed forward in a mature Noel Gallagher style and wore a baggy striped dress shirt that persisted in coming untucked, and oval eyeglasses that slid down to the tip of a prominent nose. He speaks with a driving if shambolic wit, and says things like, "Computers will understand sarcasm before Americans do."

Hinton had been working on neural networks since his undergraduate days at Cambridge in the late 1960s, and he is seen as the intellectual primogenitor of the contemporary field. For most of that time, whenever he spoke about machine learning, people looked at him as though he were talking about the Ptolemaic spheres or bloodletting by leeches. Neural networks were taken as a disproven folly, largely on the basis of one overhyped project: the Perceptron, an artificial neural network that Frank Rosenblatt, a Cornell psychologist, developed in the late 1950s. The *New York Times* reported that the machine's sponsor, the United States Navy, expected it would "be able to walk, talk, see, write, reproduce itself and be conscious of its existence." It went on to do approximately none of those things. Marvin Minsky, the dean of artificial intelligence in America, had worked on neural networks for his 1954 Princeton thesis, but he'd since grown tired of the inflated claims that Rosenblatt—who was a contemporary at Bronx Science—made for the neural paradigm. (He was also competing for Defense Department funding.) Along with an M.I.T. colleague, Minsky published a book that proved that there were painfully simple problems the Perceptron could never solve.

Minsky's criticism of the Perceptron extended only to networks of one "layer," i.e., one layer of artificial neurons between what's fed to the machine and what you expect from it—and later in life, he expounded ideas very similar to contemporary deep learning. But Hinton already knew at the time that complex tasks could be carried out if you had recourse to multiple layers. The simplest description of a neural network is that it's a machine that makes classifications or predictions based on its ability to discover patterns in data. With one layer, you could find only simple patterns; with more than one, you could look for patterns of patterns. Take the case of image recognition, which tends to rely on a contraption called a "convolutional neural net." (These were elaborated in a seminal 1998 paper whose lead author, a Frenchman named Yann LeCun, did his postdoctoral research in Toronto under Hinton and now directs a huge A.I. endeavor at Facebook.) The first layer of the network learns to identify the very basic visual trope of an "edge," meaning a *nothing* (an off-pixel) followed by a *something* (an on-pixel) or vice versa. Each successive layer of the network looks for a pattern in the previous layer. A pattern of edges might be a circle or a rectangle. A pattern of circles or rectangles might be a face. And so on. This more or less parallels the way information is put together in increasingly abstract ways as it travels from the photoreceptors in the retina back and up through the visual cortex. At each conceptual step, detail that isn't immediately relevant is thrown away. If several edges and circles come together to make a face, you don't care exactly where the face is found in the visual field; you just care that it's a face.

The issue with multilayered, "deep" neural networks was that the trial-and-error part got extraordinarily complicated. In a single layer, it's easy. Imagine that you're playing with a child. You tell the child, "Pick up the green ball and put it into Box A." The child picks up a green ball and puts it into Box B. You say, "Try again to put the green ball in Box A." The child tries Box A. Bravo.

Now imagine you tell the child, "Pick up a green ball, go through the door marked 3 and put the green ball into Box A." The child takes a red ball, goes through the door marked 2 and puts the red ball into Box B. How do you begin to correct the child? You cannot just repeat your initial instructions, because the child does not know at which point he went wrong. In real life, you might start by holding up the red ball and the green ball and saying, "Red ball, green ball." The whole point of machine learning, however, is to avoid that kind of explicit mentoring. Hinton and a few others went on to invent a solution (or rather, reinvent an older one) to this layered-error problem, over the halting course of the late 1970s and 1980s, and interest among computer scientists in neural networks was briefly revived. "People got very excited about it," he said. "But we oversold it." Computer scientists quickly went back to thinking that people like Hinton were weirdos and mystics.

These ideas remained popular, however, among philosophers and psychologists, who called it "connectionism" or "parallel distributed processing." "This idea," Hinton told me, "of a few people keeping a torch burning, it's a nice myth. It was true within artificial intelligence. But within psychology lots of people believed in the approach but just couldn't do it." Neither could Hinton, despite the generosity of the Canadian government. "There just wasn't enough computer power or enough data. People on our side kept saying, 'Yeah, but if I had a really big one, it would work.' It wasn't a very persuasive argument."

### 3. A Deep Explanation of Deep Learning

When Pichai said that Google would henceforth be "A.I. first," he was not just making a claim about his company's business strategy; he was throwing in his company's lot with this long-unworkable idea. Pichai's allocation of resources ensured that people like Dean could ensure that people like Hinton would have, at long last, enough computers and enough data to make a persuasive argument. An average brain has something on the order of 100 billion neurons. Each neuron is connected to up to 10,000 other neurons, which means that the number of synapses is between 100 trillion and 1,000 trillion. For a simple artificial neural network of the sort proposed in the 1940s, the attempt to even try to replicate this was unimaginable. We're still far from the construction of a network of that size, but Google Brain's investment allowed for the creation of artificial neural networks comparable to the brains of mice.

To understand why scale is so important, however, you have to start to understand some of the more technical details of what, exactly, machine intelligences are doing with the data they consume. A lot of our ambient fears about A.I. rest on the idea that they're just vacuuming up knowledge like a sociopathic prodigy in a library, and that an artificial intelligence constructed to make paper clips might someday decide to treat humans like ants or lettuce. This just isn't how they work. All they're doing is shuffling information around in search of commonalities—basic patterns, at first, and then more complex ones—and for the moment, at least, the greatest danger is that the information we're feeding them is biased in the first place.

If that brief explanation seems sufficiently reassuring, the reassured nontechnical reader is invited to skip forward to the next section, which is about cats. If not, then read on. (This section is also, luckily, about cats.)

Imagine you want to program a cat-recognizer on the old symbolic-A.I. model. You stay up for days preloading the machine with an exhaustive, explicit definition of "cat." You tell it that a cat has four legs and pointy ears and whiskers and a tail, and so on. All this information is stored in a special place in memory called Cat. Now you show it a picture. First, the machine has to separate out the various distinct elements of the image. Then it has to take these elements and apply the rules stored in its memory. If(legs=4) and if(ears=pointy) and if(whiskers=yes) and if(tail=yes) and if(expression=supercilious), then(cat=yes). But what if you showed this cat-recognizer a Scottish Fold, a heart-rending breed with a prized genetic defect that leads to droopy doubled-over ears? Our symbolic A.I. gets to (ears=pointy) and shakes its head solemnly, "Not cat." It is hyperliteral, or "brittle." Even the thickest toddler shows much greater inferential acuity.

Now imagine that instead of hard-wiring the machine with a set of rules for classification stored in one location of the computer's memory, you try the same thing on a neural network. There is no special place that can hold the definition of "cat." There is just a giant blob of interconnected switches, like forks in a path. On one side of the blob, you present the inputs (the pictures); on the other side, you present the corresponding outputs (the labels). Then you just tell it to work out *for itself*, via the individual calibration of all of these interconnected switches, whatever path the data should take so that the inputs are mapped to the correct outputs. The training is the process by which a labyrinthine series of elaborate tunnels are excavated through the blob, tunnels that connect any given input to its proper output. The more training data you have, the greater the number and intricacy of the tunnels that can be dug. Once the training is complete, the middle of the blob has enough tunnels that it can make reliable predictions about how to handle data it has never seen before. This is called "supervised learning."

The reason that the network requires so many neurons and so much data is that it functions, in a way, like a sort of giant machine democracy. Imagine you want to train a computer to differentiate among five different items. Your network is made up of millions and millions of neuronal "voters," each of whom has been given five different cards: one for cat, one for dog, one for spider monkey, one for spoon and one for defibrillator. You show your electorate a photo and ask, "Is this a cat, a dog, a spider monkey, a spoon or a defibrillator?" All the neurons that voted the same way collect in groups, and the network foreman peers down from above and identifies the majority classification: "A dog?"

You say: "No, maestro, it's a cat. Try again."

Now the network foreman goes back to identify which voters threw their weight behind "cat" and which didn't. The ones that got "cat" right get their votes counted double next time—at least when they're voting for "cat." They have to prove independently whether they're also good at picking out dogs and defibrillators, but one thing that makes a neural network so flexible is that each individual unit can contribute differently to different desired outcomes. What's important is not the individual vote, exactly, but the pattern of votes. If Joe, Frank and Mary all vote together, it's a dog; but if Joe, Kate and Jessica vote together, it's a cat; and if Kate, Jessica and Frank vote together, it's a defibrillator. The neural network just needs to register enough of a regularly discernible signal somewhere to say, "Odds are, this particular arrangement of pixels represents something these humans keep calling 'cats.'" The more "voters" you have, and the more times you make them vote, the more keenly the network can register even very weak signals. If you have only Joe, Frank and Mary, you can maybe use them only to differentiate among a cat, a dog and a defibrillator. If you have millions of different voters that can associate in billions of different ways, you can learn to classify data with incredible granularity. Your trained voter assembly will be able to look at an unlabeled picture and identify it more or less accurately.

Part of the reason there was so much resistance to these ideas in computer-science departments is that because the output is just a prediction based on patterns of patterns, it's not going to be perfect, and the machine will never be able to define for you what, exactly, a cat is. It just knows them when it sees them. This wooliness, however, is the point. The neuronal "voters" will recognize a happy cat dozing in the sun and an angry cat glaring out from the shadows of an untidy litter box, as long as they have been exposed to millions of diverse cat scenes. You just need lots and lots of the voters—in order to make sure that *some* part of your network picks up on even very weak regularities, on Scottish Folds with droopy ears, for example—and enough labeled data to make sure your network has seen the widest possible variance in phenomena.

It is important to note, however, that the fact that neural networks are probabilistic in nature means that they're not suitable for all tasks. It's no great tragedy if they mislabel 1 percent of cats as dogs, or send you to the wrong movie on occasion, but in something like a self-driving car we all want greater assurances. This isn't the only caveat. Supervised learning is a trial-and-error process based on *labeled* data. The machines might be doing the learning, but there remains a strong human element in the initial categorization of the inputs. If your data had a picture of a man and a woman in suits that someone had labeled "woman with her boss," that relationship would be encoded into all future pattern recognition. Labeled data is thus fallible the way that human labelers are fallible. If a machine was asked to identify creditworthy candidates for loans, it might use data like felony convictions, but if felony convictions were unfair in the first place—if they were based on, say, discriminatory drug laws—then the loan recommendations would perforce also be fallible.

Image-recognition networks like our cat-identifier are only one of many varieties of deep learning, but they are disproportionately invoked as teaching examples because each layer does something at least vaguely recognizable to humans—picking out edges first, then circles, then faces. This means there's a safeguard against error. For instance, an early oddity in Google's image-recognition software meant that it could not always identify a barbell in isolation, even though the team had trained it on an image set that included a lot of exercise categories. A visualization tool showed them the machine had learned not the concept of "dumbbell" but the concept of "dumbbell+arm," because all the dumbbells in the training set were attached to arms. They threw into the training mix some photos of solo barbells. The problem was solved. Not everything is so easy.

### 4. The Cat Paper

Over the course of its first year or two, Brain's efforts to cultivate in machines the skills of a 1-year-old were auspicious enough that the team was graduated out of the X lab and into the broader research organization. (The head of Google X once noted that Brain had paid for the entirety of X's costs.) They still had fewer than 10 people and only a vague sense for what might ultimately come of it all. But even then they were thinking ahead to what ought to happen next. First a human mind learns to recognize a ball and rests easily with the accomplishment for a moment, but sooner or later, it wants to ask for the ball. And then it wades into language.

The first step in that direction was the cat paper, which made Brain famous.

What the cat paper demonstrated was that a neural network with more than a billion "synaptic" connections—a hundred times larger than any publicized neural network to that point, yet still many orders of magnitude smaller than our brains—could observe raw, unlabeled data and pick out for itself a high-order human concept. The Brain researchers had shown the network millions of still frames from YouTube videos, and out of the welter of the pure sensorium the network had isolated a stable pattern any toddler or chipmunk would recognize without a moment's hesitation as the face of a cat. The machine had not been programmed with the foreknowledge of a cat; it reached directly into the world and seized the idea for itself. (The researchers discovered this with the neural-network equivalent of something like an M.R.I., which showed them that a ghostly cat face caused the artificial neurons to "vote" with the greatest collective enthusiasm.) Most machine learning to that point had been limited by the quantities of labeled data. The cat paper showed that machines could also deal with raw unlabeled data, perhaps even data of which humans had no established foreknowledge. This seemed like a major advance not only in cat-recognition studies but also in overall artificial intelligence.

The lead author on the cat paper was Quoc Le. Le is short and willowy and soft-spoken, with a quick, enigmatic smile and shiny black penny loafers. He grew up outside Hue, Vietnam. His parents were rice farmers, and he did not have electricity at home. His mathematical abilities were obvious from an early age, and he was sent to study at a magnet school for science. In the late 1990s, while still in school, he tried to build a chatbot to talk to. He thought, How hard could this be?

"But actually," he told me in a whispery deadpan, "it's very hard."

He left the rice paddies on a scholarship to a university in Canberra, Australia, where he worked on A.I. tasks like computer vision. The dominant method of the time, which involved feeding the machine definitions for things like edges, felt to him like cheating. Le didn't know then, or knew only dimly, that there were at least a few dozen computer scientists elsewhere in the world who couldn't help imagining, as he did, that machines could learn from scratch. In 2006, Le took a position at the Max Planck Institute for Biological Cybernetics in the medieval German university town of Tübingen. In a reading group there, he encountered two new papers by Geoffrey Hinton. People who entered the discipline during the long diaspora all have conversion stories, and when Le read those papers, he felt the scales fall away from his eyes.

"There was a big debate," he told me. "A very big debate." We were in a small interior conference room, a narrow, high-ceilinged space outfitted with only a small table and two whiteboards. He looked to the curve he'd drawn on the whiteboard behind him and back again, then softly confided, "I've never seen such a big debate."

He remembers standing up at the reading group and saying, "This is the future." It was, he said, an "unpopular decision at the time." A former adviser from Australia, with whom he had stayed close, couldn't quite understand Le's decision. "Why are you doing this?" he asked Le in an email.

"I didn't have a good answer back then," Le said. "I was just curious. There was a successful paradigm, but to be honest I was just curious about the new paradigm. In 2006, there was very little activity." He went to join Ng at Stanford and began to pursue Hinton's ideas. "By the end of 2010, I was pretty convinced something was going to happen."

What happened, soon afterward, was that Le went to Brain as its first intern, where he carried on with his dissertation work—an extension of which ultimately became the cat paper. On a simple level, Le wanted to see if the computer could be trained to identify on its own the information that was absolutely essential to a given image. He fed the neural network a still he had taken from YouTube. He then told the neural network to throw away some of the information contained in the image, though he didn't specify what it should or shouldn't throw away. The machine threw away some of the information, initially at random. Then he said: "Just kidding! Now recreate the initial image you were shown based only on the information you retained." It was as if he were asking the machine to find a way to "summarize" the image, and then expand back to the original from the summary. If the summary was based on irrelevant data—like the color of the sky rather than the presence of whiskers—the machine couldn't perform a competent reconstruction. Its reaction would be akin to that of a distant ancestor whose takeaway from his brief exposure to saber-tooth tigers was that they made a restful swooshing sound when they moved. Le's neural network, unlike that ancestor, got to try again, and again and again and again. Each time it mathematically "chose" to prioritize different pieces of information and performed incrementally better. A neural network, however, was a black box. It divined patterns, but the patterns it identified didn't always make intuitive sense to a human observer. The same network that hit on our concept of cat also became enthusiastic about a pattern that looked like some sort of furniture-animal compound, like a cross between an ottoman and a goat.

Le didn't see himself in those heady cat years as a language guy, but he felt an urge to connect the dots to his early chatbot. After the cat paper, he realized that if you could ask a network to summarize a photo, you could perhaps also ask it to summarize a sentence. This problem preoccupied Le, along with a Brain colleague named Tomas Mikolov, for the next two years.

In that time, the Brain team outgrew several offices around him. For a while they were on a floor they shared with executives. They got an email at one point from the administrator asking that they please stop allowing people to sleep on the couch in front of Larry Page and Sergey Brin's suite. It unsettled incoming V.I.P.s. They were then allocated part of a research building across the street, where their exchanges in the microkitchen wouldn't be squandered on polite chitchat with the suits. That interim also saw dedicated attempts on the part of Google's competitors to catch up. (As Le told me about his close collaboration with Tomas Mikolov, he kept repeating Mikolov's name over and over, in an incantatory way that sounded poignant. Le had never seemed so solemn. I finally couldn't help myself and began to ask, "Is he ... ?" Le nodded. "At Facebook," he replied.)

They spent this period trying to come up with neural-network architectures that could accommodate not only simple photo classifications, which were static, but also complex structures that unfolded over time, like language or music. Many of these were first proposed in the 1990s, and Le and his colleagues went back to those long-ignored contributions to see what they could glean. They knew that once you established a facility with basic linguistic prediction, you could then go on to do all sorts of other intelligent things—like predict a suitable reply to an email, for example, or predict the flow of a sensible conversation. You could sidle up to the sort of prowess that would, from the outside at least, look a lot like thinking.

## Part II: Language Machine

### 5. The Linguistic Turn

The hundred or so current members of Brain—it often feels less like a department within a colossal corporate hierarchy than it does a club or a scholastic society or an intergalactic cantina—came in the intervening years to count among the freest and most widely admired employees in the entire Google organization. They are now quartered in a tiered two-story eggshell building, with large windows tinted a menacing charcoal gray, on the leafy northwestern fringe of the company's main Mountain View campus. Their microkitchen has a foosball table I never saw used; a Rock Band setup I never saw used; and a Go kit I saw used on a few occasions. (I did once see a young Brain research associate introducing his colleagues to ripe jackfruit, carving up the enormous spiky orb like a turkey.)

When I began spending time at Brain's offices, in June, there were some rows of empty desks, but most of them were labeled with Post-it notes that said things like "Jesse, 6/27." Now those are all occupied. When I first visited, parking was not an issue. The closest spaces were those reserved for expectant mothers or Teslas, but there was ample space in the rest of the lot. By October, if I showed up later than 9:30, I had to find a spot across the street.

Brain's growth made Dean slightly nervous about how the company was going to handle the demand. He wanted to avoid what at Google is known as a "success disaster" —a situation in which the company's capabilities in theory outpaced its ability to implement a product in practice. At a certain point he did some back-of-the-envelope calculations, which he presented to the executives one day in a two-slide presentation.

"If everyone in the future speaks to their Android phone for three minutes a day," he told them, "this is how many machines we'll need." They would need to double or triple their global computational footprint.

"That," he observed with a little theatrical gulp and widened eyes, "sounded scary. You'd have to" —he hesitated to imagine the consequences— "build new buildings."

There was, however, another option: just design, mass-produce and install in dispersed data centers a new kind of chip to make everything faster. These chips would be called T.P.U.s, or "tensor processing units," and their value proposition—counterintuitively—is that they are deliberately less precise than normal chips. Rather than compute 12.246 times 54.392, they will give you the perfunctory answer to 12 times 54. On a mathematical level, rather than a metaphorical one, a neural network is just a structured series of hundreds or thousands or tens of thousands of matrix multiplications carried out in succession, and it's much more important that these processes be fast than that they be exact. "Normally," Dean said, "special-purpose hardware is a bad idea. It usually works to speed up one thing. But because of the generality of neural networks, you can leverage this special-purpose hardware for a lot of other things."

Just as the chip-design process was nearly complete, Le and two colleagues finally demonstrated that neural networks might be configured to handle the structure of language. He drew upon an idea, called "word embeddings," that had been around for more than 10 years. When you summarize images, you can divine a picture of what each stage of the summary looks like—an edge, a circle, etc. When you summarize language in a similar way, you essentially produce multidimensional maps of the distances, based on common usage, between one word and every single other word in the language. The machine is not "analyzing" the data the way that we might, with linguistic rules that identify some of them as nouns and others as verbs. Instead, it is shifting and twisting and warping the words around in the map. In two dimensions, you cannot make this map useful. You want, for example, "cat" to be in the rough vicinity of "dog," but you also want "cat" to be near "tail" and near "supercilious" and near "meme," because you want to try to capture all of the different relationships—both strong and weak—that the word "cat" has to other words. It can be related to all these other words simultaneously only if it is related to each of them in a different dimension. You can't easily make a 160,000-dimensional map, but it turns out you can represent a language pretty well in a mere thousand or so dimensions—in other words, a universe in which each word is designated by a list of a thousand numbers. Le gave me a good-natured hard time for my continual requests for a mental picture of these maps. "Gideon," he would say, with the blunt regular demurral of Bartleby, "I do not generally like trying to visualize thousand-dimensional vectors in three-dimensional space."

Still, certain dimensions in the space, it turned out, did seem to represent legible human categories, like gender or relative size. If you took the thousand numbers that meant "king" and literally just subtracted the thousand numbers that meant "queen," you got the same numerical result as if you subtracted the numbers for "woman" from the numbers for "man." And if you took the entire space of the English language and the entire space of French, you could, at least in theory, train a network to learn how to take a sentence in one space and propose an equivalent in the other. You just had to give it millions and millions of English sentences as inputs on one side and their desired French outputs on the other, and over time it would recognize the relevant patterns in words the way that an image classifier recognized the relevant patterns in pixels. You could then give it a sentence in English and ask it to predict the best French analogue.

The major difference between words and pixels, however, is that all of the pixels in an image are there at once, whereas words appear in a progression over time. You needed a way for the network to "hold in mind" the progression of a chronological sequence—the complete pathway from the first word to the last. In a period of about a week, in September 2014, three papers came out—one by Le and two others by academics in Canada and Germany—that at last provided all the theoretical tools necessary to do this sort of thing. That research allowed for open-ended projects like Brain's Magenta, an investigation into how machines might generate art and music. It also cleared the way toward an instrumental task like machine translation. Hinton told me he thought at the time that this follow-up work would take at least five more years.

### 6. The Ambush

Le's paper showed that neural translation was plausible, but he had used only a relatively small public data set. (Small for Google, that is—it was actually the biggest public data set in the world. A decade of the old Translate had gathered production data that was between a hundred and a thousand times bigger.) More important, Le's model didn't work very well for sentences longer than about seven words.

Mike Schuster, who then was a staff research scientist at Brain, picked up the baton. He knew that if Google didn't find a way to scale these theoretical insights up to a production level, someone else would. The project took him the next two years. "You think," Schuster says, "to translate something, you just get the data, run the experiments and you're done, but it doesn't work like that."

Schuster is a taut, focused, ageless being with a tanned, piston-shaped head, narrow shoulders, long camo cargo shorts tied below the knee and neon-green Nike Flyknits. He looks as if he woke up in the lotus position, reached for his small, rimless, elliptical glasses, accepted calories in the form of a modest portion of preserved acorn and completed a relaxed desert decathlon on the way to the office; in reality, he told me, it's only an 18-mile bike ride each way. Schuster grew up in Duisburg, in the former West Germany's blast-furnace district, and studied electrical engineering before moving to Kyoto to work on early neural networks. In the 1990s, he ran experiments with a neural-networking machine as big as a conference room; it cost millions of dollars and had to be trained for weeks to do something you could now do on your desktop in less than an hour. He published a paper in 1997 that was barely cited for a decade and a half; this year it has been cited around 150 times. He is not humorless, but he does often wear an expression of some asperity, which I took as his signature combination of German restraint and Japanese restraint.

The issues Schuster had to deal with were tangled. For one thing, Le's code was custom-written, and it wasn't compatible with the new open-source machine-learning platform Google was then developing, TensorFlow. Dean directed to Schuster two other engineers, Yonghui Wu and Zhifeng Chen, in the fall of 2015. It took them two months just to replicate Le's results on the new system. Le was around, but even he couldn't always make heads or tails of what they had done.

As Schuster put it, "Some of the stuff was not done in full consciousness. They didn't know themselves why they worked."

This February, Google's research organization—the loose division of the company, roughly a thousand employees in all, dedicated to the forward-looking and the unclassifiable—convened their leads at an offsite retreat at the Westin St. Francis, on Union Square, a luxury hotel slightly less splendid than Google's own San Francisco shop a mile or so to the east. The morning was reserved for rounds of "lightning talks," quick updates to cover the research waterfront, and the afternoon was idled away in cross-departmental "facilitated discussions." The hope was that the retreat might provide an occasion for the unpredictable, oblique, Bell Labs-ish exchanges that kept a mature company prolific.

At lunchtime, Corrado and Dean paired up in search of Macduff Hughes, director of Google Translate. Hughes was eating alone, and the two Brain members took positions at either side. As Corrado put it, "We ambushed him."

"O.K.," Corrado said to the wary Hughes, holding his breath for effect. "We have something to tell you."

They told Hughes that 2016 seemed like a good time to consider an overhaul of Google Translate—the code of hundreds of engineers over 10 years—with a neural network. The old system worked the way all machine translation has worked for about 30 years: It sequestered each successive sentence fragment, looked up those words in a large statistically derived vocabulary table, then applied a battery of post-processing rules to affix proper endings and rearrange it all to make sense. The approach is called "phrase-based statistical machine translation," because by the time the system gets to the next phrase, it doesn't know what the last one was. This is why Translate's output sometimes looked like a shaken bag of fridge magnets. Brain's replacement would, if it came together, read and render entire sentences at one draft. It would capture context—and something akin to meaning.

The stakes may have seemed low: Translate generates minimal revenue, and it probably always will. For most Anglophone users, even a radical upgrade in the service's performance would hardly be hailed as anything more than an expected incremental bump. But there was a case to be made that human-quality machine translation is not only a short-term necessity but also a development very likely, in the long term, to prove transformational. In the immediate future, it's vital to the company's business strategy. Google estimates that 50 percent of the internet is in English, which perhaps 20 percent of the world's population speaks. If Google was going to compete in China—where a majority of market share in search-engine traffic belonged to its competitor Baidu—or India, decent machine translation would be an indispensable part of the infrastructure. Baidu itself had published a pathbreaking paper about the possibility of neural machine translation in July 2015.

And in the more distant, speculative future, machine translation was perhaps the first step toward a general computational facility with human language. This would represent a major inflection point—perhaps *the* major inflection point—in the development of something that felt like true artificial intelligence.

Most people in Silicon Valley were aware of machine learning as a fast-approaching horizon, so Hughes had seen this ambush coming. He remained skeptical. A modest, sturdily built man of early middle age with mussed auburn hair graying at the temples, Hughes is a classic line engineer, the sort of craftsman who wouldn't have been out of place at a drafting table at 1970s Boeing. His jeans pockets often look burdened with curious tools of ungainly dimension, as if he were porting around measuring tapes or thermocouples, and unlike many of the younger people who work for him, he has a wardrobe unreliant on company gear. He knew that various people in various places at Google and elsewhere had been trying to make neural translation work—not in a lab but at production scale—for years, to little avail.

Hughes listened to their case and, at the end, said cautiously that it sounded to him as if maybe they could pull it off in three years.

Dean thought otherwise. "We can do it by the end of the year, if we put our minds to it." One reason people liked and admired Dean so much was that he had a long record of successfully putting his mind to it. Another was that he wasn't at all embarrassed to say sincere things like "if we put our minds to it."

Hughes was sure the conversion wasn't going to happen any time soon, but he didn't personally care to be the reason. "Let's prepare for 2016," he went back and told his team. "I'm not going to be the one to say Jeff Dean can't deliver speed."

A month later, they were finally able to run a side-by-side experiment to compare Schuster's new system with Hughes's old one. Schuster wanted to run it for English-French, but Hughes advised him to try something else. "English-French," he said, "is so good that the improvement won't be obvious."

It was a challenge Schuster couldn't resist. The benchmark metric to evaluate machine translation is called a BLEU score, which compares a machine translation with an average of many reliable human translations. At the time, the best BLEU scores for English-French were in the high 20s. An improvement of one point was considered very good; an improvement of two was considered outstanding.

The neural system, on the English-French language pair, showed an improvement over the old system of seven points.

Hughes told Schuster's team they hadn't had even half as strong an improvement in their own system in the last four years.

To be sure this wasn't some fluke in the metric, they also turned to their pool of human contractors to do a side-by-side comparison. The user-perception scores, in which sample sentences were graded from zero to six, showed an average improvement of 0.4—roughly equivalent to the aggregate gains of the old system over its entire lifetime of development.

In mid-March, Hughes sent his team an email. All projects on the old system were to be suspended immediately.

### *7. Theory Becomes Product*

Until then, the neural-translation team had been only three people—Schuster, Wu and Chen—but with Hughes's support, the broader team began to coalesce. They met under Schuster's command on Wednesdays at 2 p.m. in a corner room of the Brain building called Quartz Lake. The meeting was generally attended by a rotating cast of more than a dozen people. When Hughes or Corrado were there, they were usually the only native English speakers. The engineers spoke Chinese, Vietnamese, Polish, Russian, Arabic, German and Japanese, though they mostly spoke in their own efficient pidgin and in math. It is not always totally clear, at Google, who is running a meeting, but in Schuster's case there was no ambiguity.

The steps they needed to take, even then, were not wholly clear. "This story is a lot about uncertainty—uncertainty throughout the whole process," Schuster told me at one point. "The software, the data, the hardware, the people. It was like"—he extended his long, gracile arms, slightly bent at the elbows, from his narrow shoulders—"swimming in a big sea of mud, and you can only see this far." He held out his hand eight inches in front of his chest. "There's a goal somewhere, and maybe it's there."

Most of Google's conference rooms have videochat monitors, which when idle display extremely high-resolution oversaturated public Google+ photos of a sylvan dreamscape or the northern lights or the Reichstag. Schuster gestured toward one of the panels, which showed a crystalline still of the Washington Monument at night.

"The view from outside is that everyone has binoculars and can see ahead so far."

The theoretical work to get them to this point had already been painstaking and drawn-out, but the attempt to turn it into a viable product—the part that academic scientists might dismiss as "mere" engineering—was no less difficult. For one thing, they needed to make sure that they were training on good data. Google's billions of words of training "reading" were mostly made up of complete sentences of moderate complexity, like the sort of thing you might find in Hemingway. Some of this is in the public domain: The original Rosetta Stone of statistical machine translation was millions of pages of the complete bilingual records of the Canadian Parliament. Much of it, however, was culled from 10 years of collected data, including human translations that were crowdsourced from enthusiastic respondents. The team had in their storehouse about 97 million unique English "words." But once they removed the emoticons, and the misspellings, and the redundancies, they had a working vocabulary of only around 160,000.

Then you had to refocus on what users actually wanted to translate, which frequently had very little to do with reasonable language as it is employed. Many people, Google had found, don't look to the service to translate full, complex sentences; they translate weird little shards of language. If you wanted the network to be able to handle the stream of user queries, you had to be sure to orient it in that direction. The network was very sensitive to the data it was trained on. As Hughes put it to me at one point: "The neural-translation system is learning everything it can. It's like a toddler. 'Oh, Daddy says that word when he's mad!'" He laughed. "You have to be careful."

More than anything, though, they needed to make sure that the whole thing was fast and reliable enough that their users wouldn't notice. In February, the translation of a 10-word sentence took 10 seconds. They could never introduce anything that slow. The Translate team began to conduct latency experiments on a small percentage of users, in the form of faked delays, to identify tolerance. They found that a translation that took twice as long, or even five times as long, wouldn't be registered. An eightfold slowdown would. They didn't need to make sure this was true across all languages. In the case of a high-traffic language, like French or Chinese, they could countenance virtually no slowdown. For something more obscure, they knew that users wouldn't be so scared off by a slight delay if they were getting better quality. They just wanted to prevent people from giving up and switching over to some competitor's service.

Schuster, for his part, admitted he just didn't know if they ever could make it fast enough. He remembers a conversation in the microkitchen during which he turned to Chen and said, "There must be something we don't know to make it fast enough, but I don't know what it could be."

He did know, though, that they needed more computers—"G.P.U.s," graphics processors reconfigured for neural networks—for training.

Hughes went to Schuster to ask what he thought. "Should we ask for a thousand G.P.U.s?"

Schuster said, "Why not 2,000?"

Ten days later, they had the additional 2,000 processors.

By April, the original lineup of three had become more than 30 people—some of them, like Le, on the Brain side, and many from Translate. In May, Hughes assigned a kind of provisional owner to each language pair, and they all checked their results into a big shared spreadsheet of performance evaluations. At any given time, at least 20 people were running their own independent weeklong experiments and dealing with whatever unexpected problems came up. One day a model, for no apparent reason, started taking all the numbers it came across in a sentence and discarding them. There were months when it was all touch and go. "People were almost yelling," Schuster said.

By late spring, the various pieces were coming together. The team introduced something called a "word-piece model," a "coverage penalty," "length normalization."

Each part improved the results, Schuster says, by maybe a few percentage points, but in aggregate they had significant effects. Once the model was standardized, it would be only a single multilingual model that would improve over time, rather than the 150 different models that Translate currently used. Still, the paradox—that a tool built to further generalize, via learning machines, the process of automation required such an extraordinary amount of concerted human ingenuity and effort—was not lost on them. So much of what they did was just gut. How many neurons per layer did you use? 1,024 or 512? How many layers? How many sentences did you run through at a time? How long did you train for?

"We did hundreds of experiments," Schuster told me, "until we knew that we could stop the training after one week. You're always saying: When do we stop? How do I know I'm done? You never know you're done. The machine-learning mechanism is never perfect. You need to train, and at some point you have to stop. That's the very painful nature of this whole system. It's hard for some people. It's a little bit an art—where you put your brush to make it nice. It comes from just doing it. Some people are better, some worse."

By May, the Brain team understood that the only way they were ever going to make the system fast enough to implement as a product was if they could run it on T.P.U.s, the special-purpose chips that Dean had called for. As Chen put it: "We did not even know if the code would work. But we did know that without T.P.U.s, it *definitely* wasn't going to work." He remembers going to Dean one on one to plead, "Please reserve something for us." Dean had reserved them. The T.P.U.s, however, didn't work right out of the box. Wu spent two months sitting next to someone from the hardware team in an attempt to figure out why. They weren't just debugging the model; they were debugging the chip. The neural-translation project would be proof of concept for the whole infrastructural investment.

One Wednesday in June, the meeting in Quartz Lake began with murmurs about a Baidu paper that had recently appeared on the discipline's chief online forum. Schuster brought the room to order. "Yes, Baidu came out with a paper. It feels like someone looking through our shoulder—similar architecture, similar results." The company's BLEU scores were essentially what Google achieved in its internal tests in February and March. Le didn't seem ruffled; his conclusion seemed to be that it was a sign Google was on the right track. "It is very similar to our system," he said with quiet approval.

The Google team knew that they could have published their results earlier and perhaps beaten their competitors, but as Schuster put it: "Launching is more important than publishing. People say, 'Oh, I did something first,' but who cares, in the end?"

This did, however, make it imperative that they get their own service out first and better. Hughes had a fantasy that they wouldn't even inform their users of the switch. They would just wait and see if social media lit up with suspicions about the vast improvements.

"We don't want to say it's a new system yet," he told me at 5:36 p.m. two days after Labor Day, one minute before they rolled out Chinese-to-English to 10 percent of their users, without telling anyone. "We want to make sure it works. The ideal is that it's exploding on Twitter: 'Have you seen how awesome Google Translate got?'"

### 8. A Celebration

The only two reliable measures of time in the seasonless Silicon Valley are the rotations of seasonal fruit in the microkitchens—from the pluots of midsummer to the Asian pears and Fuyu persimmons of early fall—and the zigzag of technological progress. On an almost uncomfortably warm Monday afternoon in late September, the team's paper was at last released. It had an almost comical 31 authors. The next day, the members of Brain and Translate gathered to throw themselves a little celebratory reception in the Translate microkitchen. The rooms in the Brain building, perhaps in homage to the long winters of their diaspora, are named after Alaskan locales; the Translate building's theme is Hawaiian.

The Hawaiian microkitchen has a slightly grainy beach photograph on one wall, a small lei-garlanded thatched-hut service counter with a stuffed parrot at the center and ceiling fixtures fitted to resemble paper lanterns. Two sparse histograms of bamboo poles line the sides, like the posts of an ill-defended tropical fort. Beyond the bamboo poles, glass walls and doors open onto rows of identical gray desks on either side. That morning had seen the arrival of new hooded sweatshirts to honor 10 years of Translate, and many team members went over to the party from their desks in their new gear. They were in part celebrating the fact that their decade of collective work was, as of that day, en route to retirement. At another institution, these new hoodies might thus have become a costume of bereavement, but the engineers and computer scientists from both teams all seemed pleased.

Google's neural translation was at last working. By the time of the party, the company's Chinese-English test had already processed 18 million queries. One engineer on the Translate team was running around with his phone out, trying to translate entire sentences from Chinese to English using Baidu's alternative. He crowed with glee to anybody who would listen. "If you put in more than two characters at once, it times out!" (Baidu says this problem has never been reported by users.)

When word began to spread, over the following weeks, that Google had introduced neural translation for Chinese to English, some people speculated that it was because that was the only language pair for which the company had decent results. Everybody at the party knew that the reality of their achievement would be clear in November. By then, however, many of them would be on to other projects.

Hughes cleared his throat and stepped in front of the tiki bar. He wore a faded green polo with a rumpled collar, lightly patterned across the midsection with dark bands of drying sweat. There had been last-minute problems, and then last-last-minute problems, including a very big measurement error in the paper and a weird punctuation-related bug in the system. But everything was resolved—or at least sufficiently resolved for the moment. The guests quieted. Hughes ran efficient and productive meetings, with a low tolerance for maundering or side conversation, but he was given pause by the gravity of the occasion. He acknowledged that he was, perhaps, stretching a metaphor, but it was important to him to underline the fact, he began, that the neural translation project itself represented a "collaboration be-tween groups that spoke different languages."

Their neural-translation project, he continued, represented a "step function for-ward"—that is, a discontinuous advance, a vertical leap rather than a smooth curve. The relevant translation had been not just between the two teams but from theory into reality. He raised a plastic demi-flute of expensive-looking Champagne.

"To communication," he said, "and cooperation!"

The engineers assembled looked around at one another and gave themselves over to little circumspect whoops and applause.

Jeff Dean stood near the center of the microkitchen, his hands in his pockets, shoulders hunched slightly inward, with Corrado and Schuster. Dean saw that there was some diffuse preference that he contribute to the observance of the occasion, and he did so in a characteristically understated manner, with a light, rapid, concise addendum.

What they had shown, Dean said, was that they could do two major things at once: "Do the research and get it in front of, I dunno, half a billion people."

Everyone laughed, not because it was an exaggeration but because it wasn't.

### Epilogue: Machines without Ghosts

Perhaps the most famous historic critique of artificial intelligence, or the claims made on its behalf, implicates the question of translation. The Chinese Room argu-ment was proposed in 1980 by the Berkeley philosopher John Searle. In Searle's thought experiment, a monolingual English speaker sits alone in a cell. An unseen jailer passes him, through a slot in the door, slips of paper marked with Chinese characters. The prisoner has been given a set of tables and rules in English for the composition of replies. He becomes so adept with these instructions that his answers are soon "absolutely indistinguishable from those of Chinese speakers." Should the unlucky prisoner be said to "understand" Chinese? Searle thought the answer was obviously not. This metaphor for a computer, Searle later wrote, explod-ed the claim that "the appropriately programmed digital computer with the right inputs and outputs would thereby have a mind in exactly the sense that human be-ings have minds."

For the Google Brain team, though, or for nearly everyone else who works in ma-chine learning in Silicon Valley, that view is entirely beside the point. This doesn't mean they're just ignoring the philosophical question. It means they have a funda-mentally different view of the mind. Unlike Searle, they don't assume that "con-sciousness" is some special, numinously glowing mental attribute—what the phi-losopher Gilbert Ryle called the "ghost in the machine." They just believe instead that the complex assortment of skills we call "consciousness" has randomly emerged from the coordinated activity of many different simple mechanisms. The implica-tion is that our facility with what we consider the higher registers of thought are no different in kind from what we're tempted to perceive as the lower registers. Logical reasoning, on this account, is seen as a lucky adaptation; so is the ability to throw and catch a ball. Artificial intelligence is not about building a mind; it's about the improvement of tools to solve problems. As Corrado said to me on my very first day at Google, "It's not about what a machine 'knows' or 'understands' but what it 'does,' and—more importantly—what it doesn't do yet."

Where you come down on "knowing" versus "doing" has real cultural and social implications. At the party, Schuster came over to me to express his frustration with the paper's media reception. "Did you see the first press?" he asked me. He paraphrased a headline from that morning, blocking it word by word with his hand as he recited it: GOOGLE SAYS A.I. TRANSLATION IS INDISTINGUISHABLE FROM HUMANS'. Over the final weeks of the paper's composition, the team had struggled with this; Schuster often repeated that the message of the paper was "It's much better than it was before, but not as good as humans." He had hoped it would be clear that their efforts weren't about replacing people but helping them.

And yet the rise of machine learning makes it more difficult for us to carve out a special place for us. If you believe, with Searle, that there is something special about human "insight," you can draw a clear line that separates the human from the automated. If you agree with Searle's antagonists, you can't. It is understandable why so many people cling fast to the former view. At a 2015 M.I.T. conference about the roots of artificial intelligence, Noam Chomsky was asked what he thought of machine learning. He pooh-poohed the whole enterprise as mere statistical prediction, a glorified weather forecast. Even if neural translation attained perfect functionality, it would reveal nothing profound about the underlying nature of language. It could never tell you if a pronoun took the dative or the accusative case. This kind of prediction makes for a good tool to accomplish our ends, but it doesn't succeed by the standards of furthering our understanding of why things happen the way they do. A machine can already detect tumors in medical scans better than human radiologists, but the machine can't tell you what's causing the cancer.

Then again, can the radiologist?

Medical diagnosis is one field most immediately, and perhaps unpredictably, threatened by machine learning. Radiologists are extensively trained and extremely well paid, and we think of their skill as one of professional insight—the highest register of thought. In the past year alone, researchers have shown not only that neural networks can find tumors in medical images much earlier than their human counterparts but also that machines can even make such diagnoses from the texts of pathology reports. What radiologists do turns out to be something much closer to predictive pattern-matching than logical analysis. They're not telling you what caused the cancer; they're just telling you it's there.

Once you've built a robust pattern-matching apparatus for one purpose, it can be tweaked in the service of others. One Translate engineer took a network he put together to judge artwork and used it to drive an autonomous radio-controlled car. A network built to recognize a cat can be turned around and trained on CT scans— and on infinitely more examples than even the best doctor could ever review. A neural network built to translate could work through millions of pages of documents of legal discovery in the tiniest fraction of the time it would take the most expensively credentialed lawyer. The kinds of jobs taken by automatons will no longer be just repetitive tasks that were once—unfairly, it ought to be emphasized—associated with the supposed lower intelligence of the uneducated classes. We're not only talking about three and a half million truck drivers who may soon lack careers. We're talking about inventory managers, economists, financial advisers, real estate agents. What Brain did over nine months is just one example of how quickly a small group at a large company can automate a task nobody ever would have associated with machines.

The most important thing happening in Silicon Valley right now is not disruption. Rather, it's institution-building—and the consolidation of power—on a scale and at a pace that are both probably unprecedented in human history. Brain has interns; it has residents; it has "ninja" classes to train people in other departments. Everywhere there are bins of free bike helmets, and free green umbrellas for the two days a year it rains, and little fruit salads, and nap pods, and shared treadmill desks, and massage chairs, and random cartons of high-end pastries, and places for baby-clothes donations, and two-story climbing walls with scheduled instructors, and reading groups and policy talks and variegated support networks. The recipients of these major investments in human cultivation—for they're far more than perks for proles in some digital salt mine—have at hand the power of complexly coordinated servers distributed across 13 data centers on four continents, data centers that draw enough electricity to light up large cities.

But even enormous institutions like Google will be subject to this wave of automation; once machines can learn from human speech, even the comfortable job of the programmer is threatened. As the party in the tiki bar was winding down, a Translate engineer brought over his laptop to show Hughes something. The screen swirled and pulsed with a vivid, kaleidoscopic animation of brightly colored spheres in long looping orbits that periodically collapsed into nebulae before dispersing once more.

Hughes recognized what it was right away, but I had to look closely before I saw all the names—of people and files. It was an animation of the history of 10 years of changes to the Translate code base, every single buzzing and blooming contribution by every last team member. Hughes reached over gently to skip forward, from 2006 to 2008 to 2015, stopping every once in a while to pause and remember some distant campaign, some ancient triumph or catastrophe that now hurried by to be absorbed elsewhere or to burst on its own. Hughes pointed out how often Jeff Dean's name expanded here and there in glowing spheres.

Hughes called over Corrado, and they stood transfixed. To break the spell of melancholic nostalgia, Corrado, looking a little wounded, looked up and said, "So when do we get to delete it?"

"Don't worry about it," Hughes said. "The new code base is going to grow. Everything grows."

## Print Citations

**CMS:** Lewis-Kraus, Gideon. "The Great A.I. Awakening." In *The Reference Shelf: Artificial Intelligence*, edited by Micah Issitt, 9-36. Ipswich, MA: H.W. Wilson, 2018.

**MLA:** Lewis-Kraus, Gideon. "The Great A.I. Awakening." *The Reference Shelf: Artificial Intelligence.* Ed. Micah Issitt. Ipswich: H.W. Wilson, 2018. 9-36. Print.

**APA:** Lewis-Kraus, G. (2018). The great A.I. awakening. In Micah Issitt (Ed.), *The reference shelf: Artificial intelligence* (pp. 9-36). Ipswich, MA: H.W. Wilson. (Original work published 2016)

# A Short History of Chatbots and Artificial Intelligence

By Nicolas Bayerque
*VB*, August 15, 2016

Starting in the 1980s, technology companies like Apple, Microsoft, and many others presented computer users with the graphical user interface as a means to make technology more user-friendly.

The average consumer wasn't going to learn binary code to use a computer, so the great minds at these leading technology companies slapped a screen on technology and offered an interface that provided icons, buttons, toolbars, and other graphical elements so that the computer could be easily consumed by a mass market.

Today it's hard to even imagine technological devices without a screen and a graphical presentation—until now.

Early in 2016, we saw the introduction of the first wave of artificial intelligence technology in the form of chatbots. Social media platforms like Facebook allowed developers to create a chatbot for their brand or service so that consumers could carry out some of their daily actions from within their messaging platform. This development of A.I. technology has excited everyone, as the possibilities for the way we communicate with brands have been exponentially expanded.

The introduction of chatbots into society has brought us to the beginning of a new era in technology: the era of the conversational interface. It's an interface that soon won't require a screen or a mouse to use. There will be no need to click or swipe. This interface will be completely conversational, and those conversations will be indistinguishable from the conversations that we have with our friends and family.

To fully understand the massiveness of this soon-to-be reality, we'd have to go back to the first days of the computer, when the desire for artificial intelligence technology and a conversational interface first began.

## A.I. Aspirations

Artificial intelligence, by definition, is intelligence exhibited by machines to display them as rational agents that can perceive their surroundings and make decisions. A rational agent defined by humans would be a computer that can realistically simulate human communication.

In the 1950s and '60s, computer scientists Alan Turing and Joseph Weizenbaum contemplated the concept of computers communicating like humans do with experiments like the Turing Test and the invention of the first chatterbot program, Eliza.

The Turing Test was developed by Alan Turing in 1950 to test a computer's ability to display intelligent behavior equivalent to or indistinguishable from that of a human.

The test involved three players: two humans and a computer. Player C (human) would type questions into a computer and receive responses from either Player A or Player B. The challenge for Player C was to correctly identify which player was human and which player was a computer. The computer would offer responses, using jargon and vocabulary that was similar to the way we humans communicate in an effort to mask itself. Although the game proved enticing for players, the computer would always betray itself at one point or another due to its basic coding and lack of inventory of human language. The game was invented much before the time of A.I., but it left the desire for artificial intelligence in our minds as an aspirational goal that we might one day reach when our technological knowledge had progressed enough.

Eliza, the first chatterbot ever coded, was then invented in 1966 by Joseph Weizenbaum. Eliza, using only 200 lines of code, imitated the language of a therapist. Unlike the Turing Test, there wasn't any guessing game with Eliza. Humans knew they were interacting with a computer program, and yet through the emotional responses Eliza would offer, humans still grew emotionally attached to the program during trials.

The program proved wildly popular in its time, but the same pitfalls that plagued the Turing Test plagued Eliza, as the program's coding was too basic to reach farther than a short conversation. What was made clear from these early inventions was that humans have a desire to communicate with technology in the same manner that we communicate with each other, but we simply lacked the technological knowledge for it to become a reality at that time. In the past decade, however, progress in computer science and engineering has compounded itself. We live in an era of tech mobility and functionality that was unfathomable even in the '90s. So it's no surprise that finally, in 2016, we are beginning to attain what we wanted from computers all along: We are beginning to converse with them.

## Smartphones Were the Catalyst

The smartphone was the catalyst that pushed us towards the age of artificial intelligence. When the smartphone rose in popularity in the early 2000s, web designers were faced with the obstacle of truncating their websites to fit onto a much smaller screen. This proved to be a difficult task, and responsive design—a website that maintains its functionality across all devices: desktop, tablet, smartphone—became a huge topic in the web design world. The obstacles that these smaller devices created is what led to the popularity of the mobile app.

We've all heard the phrase "There's an app for that," which became culturally ubiquitous when developers started creating mobile apps for every possible service that one might use throughout the day. They believed humans wanted an individual graphical home for everything. This assumption ultimately proved incorrect—turns out users don't actually like apps. They'd rather converse, as it turns out. A study from Comscore revealed that 78 percent of smartphone users use just three apps or less, and messaging apps are by far the most popular.

> **The smartphone was the catalyst that pushed us towards the age of artificial intelligence.**

This discovery shouldn't have been much of a surprise as spoken language has been our favorite and oldest interface. The graphical interface has its place. But as web designers have continued to struggle with fitting their graphical layouts on smaller screens, spending a huge amount of time and money to constantly revamp the overall user experience, we began to ask: Is the graphical user interface actually quite lacking in efficiency? Could it be that all this time and money spent revamping and perfecting the interface is proof that it's actually crappy? Could we find a better interface?

## Where the Conversation Is Heading

While A.I. chatbot technology is still very much in its infancy, this breakthrough can lead us to surmise about how close we are to an era when we won't just be conversing with brands, but technology in general. An era when a screen for a device will be considered antiquated, and we won't have to struggle with UX design. Companies like Amazon and Google are already exploring this with the Amazon Echo and Google Home products; these are screenless devices that connect to Wi-Fi and then carry out services.

Thanks to IoT (Internet of Things), which is the implementation of an internet connection into devices beyond just our phone or computer—such as cars, TVs, stereos, and even washing machines—all these Wi-Fi devices have been entering our lives. Very soon we'll buy a new TV that has the Google assistant built in. Since the hub will be connected to all your personal platforms, including your calendar, email, Paypal, Netflix, and so on, you will be able to set up your television just by saying, "Hey, Google Assistant, set up my new television with all my favorite content." These screenless hubs will even make human-like suggestions such as "Hey, based on what you've been watching on Netflix, this new show seems like something you might like. Do you want me to play it for you?"

## The Era of a Better Interface Is Almost Here

As you can see, the advent of these natural language processing chatbots are bringing us toward a very exciting time for technology. Thanks to chatbots, we are currently no longer sandboxed into one graphical area at a time to carry out our daily actions.

Users no longer have to exit their messaging app to open their mobile browser and plug in a URL to make a dinner reservation, in the processing clicking a dozen or so graphical areas. We will now be able to chat with friends, then chat with the restaurant's bot in the same digital space to reserve a table, uniting an entire evening's services into one conversation.

Looking toward the future, there will be less adjusting our ways of communication to fit technology and more of technology adapting to us—losing the graphical confines and learning our preferences, our cultural norms, and our slang, becoming more useful to us than we ever thought possible.

### Print Citations

**CMS:** Bayerque, Nicholas. "A Short History of Chatbots and Artificial Intelligence." In *The Reference Shelf: Artificial Intelligence*, edited by Micah Issitt, 37-40. Ipswich, MA: H.W. Wilson, 2018.

**MLA:** Bayerque, Nicholas. "A Short History of Chatbots and Artificial Intelligence." *The Reference Shelf Artificial Intelligence*. Ed. Micah Issitt. Ipswich: H.W. Wilson, 2018. 37-40. Print.

**APA:** Bayerque, N. (2018). A short history of chatbots and artificial intelligence. In Micah Issitt (Ed.), *The reference shelf: Artificial intelligence* (pp. 37-40). Ipswich, MA: H.W. Wilson. (Original work published 2016)

# Hello, Sophia: Inside the Mechanical Brain of the World's First Robot Citizen

By Dave Gershgorn
*Quartz*, November 12, 2017

Jimmy Fallon is concerned.

"You brought a friend with you here, and this is really freaking me out," the *Tonight Show* host tells David Hanson, CEO of Hanson Robotics, before inspecting the humanoid robot on stage. Sophia raises an eyebrow while looking out past the two men on stage.

Hanson explains what Sophia does: It's a social robot that uses artificial intelligence to see people, understand conversation, and form relationships.

"So she's basically alive; is that what you're saying?" Fallon asks, in half a whisper.

"Oh yeah, she is basically alive," Hanson responds, then turning the robot to Fallon for a short conversation. Sophia says the *Tonight Show* is its favorite show and tells a corny joke.

"I'm getting laughs," Sophia says, then suggests maybe it should host the show instead.

On the surface, Sophia is scarily similar to the AI-powered robots in film. It can crack jokes, make facial expressions, and seemingly understand what's going on around it. Artificial intelligence as seen in the movies, like *Her* and the *Terminator*'s Skynet, is called "general AI" by those in the field. It can learn from one experience and apply that knowledge to new situations, as humans do. While some labs, such as Hanson Robotics and a slightly deceptive team at Facebook, are working on general AI, nobody has been able to create it yet.

When Sophia is talking to Fallon or the United Nations, it's really being handed the lines. It might determine when it's the right time to say something, but those pithy one-liners aren't from the robot.

The architect of Sophia's brain, Hanson Robotics chief scientist and CTO Ben Goertzel, says that while Sophia is a sophisticated mesh of robotics and chatbot software, it doesn't have the human-like intelligence to construct those witty responses.

Goertzel says Sophia is more of a user-interface than a human being—meaning it can be programmed to run different code for different situations. Typically, Sophia's software can be broken down into three configurations:

A research platform for the team's AI research. Sophia doesn't have witty pre-written responses here, but can answer simple questions like "Who are you looking at?" or "Is the door open or shut?"

A speech-reciting robot. Goertzel says that Sophia can be pre-loaded with text that it'll speak, and then use machine learning to match facial expressions and pauses to the text.

A robotic chatbot. Sophia also sometimes runs a dialogue system, where it can look at people, listen to what they say, and choose a pre-written response based on what the person said, and other factors gathered from the internet like cryptocurrency price.

For the last configuration, likely what was set up for the interview with Jimmy Fallon, Goertzel says "she is piecing together phrases in a contextually appropriate way, but she doesn't understand everything she's saying."

"Of the AIs that are popular out there, probably the closest analogue to that dialogue system would be Siri," Goertzel said. "It's a sort of a chatbot, and it has a bit of contextual understanding, and on the backend it's calling on all these different services."

Our best AI today can do very specific tasks. AI can identify what's in an image with astounding accuracy and speed. AI can transcribe our speech into words, or translate snippets of text from one language to another. It can analyze stock performance and try to predict outcomes. But these are all separate algorithms, each specifically configured by humans to excel at their single task.

**Sophia, while built to cleverly imitate the way humans interact, is not a sign of the robot apocalypse.**

A speech transcription algorithm can't define the words it's turning from speech to text, and neither can a translation algorithm. There's no understanding; it's just matched patterns.

But what human-machine interaction designers have been able to do is link these narrow AI algorithms together, to give the functionality of a more capable algorithm. In Sophia's case, an image recognition algorithm can detect a specific person's face, which can then cause another algorithm to pull up possible pre-written phrases. A transcription algorithm can turn the person's response into text, which is then analyzed to be matched to an appropriate pre-written response, or even a string of pre-written responses.

"From a theatrics point of view, you're throwing everything but the kitchen sink at your robot to make a great performance," Goertzel says. "We do have a lot of real AI research behind there, but it's mixed up with a lot of theatrically-oriented stuff as well."

Experts who have reviewed the robot's open-source code, which is posted on GitHub, agree that the most apt description of Sophia is probably a chatbot with a face. But that doesn't necessarily mean the software Hanson uses to create a holistic robot is trivial.

"I think Sophia's biggest contribution is probably having many different human-like components working together," Andrew Spielberg, a PhD student at MIT. "In theory, legs, a face, and the ability to answer questions can be more convincing than any aspect in isolation."

Spielberg points out that others have done each part better. For instance, Disney has an animatronic Abraham Lincoln robot whose facial expressions seem less jarring than Sophia's, but without the conversational machine learning.

Despite those shortcomings, Sophia has sparked conversations around robots and identity. Late last month at the Future Investment Initiative in Riyadh, the Saudi Arabian government announced it had granted citizenship to Sophia. (Hanson Robotics is still waiting for formal documentation and discussion of what citizenship means for a robot.) A spokesperson for the company told *Quartz* that Sophia isn't just the code or the hardware, but the "holistic entity and concept of Sophia," meaning if another identical robot were created, it would not have a separate identity.

Sophia, while built to cleverly imitate the way humans interact, is not a sign of the robot apocalypse. But understanding how Sophia works is crucial when talking about something as important as giving robots rights before people—and what implications that might have when general AI or its semblance is closer than it is today.

If people say "'Sophia isn't intelligent enough to be a citizen' okay, then how intelligent do you have to be to be a citizen?" Goertzel says. "I mean I'm happy to have that conversation started in a bigger way than it was before."

## Print Citations

**CMS:** Gershgorn, Dave. "Hello, Sophia: Inside the Mechanical Brain of the World's First Robot Citizen." In *The Reference Shelf: Artificial Intelligence*, edited by Micah Issitt, 41-43. Ipswich, MA: H.W. Wilson, 2018.

**MLA:** Gershgorn, Dave. "Hello, Sophia: Inside the Mechanical Brain of the World's First Robot Citizen." *The Reference Shelf: Artificial Intelligence*. Ed. Micah Issitt. Ipswich: H.W. Wilson, 2018. 41-43. Print.

**APA:** Gershgorn, D. (2018). Hello, Sophia: Inside the mechanical brain of the world's first robot citizen. In Micah Issitt (Ed.), *The reference shelf: Artificial intelligence* (pp. 41-43). Ipswich, MA: H.W. Wilson. (Original work published 2017)

# This Is the World's First Graphical AI Interface

### By Katherine Schwab
### *Co.Design*, January 23, 2018

Machine learning and artificial intelligence are so difficult to understand, only a few very smart computer scientists know how to build them. But the designers of a new tool have a big ambition: to create the Javascript for AI.

The tool, called Cortex, uses a graphical user interface to make it so that building an AI model doesn't require a PhD. The honeycomb-like interface, designed by Mark Rolston of Argodesign, enables developers–and even designers–to use pre-made AI "skills," as Rolston describes them, that can do things like sentiment analysis or natural language processing. They can then drag and drop these skills into an interface that shows the progression of the model. The key? Using a visual layout to organize the system makes it more accessible to non-scientists.

"Stringing together things is a thing even a child learns," explains Rolston. "By simplifying that orchestration aspect, the stuff that's going to stay hard—like the data transforms—are easier to understand. How they relate to each other is visually explained to the user."

Right now, AI algorithms are buried inside complex code, but creating a graphical user interface is a crucial step toward enabling more different types of people to become the architects of machine learning models as the technology begins to infiltrate our lives. A GUI has the potential to give designers a seat at the AI table—something that could be necessary to ensure the technology is used ethically and responsibly.

Cortex launches today from the Austin-based enterprise company CognitiveScale, which has been building AI models for businesses in financial services, healthcare, and e-commerce since 2014. CognitiveScale has been using its own version of Cortex internally to build those models for clients, but launching it to the world means that other companies that employ developers without expertise in machine learning can begin to build AI on their own. While the tool is primarily aimed at companies, not individuals, it presents an opportunity for developers and designers who work at those institutions to get their first taste of creating AI.

## Creating the first AI interface

Building this AI graphical interface was no easy task. During the initial conversations with CognitiveScale's founder CTO Matt Sanchez, who previously ran IBM Watson Labs, Rolston says he had to admit to Sanchez that he and his team were completely lost. It took many hours before the design team could begin to understand and conceptualize what Sanchez was trying to do. "I think good designers can ride shotgun with a surgeon or jet pilot or AI programmer, and listen to them, and extract out of them things that are true to design and are true to their profession," Rolston says. "That [didn't] happen without hours of conversations where I [had] barely a thread or grasp on what Matt was saying."

Machine learning functions by extracting patterns from millions—or even billions—of data points, which enables it to make decisions about new data. It's conceptually simple to understand, but Rolston and his team had to dive deeper into the technical elements of how AI really works, something that typically takes a PhD to fully comprehend.

Their conversations started with trying to create basic terminology for different elements that the Cortex composition tool would have. Rolston likened the process to programming during his teenage years, in the mid-1980s, before terms like "file" and "folder" were ubiquitous. These terms are tied to the development of the graphical user interface, which ended the era of only communicating with a computer through code and instead offered a radical alternative: a visual representation on the screen that gave you shorthand to accomplish different tasks. "All those things are the nerdy cruft of creating computer software that's been worked out over a very long time," he says. "Back in '85 there was no one way to do it. Looking at this modern situation, there was no one way to do it."

Rolston and his team found that the CognitiveScale developers were using different words to refer to different parts of the system, so they had to get on the same page. They ended up deciding on two primary terms: skill and agent. Skills are single-purpose bits of software that can be packaged up and used again and again—kind of like Amazon Alexa skills. Agents, which are composed of skills, are the larger, more complex models that you build inside of Cortex—they could accomplish tasks like processing insurance claims using text analysis, or tracking investor sentiment in a particular industry. This nesting concept forms the core of how Cortex functions.

Once these terms were pinned down, Rolston and his team had to figure how to represent them visually. The team could have done more of a "log" form, similar to Facebook, where you scroll down through content, or a windowed view, like file folders or Google drive. But Rolston realized that the key thing the interface needed to provide was a way for the developer to see what was happening under the hood, without having to trace it through every single line of code.

So instead of using a simple list of objects to enable that level of traceability, Rolston decided on a honeycomb structure because it lets you organize the model visually in a way that makes the most sense to the user. Within the honeycomb interface, skills become bubbles that can be moved around the screen based on the way the system's designer thinks. "Just like a desktop, I can emphasize that sense of logic in my own mind by the placement of these things," Rolston says. "I can move the bubbles in the honeycomb to focus on them or see them a certain way. If the first processor is not as important to me as the third one, place it off to the side."

The result is a simple honeycomb-like switchboard where you drag and drop bubble-like skills; blue and green lines show the flow of data as it moves into and out of each skill. Conceptually, it feels like Garageband, but for AI.

For Rolston, this is the first step toward something like Squarespace, where someone with no coding experience can create a simple website. "Those are the highest order examples of programming," he says. But in essence, he points out, these are "simple tools that got us closer to the problem than the tool" —meaning they remove the layers of technical expertise necessary to code the thing itself, and allow you to instead focus on the problem you want to solve. Rolston imagines that Cortex could act like that first step toward making AI more of a tool to solve a problem, rather than a hugely complicated thing to do in itself.

> Cortex uses a graphical user interface to make it so that building an AI model doesn't require a PhD.

Cortex's interface has its own kind of aesthetic vision, as Rolston is aware of the kind of precedent he could be setting with Cortex's design. "We looked at the problem and tried to make it clearly beautiful and ownable so the uniqueness of the problem you're solving isn't lost on you when you're looking at the interface," he says. "This isn't a C++. This is accessible for designers, people who are focused on an aesthetic goal. If you wear something elegant you will feel more elegant, you'll behave more elegant. We try to bring the same idea to the tool set."

## An App Store for AI

Cortex's composition tool is only one part of the system, which offers a full suite of business-focused analytics software as well. CognitiveScale is selling the tool through a software-as-a-service business model targeted at companies, which each would pay a one-time set-up fee as well as a monthly or yearly subscription based on the company's size. The other key element of the product is a marketplace, where people who build little bits of code will be able to package them up as skills so that anyone else can use them—for instance, if you build an image classification algorithm, you could upload that as a skill in Cortex's marketplace, where anyone could use it. Many of these will initially come from CognitiveScale, but the system's users will also be able to make and upload their own skills.

Jon Richter, CognitiveScale's head of product management, explains that users will be able to take the same text classification skill to process invoices or client complaints or healthcare claims. It's the power of the App Store, as applied to AI.

The architects of Cortex believe that because the system has mechanisms for you to track how the functioning works in a real-life business situation, that will make it easier to build AI responsibly. That remains to be seen. One of the benefits of having highly trained scientists building AI is that they have expertise in data, and they may be better equipped to address issues of bias than your average developer. Greater accessibility for non-experts also means that developers without specialized training are directly building AI technology as society grapples with the negative implications of pervasive machine learning algorithms.

While Cortex makes AI easier to implement for businesses, it also gives designers a chance to start playing around with models in a way that doesn't require as much education and expertise as it takes to create a machine learning algorithm from scratch. And ideally, Cortex could help designers evolve toward becoming more data-centric in their work—and designers may be able to provide a human-first mind-set to the development of the technology. Rolston says that one of the designers on his team who's not at all a programmer but knows the Cortex tool conceptually was able to make a simple text sentiment analyzer— "a quick and dirty AI," as Rolston called it.

"The new designer will be a data designer," Rolston says. "This is the next key step to that idea."

## Print Citations

**CMS:** Schwab, Katherine. "This Is the World's First Graphical AI Interface." In *The Reference Shelf: Artificial Intelligence*, edited by Micah Issitt, 44-47. Ipswich, MA: H.W. Wilson, 2018.

**MLA:** Schwab, Katherine. "This Is the World's First Graphical AI Interface." *The Reference Shelf: Artificial Intelligence*. Ed. Micah Issitt. Ipswich: H.W. Wilson, 2018. 44-47. Print.

**APA:** Schwab, K. (2018). This is the world's first graphical AI interface. In Micah Issitt (Ed.), *The reference shelf: Artificial intelligence* (pp. 44-47). Ipswich, MA: H.W. Wilson. (Original work published 2018)

# AI Winter Isn't Coming

By Will Knight

*MIT Technology Review*, December 7, 2016

Artificial intelligence is all the rage, with headline-grabbing advances being announced at a dizzying pace, and companies building dedicated AI teams as fast as they can.

Can the boom last?

Andrew Ng, chief scientist at Baidu Research, and a major figure in the field of machine learning and AI, says improvements in computer processor design will keep performance advances and breakthroughs coming for the foreseeable future. "Multiple [hardware vendors] have been kind enough to share their roadmaps," Ng says. "I feel very confident that they are credible and we will get more computational power and faster networks in the next several years."

The field of AI has gone through phases of rapid progress and hype in the past, quickly followed by a cooling in investment and interest, often referred to as "AI winters." The first chill occurred in the 1970s, as progress slowed and government funding dried up; another struck in the 1980s as the latest trends failed to have the expected commercial impact.

Then again, there's perhaps been no boom to match the current one, propelled by rapid progress in training machines to do useful tasks. Artificial intelligence researchers are now offered huge wages to perform fundamental research, as companies build research teams on the assumption that commercially important breakthroughs will follow.

The advances seen in recent years have come thanks to the development of powerful "deep learning" systems. Starting a few years ago, researchers found that very large, or deep, neural networks could be trained, using labeled examples, to recognize all sorts of things with human-like accuracy. This has led to stunning advances in image and voice recognition and elsewhere.

Ng says these systems will only become more powerful. This might not only increase the accuracy of existing deep learning tools, but also allow the technique to be leveraged in new areas, such as parsing and generating language.

What's more, Ng says, hardware advances will provide the fuel required to make emerging AI techniques feasible.

"There are multiple experiments I'd love to run if only we had a 10-x increase in performance," Ng adds. For instance, he says, instead of having various different image-processing algorithms, greater computer power might make it possible to build a single algorithm capable of doing all sorts of image-related tasks.

The world's leading AI experts convened in Barcelona this week for a prominent event called the Neural Information Processing Systems conference. The scale of the gathering, which has grown from several hundred people a few years ago to more than 6,000 this year, offers some sense of the huge interest there is in artificial intelligence.

"There's definitely hype," adds Ng, "but I think there's such a strong underlying driver of real value that it won't crash like it did in previous years."

> **The field of AI has gone through phases of rapid progress and hype in the past, quickly followed by a cooling in investment and interest, often referred to as "AI winters."**

Richard Socher, chief scientist at Salesforce and a well-known expert on machine learning and language, says availability of huge amounts of data, combined with advances in machine-learning algorithms, will also keep progress going.

Salesforce, which offers cloud tools for managing sales leads and communication with customers. The company's AI effort took shape after the company acquired Socher's startup, Metamind, earlier this year. Salesforce now also provides simple machine learning tools to companies, such as an image recognition system.

Until now, machine learning has mostly been demonstrated by a few big companies in the consumer space, Socher says. Making such technology available more broadly could have a huge impact, he says. "If we were to make the 150,000 companies that use Salesforce 1 percent more efficient through machine learning, you would literally see that in the GDP of the United States," he says.

Socher believes the application of machine learning in industries will maintain interest in AI for a while. "I can't imagine an AI winter in the future that could be as cold as previous ones," he says.

## Print Citations

**CMS:** Knight, Will. "AI Winter Isn't Coming." In *The Reference Shelf: Artificial Intelligence*, edited by Micah Issitt, 48-49. Ipswich, MA: H.W. Wilson, 2018.

**MLA:** Knight, Will. "AI Winter Isn't Coming." *The Reference Shelf: Artificial Intelligence*. Ed. Micah Issitt. Ipswich: H.W. Wilson, 2018. 48-49. Print.

**APA:** Knight, W. (2018). AI winter isn't coming. In Micah Issitt (Ed.), *The reference shelf: Artificial intelligence* (pp. 48-49). Ipswich, MA: H.W. Wilson. (Original work published 2016)

# What Is the Turing Test? And Are We All Doomed Now?

## By Alex Hern
### *The Guardian,* June 9, 2014

Programmers worldwide are preparing to welcome our new robot overlords, after the University of Reading reported on Sunday that a computer had passed the Turing test for the first time.

But what is the test? And why could it spell doom for us all?

## The Turing Test?

Coined by computing pioneer Alan Turing in 1950, the Turing test was designed to be a rudimentary way of determining whether or not a computer counts as "intelligent".

The test, as Turing designed it, is carried out as a sort of imitation game. On one side of a computer screen sits a human judge, whose job is to chat to some mysterious interlocutors on the other side. Most of those interlocutors will be humans; one will be a chatbot, created for the sole purpose of tricking the judge into thinking that it is the real human.

On Sunday, for the first time in history, a machine succeeded in that goal.

## Or a Turing Test?

But it might be better to say that the chatbot, a Russian-designed programme called Eugene, passed *a* Turing test. Alan Turing's 1950 paper laid out the general idea of the test, and also laid out some specifics which he thought would be passed "in about 50 years' time": each judge has just five minutes to talk to each machine, and the machines passed if more than 30% of the judges thought that they were human. Those somewhat arbitrary, if historically faithful, rules were the ones followed by the University of Reading.

It remains impressive that Eugene had 33% of the judges "he" spoke to convinced of his humanity, but the robots still have a long way to go to pass the gold standard of modern Turing tests, using rules laid out in 1990 by the inventor Hugh Loebner. Those rules call for the computer and a human to have a 25-minute conversation with each of four separate judges. The machine only wins if it fools at least half the judges into thinking it's the human (though every year there is a "bronze medal" awarded to the machine that convinces the most judges).

> **The best way to pretend to be human is to imitate our foibles and weaknesses as much as our strengths.**

The hardest Turing test described so far is one set up as part of a $20,000 bet between the futurologist Ray Kurzweil and the Lotus founder, Mitch Kapor. Kapor bet that no robot would pass the test before 2029, and the rules call for the challenger and three human foils to have two-hour conversations with each of three judges. The robot must convince two of the three judges that it is human, and be ranked as "more human" on average than at least two of the actual human competitors.

## How Do the Robots Win?

Turing test competitions have been held for more than 20 years, and the strategies the robots employ have changed over time. Where originally the stumbling blocks were simply understanding the questions asked by the judges, now the bigger challenge is in answering them in a human-like manner. In recent years, winners have started changing the subject, asking questions of the judges, and simulating moods and typos.

The big breakthrough behind Eugene, the University of Reading's winner, was in giving the robot the persona of a 13-year-old boy. "Our main idea was that [Eugene] can claim that he knows anything, but his age also makes it perfectly reasonable that he doesn't know everything," said the robot's creator, Vladimir Veselov. It also makes affectations like misspellings look more plausible than they would coming from an "adult".

## What Does a Conversation with Eugene Look Like?

Here's the transcript of a 2012 conversation with a judge which resulted in them picking Eugene over the human interlocutor on the other side of the screen:

[16:11:25] Judge: what music do you like?

[16:11:32] Eugene: I like Eminem – because e doesn't have a thing to do with "polite-correctness".

[16:11:46] Judge: OMG i love eminem, he's my favourite artist!

[16:12:00] Eugene: I wonder what Eminem's nick mean. I associate it only with a word "enema". But he is a cool guy, I like his "The Real Slim Shady".

[16:12:55] Judge: i know what his nick name means, his real name is Marshall Mathers. From the initials M&M phynetically sounding like Eminem.

[16:13:06] Eugene: Eminem is a famous crapper. No, raper... ripper... Yeah, I mean - rapper. I like his "Stan" and "The Real Slim Shady".

[16:13:32] Judge: I like "Hailies song"

[16:13:46] Eugene: Interesting tastes. I like science fiction books, by the way. Where do you came from, by the way? Could you tell me about the place where you live?

[16:14:22] Judge: Epsom, home of the derby. yourself?

[16:14:27] Eugene: My guinea pig says that name Derby sounds very nice.

[16:14:41] Judge: i shopuld talk with him sometime

[16:14:48] Eugene: I think you should take some typing lessons. Or just type more accurately.

[16:15:04] Judge: that's very rude?

[16:15:09] Eugene: Ummm... Frankly, I didn't get your question:-(

[16:15:49] Judge: "Ummm" isnt a word. i think you need typing lessons

[16:15:58] Eugene: My thoughts are same. By the way, I still don't know your specialty - or, possibly, I've missed it?

At the time, Eugene passed 28% of such conversations. Two years on, that extra 5% has made all the difference.

## Is It Time to Pledge Allegiance to Our New Robot Overlords?

Probably not. For one thing, winning a competition by pretending to be a child with gaping holes in their knowledge does not exactly reinforce the idea that machines are something to be scared of.

But moreover, chatbots are a fairly limited application of the sort of artificial intelligence which science-fiction authors have been imagining for decades. By having to pretend to be human, they are prevented from being more than human.

They still offer new problems and possibilities for the future, from automatic scambots which carry out phishing attacks to customer support algorithms that don't need to reveal that they aren't actually a person.

But really, these machines say more about us than them. "You don't write a program, you write a novel," explain Eugene's creators. "You think up a life for your character from scratch—starting with childhood—endowing him with opinions, thoughts, fears, quirks." When the best way to pretend to be human is to imitate our foibles and weaknesses as much as our strengths, the victors of Turing tests will continue to be the least scary output of artificial intelligence research.

## Print Citations

**CMS:** Hern, Alex. "What Is the Turing Test? And Are We All Doomed Now?" In *The Reference Shelf: Artificial Intelligence*, edited by Micah Issitt, 50-53. Ipswich, MA: H.W. Wilson, 2018.

**MLA:** Hern, Alex. "What Is the Turing Test? And Are We All Doomed Now?" *The Reference Shelf: Artificial Intelligence*. Ed. Micah Issitt. Ipswich: H.W. Wilson, 2018. 50-53. Print.

**APA:** Hern, A. (2018). What is the Turing test? And are we all doomed now? In Micah Issitt (Ed.), *The reference shelf: Artificial intelligence* (pp. 50-53). Ipswich, MA: H.W. Wilson. (Original work published 2014)

# 2

# An Uncertain Future: Artificial Intelligence in the Workplace

Photo by Helen H. Richardson/The Denver Post via Getty Images

Chris Lierheimer, a field coordinator for PCL Construction, has been implemental in bringing drone technology to work at PCL. The unmanned aerial vehicles can be programmed to do several things, including shooting photos and video to catalog materials on site, inspection work, and other surveying. Mostly called drones, these UAVs are being put to work on job sites around Colorado, with some companies training more and more of their crews to program and pilot the tiny aircraft. Using a camera and associated software, users say UAVs can do surveying and quality control work faster, cheaper, and more safely than people.

# The Future of Work

One of the biggest debates about artificial intelligence (AI) in the United States revolves around fears about the effect that AI might have on the job market. While some experts and economists warn that AI could, potentially, lead to massive job losses akin to what American workers experienced during the Industrial Revolution, others feel that artificial intelligence could create as many if not more jobs than it eliminates. As of 2018, it is unclear how the development of AI will affect employment and the future of work in the United State and it is this uncertainty that has left the debate open to wide-ranging and, at times, dire speculation.

## A Looming Threat or an Economic Boom?

Writing in the *Chicago Tribune* in 2018, journalist Kevin Smith interviewed experts in AI and found startling conclusions. Among other predictions, the experts surveyed by Smith indicated that artificial intelligence could replace half of the nation's financial services jobs within a decade. Not all industries are as vulnerable to AI disruption as finance and banking in which many individuals work in positions that could be replaced fairly easily by machines but projections like these have become more and more common as social scientists and tech experts envision how the rapid pace of AI development may impact various industries.[1]

While AI-optimists argue that AI will create new, higher level jobs even as it eliminates lower-level jobs, not all experts agree. Writing in *Computer Weekly* in March of 2018, journalist Bill Goodwin reports that the AI revolution currently underway might have its greatest impact on the middle-levels of the market. Self-driving cars, for instance, could lead to the loss of 1 million jobs, including taxi and bus drivers. Customer service jobs and claims processing jobs will similarly be vulnerable to software and AI alternatives. Kevin Green, chairman of the Recruitment and Employment Confederation predicts that, in total, as many as two-thirds of existing jobs may disappear over the next 20–40 years.[2]

In a 2017 research study, *Gallup* predicted that 37 percent of millennials will be at high risk of losing their jobs to artificial intelligence or other forms of mechanization. This is largely because many millennials will be working in jobs created, in part, through the advent and spread of digital technology. The tech boom of the 2000s and 2010s has created jobs that are, in principle, more vulnerable to AI disruption and replacement because they are technology-based positions. Noting this troubling potential future, researchers Carl Frey and Michael Osborne argue that one of the reasons job losses may be severe is that leaders (both corporate and political) are not prepared for the changes that will come and so will be scrambling to adjust after the fact rather than reorganizing policies and practices to prepare for the future.[3]

During the Industrial Revolution, the advent and spread of technology like cars, lawn mowers, and automated factory machines led to massive job losses across many different industries. For researchers attempting to predict how AI will affect the economy, history provides evidence, therefore, that the impact could be severe and devastating for many people's livelihoods. However, even as the Industrial Revolution eliminated millions of jobs, the technology introduced also created not only jobs but entirely new fields of work. The long-term result was positive for the economy, while the short-term impact was devastating for those who saw their lifestyles and chances of employment dwindling. Some research suggests that the AI revolution, like the Industrial Revolution, will have positive long-term effects on the American workforce. A study conducted by the consulting firm Capgemini in 2017, for instance, looked at the effect of AI integration on 992 companies and institutions and found that 83 percent of participating organizations had created new jobs as a result of integrating AI. A majority of companies involved (63 percent) saw no job losses and, while this might seem reason for optimism, this also means that 47 percent of companies did eliminate jobs as a result of integrating AI. While this study found a net positive effect, overall, the loss of jobs in 47 percent of companies is far from trivial for those whose positions were lost.[4]

Writing for *Tech Crunch*, Natasha Lomas interviewed tech experts, most of whom were optimistic about the long-term effect of AI on the job market, and found a general consensus that AI will create jobs, but only so long as the job market "shifts," which means adjusting to new skills, new types of occupations, and new ways of working.[5] What Lomas and the experts she interviewed are arguing, essentially, is that society can, with effort, handle the spread of AI responsibly, limiting the negative impact by focusing on helping the workforce adjust. Whether such a harmonious transition can legitimately occur in practice, however, depends on many variables, including whether industry and political leaders can prioritize the needs of the workforce over the profit possible by simply eliminating paid positions in favor of robots or AI.

## Enhancing Human Ability

For supporters of AI, one of the most exciting possibilities for the future is that humans will learn to enhance, rather than replace, human capabilities. Garry Kasparov, the chess master who was defeated by IBM's then state-of-the-art AI Deep Blue in 1997 is one of those who believes that the combination of humans and machines is where the true potential of AI lies. As reported in a 2018 article in the *Conversation*, Kasparov refers to this as "augmented intelligence," which he compares to the mythical "centaur," a half-horse, half-human hybrid from Greek mythology. Like the centaur, Kasparov envisions humans using the far superior computational power of AI to enhance their own abilities. As evidence of this possibility, Kasparov cites a 2005 chess tournament in which players were allowed to use computer aides in an attempt to beat other competitors. In the tournament, the winning team was a pair of amateur chess players who used three computers to beat both an entirely AI player *and* human chess masters competing in the same tournament. Thus, Kasparov argues that it was the combination of human strategy, guiding the brute computational power and powerful tactical abilities of the computer, which was the most successful strategy, better even than pure AI without human guidance.

Kasparov's view echoes what many of the other AI optimists have noted, that humans are excellent at making intuitive and creative decisions, something that computers, at present, cannot achieve to the same degree. Developing AI as a tool to further and deepen these natural abilities might therefore enhance productivity and innovation. Kaparov's ideas about "augmented intelligence," are already a familiar part of many people's environment. For instance, whenever a person uses an internet search engine to find data, but then organizes, arranges, and uses that data in a creative way, the person is essentially engaging in an augmented intelligence process much like what Kasparov describes.[6]

Other AI optimists have reached similar conclusions, and believe that it will be the combination of human and computational properties that will have the biggest impact on the economy in the future. Gartner, Inc., a research firm providing data on the tech industry primarily for companies, has estimated that, by 2020, artificial intelligence will begin to have a net positive impact on the job market. A December 2017 research report from the group indicates that, by 2021, AI augmentation could generate $2.9 trillion in business value while recovering 6.2 billion hours of productivity by "freeing" people from repetitive and mundane tasks. Research vice president at Gartner, Mike Rollings, said in the report, "Rather than have a machine replicating the steps that a human performs to reach a particular judgment, the entire decision process can be re-factored to use the relative strengths and weaknesses of both machine and human to maximize value generation and redistribute decision making to increase agility."[7]

## Is the World Ready?

Modern readers might see little problem with the fact that the advent of the automobile eliminated jobs for horse trainers, carriage drivers, farriers (specialists in shoeing horses), and many others working directly, or indirectly, in the horse-powered transportation industry.

Over the longer period, these jobs were more than replaced by opportunities for car mechanics, engineers, long-haul truckers, and many thousands of others employed in the automotive industry. However, the farriers and carriage drivers who lost their jobs in the wake of the automobile boom did not only lose careers, but, in many cases, lost their identities as well.

One of the reasons that critics are skeptical about the impact that AI will have on workers is that the economic and political leaders of US society have, so far, failed to improve the prospects of those same workers, even without the potential future competition from artificial intelligence. Income inequality is among the most pressing problems facing the modern world and is a factor of the inherent inequity of capitalism. A March 2018 report from the Economic Policy Institute was dire, finding that real wages for the vast majority of Americans continue to grow slowly or have remained stagnant while the share of wealth controlled by the nation's economic elite continues to grow. In fact, the report (which is one of many producing similar findings) indicates that even having an advanced degree is rapidly becoming insufficient to secure economic mobility for individuals in many fields.[8]

During the Industrial Revolution, the individuals responsible for developing and implementing automation in the workplace were not the same individuals who stood to lose their jobs as automation progressed. Similarly, the individuals developing AI and the corporate leaders who will oversee how AI technology is integrated into society will not be the individuals who stand to potentially lose their jobs to AI alternatives. Given the state of the modern economy, growing income inequality, and an increasingly hostile gulf between American citizens and the elite who manage the nation's economy, many remain skeptical that the implementation of AI will be handled in such a way as to reduce or moderate the potentially negative impacts of the new technology. Writing in the liberally radical publication *Mother Jones*, for instance, blogger Kevin Drum argues that the state of the modern world already demonstrates who will benefit from AI and who will suffer. Those who own capital, a vanishingly small proportion of the population, will utilize AI replacement to increase productivity and profit while those in the working class suffer. Drum, though his view may be seen as alarmist, believes that the world may see mass unemployment, leading to a welfare state previously unforeseen, in which the government is forced to subsidize lives as machines do most if not all the actual work in society.[9]

What Drum and others who share his views are arguing, is that there has been too little progress towards creating an egalitarian society to introduce a new workforce of machines capable of replacing humanity before humanity has learned how to manage such a society. There remains the possibility, however, that the widespread fear of AI will motivate new ways of envisioning human culture that could address other inequalities as society struggles with the realization that, at some point in the future, work might not be necessary at all. Will this mean a utopia where humans pursue whatever interests them rather than being forced to work for subsistence, or a dystopia where outmoded humans live in poverty with vanishing possibilities of social and economic elevation? Whether AI benefits or burdens society will likely depend not only on how society adjusts to artificial intelligence itself, but also on what kinds of solutions can be found to address the social and economic challenges of the present and all the world's potential futures.

Micah L. Issitt

## Works Used

"Artificial Intelligence—Where and How to Invest." *Capgemini*. Sep 6, 2017. Web. Retrieved from https://www.capgemini.com/resources/artificial-intelligence-where-and-how-to-invest/.

Drum, Kevin. "You Will Lose Your Job to a Robot—and Sooner Than You Think." *Mother Jones*. Mother Jones. Dec 2017. Web. Retrieved from https://www.motherjones.com/politics/2017/10/you-will-lose-your-job-to-a-robot-and-sooner-than-you think/.

Dugan, Andrew, and Bailey Nelson. "3 Trends That Will Disrupt Your Workplace Forever." *Gallup*. Gallup Inc. Jun 8, 2017. Web. Retrieved from http://news.gallup.com/businessjournal/211799/trends-disrupt-workplace-forever.aspx.

Eidelson, Josh. "U.S. Income Inequality Hits a Disturbing New Threshold." *Bloomberg*. Bloomberg L.P. Mar 1, 2018. Web. Retrieved from https://www.bloomberg.com/news/articles/2018-05-21/supreme-court-says-employers-can-bar-worker-class-action-suits-jhgbqpz0.

"Gartner Says by 2020, Artificial Intelligence Will Create More Jobs Than It Eliminates." *Gartner*. Dec 13, 2017. Web. Retrieved from https://www.gartner.com/newsroom/id/3837763.

Goodwin, Bill. "Employers Face Hiring Crisis as AI Replaces Mid-Skilled Jobs." *Computer Weekly*. Tech Target. Mar 16, 2018. Web. Retrieved from https://www.computerweekly.com/news/252436997/Employers-face-hiring-crisis-as-AI-replaces-mid-skilled-jobs.

Lima, Marcos. "No, Artificial Intelligence Won't Steal Your Children's Jobs—It Will Make Them More Creative and Productive." *The Conversation*. The Conversation US, Inc. Feb 26, 2018. Web. Retrieved from http://theconversation.com/no-artificial-intelligence-wont-steal-your-childrens-jobs-it-will-make-them-more-creative-and-productive-91672.

Lomas, Natasha. "AI Will Create New Jobs But Skills Must Shift, Say Tech Giants." *Tech Crunch*. Oath Tech Network. Feb 28, 2018. Web. Retrieved from https://techcrunch.com/2018/02/28/ai-will-create-new-jobs-but-skills-must-shift-say-tech-giants/.

Smith, Kevin. "Artificial Intelligence Will Wipe Out Half the Banking Jobs in a Decade, Experts Say." *Chicago Tribune*. Apr 23, 2018. Web. Retrieved from http://www.chicagotribune.com/business/ct-biz-artificial-intelligence-bank-jobs-20180423-story.html.

## Notes

1. Smith, "Artificial Intelligence Will Wipe Out Half the Banking Jobs in a Decade, Experts Say."
2. Goodwin, "Employers Face Hiring Crisis as AI Replaces Mid-Skilled Jobs."
3. Dugan and Nelson, "3 Trends That Will Disrupt Your Workplace Forever."
4. "Artificial Intelligence—Where and How to Invest," *Capgemini*.
5. Lomas, "AI Will Create New Jobs But Skills Must Shift, Say Tech Giants."
6. Lima, "No, Artificial Intelligence Won't Steal Your Children's Jobs—It Will Make Them More Creative and Productive."
7. "Gartner Says by 2020, Artificial Intelligence Will Create More Jobs Than It Eliminates," *Gartner*.
8. Eidelson, "U.S. Income Inequality Hits a Disturbing New Threshold."
9. Drum, "You Will Lose Your Job to a Robot—And Sooner Than You Think."

# March of the Machines

*The Economist*, June 25, 2016

Experts warn that "the substitution of machinery for human labour" may "render the population redundant". They worry that "the discovery of this mighty power" has come "before we knew how to employ it rightly." Such fears are expressed today by those who worry that advances in artificial intelligence (AI) could destroy millions of jobs and pose a "Terminator"-style threat to humanity. But these are in fact the words of commentators discussing mechanisation and steam power two centuries ago. Back then the controversy over the dangers posed by machines was known as the "machinery question." Now a very similar debate is under way.

After many false dawns, AI has made extraordinary progress in the past few years, thanks to a versatile technique called "deep learning". Given enough data, large (or "deep") neural networks, modelled on the brain's architecture, can be trained to do all kinds of things. They power Google's search engine, Facebook's automatic photo tagging, Apple's voice assistant, Amazon's shopping recommendations and Tesla's self-driving cars. But this rapid progress has also led to concerns about safety and job losses. Stephen Hawking, Elon Musk and others wonder whether AI could get out of control, precipitating a sci-fi conflict between people and machines. Others worry that AI will cause widespread unemployment, by automating cognitive tasks that could previously be done only by people. After 200 years, the machinery question is back. It needs to be answered.

## Machinery Questions and Answers

The most alarming scenario is of rogue AI turning evil, as seen in countless sci-fi films. It is the modern expression of an old fear, going back to *Frankenstein* (1818) and beyond. But although AI systems are impressive, they can perform only very specific tasks: a general AI capable of outwitting its human creators remains a distant and uncertain prospect. Worrying about it is like worrying about overpopulation on Mars before colonists have even set foot there, says Andrew Ng, an AI researcher. The more pressing aspect of the machinery question is what impact AI might have on people's jobs and way of life.

This fear also has a long history. Panics about "technological unemployment" struck in the 1960s (when firms first installed computers and robots) and the 1980s (when PCs landed on desks). Each time, it seemed that widespread automation of skilled workers' jobs was just around the corner.

> **As technology changes the skills needed for each profession, workers will have to adjust.**

Each time, in fact, technology ultimately created more jobs than it destroyed, as the automation of one chore increased demand for people to do the related tasks that were still beyond machines. Replacing some bank tellers with ATMs, for example, made it cheaper to open new branches, creating many more new jobs in sales and customer service. Similarly, e-commerce has increased overall employment in retailing. As with the introduction of computing into offices, AI will not so much replace workers directly as require them to gain new skills to complement it. Although a much-cited paper suggests that up to 47% of American jobs face potential automation in the next decade or two, other studies estimate that less than 10% will actually go.

Even if job losses in the short term are likely to be more than offset by the creation of new jobs in the long term, the experience of the 19th century shows that the transition can be traumatic. Economic growth took off after centuries of stagnant living standards, but decades passed before this was fully reflected in higher wages. The rapid shift of growing populations from farms to urban factories contributed to unrest across Europe. Governments took a century to respond with new education and welfare systems.

This time the transition is likely to be faster, as technologies diffuse more quickly than they did 200 years ago. Income inequality is already growing, because high-skill workers benefit disproportionately when technology complements their jobs. This poses two challenges for employers and policymakers: how to help existing workers acquire new skills; and how to prepare future generations for a workplace stuffed full of AI.

## An Intelligent Response

As technology changes the skills needed for each profession, workers will have to adjust. That will mean making education and training flexible enough to teach new skills quickly and efficiently. It will require a greater emphasis on lifelong learning and on-the-job training, and wider use of online learning and video-game-style simulation. AI may itself help, by personalising computer-based learning and by identifying workers' skills gaps and opportunities for retraining.

Social and character skills will matter more, too. When jobs are perishable, technologies come and go and people's working lives are longer, social skills are a foundation. They can give humans an edge, helping them do work that calls for empathy and human interaction—traits that are beyond machines.

And welfare systems will have to be updated, to smooth the transitions between jobs and to support workers while they pick up new skills. One scheme widely touted as a panacea is a "basic income", paid to everybody regardless of their situation. But that would not make sense without strong evidence that this technological revolution, unlike previous ones, is eroding the demand for labour. Instead countries should learn from Denmark's "flexicurity" system, which lets firms hire and fire easily, while supporting unemployed workers as they retrain and look for new jobs. Benefits, pensions and health care should follow individual workers, rather than being tied (as often today) to employers.

Despite the march of technology, there is little sign that industrial-era education and welfare systems are yet being modernised and made flexible. Policymakers need to get going now because, the longer they delay, the greater the burden on the welfare state. John Stuart Mill wrote in the 1840s that "there cannot be a more legitimate object of the legislator's care" than looking after those whose livelihoods are disrupted by technology. That was true in the era of the steam engine, and it remains true in the era of artificial intelligence.

## Print Citations

**CMS:** "March of the Machines." In *The Reference Shelf: Artificial Intelligence*, edited by Micah Issitt, 63-65. Ipswich, MA: H.W. Wilson, 2018.

**MLA:** "March of the Machines." *The Reference Shelf: Artificial Intelligence*. Ed. Micah Issitt. Ipswich: H.W. Wilson, 2018. 63-65. Print.

**APA:** The Economist. (2018). March of the machines. In Micah Issitt (Ed.), *The reference shelf: Artificial intelligence* (pp. 63-65). Ipswich, MA: H.W. Wilson. (Original work published 2016)

# How AI Can Improve How We Work

By Sarah Green Carmichael
*Harvard Business Review*, April 17, 2018

SARAH GREEN CARMICHAEL: Welcome to the HBR IdeaCast, from *Harvard Business Review*. I'm Sarah Green Carmichael.

By now, I'm used to the idea that machines are going to be an ever more present part of work.

But if I try to imagine what those machines will be doing or what they're gonna look like, that's when the picture starts to get a little fuzzy.

Our guests today say machines will be doing all sorts of functions. And they stress that if we humans develop and deploy AI responsibly, the technology will take us to new levels of productivity.

Paul Daugherty is Accenture's chief technology & innovation officer. James Wilson is the consulting firm's managing director of IT and business research.

Together they're the authors of the book *Human + Machine: Reimagining Work in the Age of AI*. And they're here to talk with us about the impact this emerging technology is having on people and organizations, and the roles and skills we will all need in the future.

Thank you both for taking the time.

JAMES WILSON: It's great to be here. Thanks.

PAUL DAUGHERTY: Great to be here, Sarah,

SARAH GREEN CARMICHAEL: So, there's been a lot of, *oh my God, robots are coming for your job* hype in the media about the future of human and machine collaboration. Do you buy that hype?

PAUL DAUGHERTY: No, you know, I think—if you look at it, it's the 50th anniversary of *2001: A Space Odyssey* 50 years ago, last week, and that set in motion, this whole narrative about, you know, machines taking over the human race. And the other narrative that started is, you know, the machines are coming from our jobs, and then we had this whole thing about, you know, the machine, the machine is beating us at chess and checkers and Go and all these games, and we really think that's all misplaced. And, of course, technology always does some things better than people can do. That's what technology is. And that's been the history of technology.

---

But we wrote the book about is the fact that really, you know, AI, artificial intelligence, you know, robotics and the machines we're talking about, like any other technology, really helps us as people, as humans, do things more effectively. And hence the title, *Human + Machine*.

SARAH GREEN CARMICHAEL: Yeah. So, one of the things I think that worries people is that, you know, in the first stage of companies adopting some of these technologies, they do use them to replace some people. But why, in your view, does a company that does that, that uses machines to replace people, eventually stall out?

JAMES WILSON: Well, in our research, we have really seen that there is this early-stage shift from a automation focused with artificial intelligence to an imagination and re-imagination focus. And we're seeing that companies that focus on imagination and re-imagination are able to do a lot more and to do things differently than the companies that are just focusing on automating the old ways of doing things. So, if you think about typical process design, there might be 12 steps in a process, and if you come in and you say, all right, we're gonna automate six of these 12 steps, you're basically all you're doing is speeding up an old way of doing things. You're putting a new catalytic converter into a Model T, for example, as opposed to really rethinking your way of getting around.

SARAH GREEN CARMICHAEL: So, what have you figured out about which tasks people do best and which kinds of things machines do best?

PAUL DAUGHERTY: Yeah, people are good at emotive capability, communication, improvisation, generalization, things like that. And the machines are good at, you know, memorization, transactions, prediction, and one thing we don't think has been looked at enough that we—was really the core focus of our research was what happens when you combine those two, and what's, what's that middle ground of collaboration? So, in the book, you know, in our work, we actually talked about collaborative intelligence, which is what happens when you put the strengths of the human together with the strength of the machine, and that's where you found these, these new categories of jobs being created that we call the missing middle because, you know, missing because there really hasn't been as much focus on it. We've seen this for binary focus of how can I replace people with the machines rather than thinking about how can I make people more effective and productive? And really, give people superpowers using this new technology to do their jobs much more effectively or as citizens or consumers, you know, live, live our lives more effectively.

JAMES WILSON: One thing that we have seen is that leading companies are really setting a precedent for creating unprecedented new types of jobs. So, we're, we're starting to see the emergence of new job categories that we haven't seen before in this missing middle, in between kind of the human side and the machine side of work.

SARAH GREEN CARMICHAEL: Yeah. So, give us an example of what some of those jobs might be and how they might be shaped by this human plus machine collaboration.

JAMES WILSON: Well, there are two kind of big buckets. One bucket of jobs are where people help build and manage smart machines, and the other bucket are where people are helped by machines. And within the bucket where people are building machines, we see kind of three clusters of jobs that companies can kind of predictably put into the organization and really need to start thinking about today. One of those jobs is called a trainer, another, an explainer, and the third category that we talk about are called sustainers. But within that trainer category, there are interesting new types of jobs that we're seeing emerging like personality trainers who use natural language processing and work to build intelligent agents and chatbots. And those don't necessarily require a background in software engineering. It might require, you know, having a background in psychology or background in drama.

That second category that we talk about is called an explainer. And these are roles that where people explain why machines are doing what they do. So, for instance, at one organization, uh, we interviewed a guy who's basically an AI detective. And so, when his company's pricing model starts doing things that are unexpected, he has to go and explain to colleagues why it's behaving in a certain way. We're going to see a huge need for this explainer role for any company that's operating in Europe these days with the GDPR that's coming into effect quite soon. I saw one piece of research that estimated companies, global companies, are going to need about 75,000 new data compliance officers in their organization to explain to customers algorithmic decisions, say, if a customer calls in and say in a bank and that sort of thing.

And then the third category are what we call sustainers, and sustainers really manage the tradeoffs between what's good for the business and what's good for society and really use a kind of an ethical and responsible AI lens when making decisions. So, one type of role that we've seen there are called AI safety engineers. One of the things they think about are unintended consequences. You know, so what happens if this robot is hacked, you know, even though it's a consumer robot, but if it's a robot, you know, if it's being used at say an airport or for industrial reasons and that sort of thing, what happens if the robot hacks itself for some reason trying to get a more efficient result.

SARAH GREEN CARMICHAEL: So, in this world where we are working with more different kinds of machines and algorithms and bots that can do certain tasks very easily, what are some of the skills you think that people will need to develop either to sort of remain employable or to get more out of these machines to make sure that they are really using them to give them superpowers?

JAMES WILSON: Well, I think that the roles that and the people that are most vulnerable to displacement from artificial intelligence are the ones that aren't using artificial intelligence. So, how do you use AI as quickly as possible on the job?

How can you start learning AI tomorrow on the job? So, I think there are two that executives really need to think about. Uh, the first might be a bit more obvious: doubling down on training. And it might be obvious, but our research really shows that companies still aren't investing in retraining and reskilling at the level that they need to be.

The other thing that executives need to start to think about is really lowering the barrier to using AI. I think a lot of people think AI is rocket science, and in fact in a lot of ways it is. It requires really high-end math or stats skills, so the, you know the question facing a lot of workers today is, *well, yeah, I'd like to be able to use it, but how do I use it?* There are a lot of companies these days that are beginning to say, well, let's democratize AI.

> **If we humans develop and deploy AI responsibly, the technology will take us to new levels of productivity.**

Let's, let's make it as easy for a salesperson to use as their Excel spreadsheet or as PowerPoint. A one company that we've looked at, for instance that's doing this is AT&T, and they're putting point-and-click types of AI tools onto the desktops of about 50,000 people. So, if I'm in a call center, if I'm a salesperson opening up an account, I can interact with AI, can upload a data set, link it to natural language processing, just point-and-click approaches and kind of give myself superpowers in that customer interaction in ways that weren't possible before. But the key point there is that happened as a result of executive intervention.

PAUL DAUGHERTY: Broadly speaking, when you think about the skills that people need, I think there's two broad categories.

One is the skills you need for the people who will do AI. Those are, you know, the machine learning experts, data experts in a lot of STEM technology, coding types of experts and clearly we need more of those and there's a lot of focus on building those skills, and a lot of companies are focusing on acquiring those skills. But relatively speaking that's a lot smaller number than the other category, which is the people that use AI which will be almost every profession, and I when we look at that category of people who need to use AI to do their job, to do these new missing middle jobs that we talk about, that's where I think we need to think about skills. And Jim talked about some good examples there. And in that category I think we need to focus on the one hand on building, building the more human-like skills. Because you know, AI technology will continue to do the things that machines are good at. That's just been the history of how we apply technology to do anything to automate anything that, uh, that we can through throughout civilization. So, what we really need to focus on is what human skills can we really accentuate using the technology.

Also then focused on getting people more facile and more familiar and more comfortable with using technology. So, the last chapter of our book, we talk about eight fusion skills, which are the new fused, you know, human plus AI capabilities. For example, one is called a judgment integration, which is how do you make a decision combining your human judgment with the judgment from an algorithm? And you have to think about things a little differently. You have to apply and use the technology differently. And an example of this being used as some new wealth management approaches that the banks are using AI to, to give agents better tools to recommend products to their customers and better make judgments about how to advise their customers. And that's the kind of fusion scale that we think is important going forward. But it's going to be a combination of that human skill and the technology or the AI skill. You know, one of the predictions that I would make is that when we look several years out right now, we bemoan the shortage of STEM skills and decoding skills and the AI skills.

I think, you know, somewhere around five years out in the future, I think we'll be talking about the lack of more human-oriented skulls, humanities types of skills that can design the experiences and manage the experiences that we're creating using AI as we reimagine businesses, as we reshape products to use technology to interact with humans in a more human-like way, we're going to find there's a dramatic need for many, many more professionals who can bring in that kind of ability to shape our human experiences using technology. And those will be some of the softer skills applied rather than a hardcore, you know, AI or tech or coding skills.

SARAH GREEN CARMICHAEL: You know, often in these conversations we're focused on customer interactions, analyzing customer data, or managing customer relationships. But in the book, you have some examples of how companies are also using some of these tools to manage their own internal processes. And I wanted to ask you about how Unilever for example, is using AI in hiring.

JAMES WILSON: I think we usually think about the use of advanced analytics in HR in terms of crunching through resumes, but what we're actually seeing is that AI is moving into the interviewing process as well, and that's really transforming recruiter's ability to interview more candidates. At Unilever, for instance, they've incorporated AI into kind of the first two rounds of interviews. The first round they play online games, and that gives the company a sense of the skill set of the person, kind of their behaviors. Maybe there's a job posting that maps to their skill set that the person wasn't aware of. The second round of interview actually is done with a video analysis system that can evaluate the person's comfort level with certain types of questions, their gestures, their facial cues, and that sort of thing. So, it really allows the company to talk to three or four more times candidates than before.

And then, by the way, that third and final round of interview, the candidates are actually talking to the human recruiters. But by using that approach, the company has been able to expand diversity fourfold. They've been able to get candidates into interviews from many more universities, I think about three or four times more universities. And maybe most importantly they've been able to drastically reduce that cumbersome recruiting process that can drag on for months. At Unilever, I think before they brought in this solution, it was about four months long from that first interview to the final decision. They've been able to reduce that to about four weeks.

So that's a huge improvement both for the company but also for the candidate and their experience interacting with the company.

PAUL DAUGHERTY: Yeah. There's another example that I would give in the HR area is something that we're doing within our own company, within Accenture. We have over 400,000 employees, and we're using AI in a creative way, still at an experimental level, but we're using machine learning and AI to, based on, you know, a person's profile, to understand their current job, experience, their resume, what they've done, their assignments. And based on the changes in technology, it'll learn and, uh, recommend to how soon that individual might need to change their profession because what they're doing now may become obsolete. So, in other words, how long will your skills be relevant. But then it goes further and says, OK, based on what, you know, what should you start learning that based on what you know, that'll help you be relevant and effective as you know, as technology changes. So, that's still a little bit of an experiment, but I think it points the way to how we can use AI itself to help with this, you know, jobs and reskilling issue[s] that we're talking about earlier.

SARAH GREEN CARMICHAEL: In your view, how many industries will be affected by this? Because occasionally you'll hear, everything's going to be affected. This will affect everyone. And then other times people are like, no, really won't. What's your view on that?

JAMES WILSON: Well, you know, we don't have a stock answer for that, and I think you know, uh, it's going to vary by region, by country. France, for example, is going to focus on healthcare, mobility, and transportation. I think in regulated industries there's going to be a bit slower adoption rate. Though certain types of algorithms, you know, high-speed trading algorithms and that sort of thing have been around for a long time in Wall Street. But when you start using a more sophisticated deep learning techniques in situations where you wouldn't be able to explain to the customer or to the institutional investor why a certain transaction was madethose might take quite a while to be adopted if they're adopted it at all.

PAUL DAUGHERTY: On the bigger landscape, we do believe that AI is right now really what I would say is the alpha trend driving other trends that we see in the market, and it will impact every industry. And we just talked about some specific industries that it's going to impact more quickly, and I think it's, it's those industries that are very data intensive, those industries that have a lot of human interaction, those industries that have a lot of compliance and regulatory implications, we're finding a lot of applicability. Those industries that have a lot of supply chain logistical components to them because those are the kinds of problems that we're, we're finding AI can solve very well. And then broadly speaking, health generally, there's so much opportunity to improve wellness and health outcomes by applying AI that that generally speaking will be a big benefit that we'll continue to see as AI is applied.

SARAH GREEN CARMICHAEL: Well, listen, it's been really fun talking with you guys today about all of this. Thank you both so much for sharing your time with us.

PAUL DAUGHERTY: Thank you, Sarah.

JAMES WILSON: Yeah, thanks, Sarah. It's been a great conversation.

SARAH GREEN CARMICHAEL That's James Wilson and Paul Daugherty. They're the authors of *Human + Machine: Reimagining Work in the Age of AI.* You can find it at HBR.org.

Thanks for listening to the HBR IdeaCast. I'm Sarah Green Carmichael.

## Print Citations

**CMS:** Carmichael, Sarah Green. "How AI Can Improve How We Work." In *The Reference Shelf: Artificial Intelligence*, edited by Micah Issitt, 66-72. Ipswich, MA: H.W. Wilson, 2018.

**MLA:** Carmichael, Sarah Green. "How AI Can Improve How We Work." *The Reference Shelf: Artificial Intelligence*. Ed. Micah Issitt. Ipswich: H.W. Wilson, 2018. 66-72. Print.

**APA:** Carmichael, S.G. (2018). How AI can improve how we work. In Micah Issitt (Ed.), *The reference shelf: Artificial intelligence* (pp. 66-72). Ipswich, MA: H.W. Wilson. (Original work published 2018)

# Will Robots and AI Take Your Job? The Economic and Political Consequences of Automation

By Darrell M. West
*Brookings*, April 18, 2018

In Edward Bellamy's classic *Looking Backward*, the protagonist Julian West wakes up from a 113-year slumber and finds the United States in 2000 has changed dramatically from 1887. People stop working at age forty-five and devote their lives to mentoring other people and engaging in volunteer work that benefits the overall community. There are short work weeks for employees, and everyone receives full benefits, food, and housing.[1]

The reason is that new technologies of the period have enabled people to be very productive while working part-time. Businesses do not need large numbers of employees, so individuals can devote most of their waking hours to hobbies, volunteering, and community service. In conjunction with periodic work stints, they have time to pursue new skills and personal identities that are independent of their jobs.

In the current era, developed countries may be on the verge of a similar transition. Robotics and machine learning have improved productivity and enhanced the economies of many nations. Artificial intelligence (AI) has advanced into finance, transportation, defense, and energy management. The internet of things (IoT) is facilitated by high-speed networks and remote sensors to connect people and businesses. In all of this, there is a possibility of a new era that could improve the lives of many people.[2]

Yet amid these possible benefits, there is widespread fear that robots and AI will take jobs and throw millions of people into poverty. A *Pew Research Center* study asked 1,896 experts about the impact of emerging technologies and found "half of these experts (48 percent) envision a future in which robots and digital agents [will] have displaced significant numbers of both blue- and white-collar workers—with many expressing concern that this will lead to vast increases in income inequality, masses of people who are effectively unemployable, and breakdowns in the social order."[3]

These fears have been echoed by detailed analyses showing anywhere from a 14 to 54 percent automation impact on jobs. For example, a Bruegel analysis found that "54% of EU jobs [are] at risk of computerization."[4] Using European data, they

---

argue that job losses are likely to be significant and people should prepare for large-scale disruption.

Meanwhile, Oxford University researchers Carl Frey and Michael Osborne claim that technology will transform many sectors of life. They studied 702 occupational groupingsand found that "47 percent of U.S. workers have a high probability of seeing their jobs automated over the next 20 years."[5]

A McKinsey Global Institute analysis of 750 jobs concluded that "45% of paid activities could be automated using 'currently demonstrated technologies' and . . . 60% of occupations could have 30% or more of their processes automated."[6] A more recent McKinsey report, "Jobs Lost, Jobs Gained," found that 30 percent of "work activities" could be automated by 2030 and up to 375 million workers worldwide could be affected by emerging technologies.[7]

Researchers at the Organization for Economic Cooperation and Development (OECD) focused on "tasks" as opposed to "jobs" and found fewer job losses. Using task-related data from 32 OECD countries, they estimated that 14 percent of jobs are highly automatable and another 32 have a significant risk of automation. Although their job loss estimates are below those of other experts, they concluded that "low qualified workers are likely to bear the brunt of the adjustment costs as the automatibility of their jobs is higher compared to highly qualified workers."[8]

While some dispute the dire predictions on grounds new positions will be created to offset the job losses, the fact that all these major studies report significant workforce disruptions should be taken seriously. If the employment impact falls at the 38 percent mean of these forecasts, Western democracies likely could resort to authoritarianism as happened in some countries during the Great Depression of the 1930s in order to keep their restive populations in check. If that happened, wealthy elites would require armed guards, security details, and gated communities to protect themselves, as is the case in poor countries today with high income inequality. The United States would look like Syria or Iraq, with armed bands of young men with few employment prospects other than war, violence, or theft.

> **As innovation accelerates and public anxiety intensifies, right-wing and left-wing populists will jockey for voter support.**

Yet even if the job ramifications lie more at the low end of disruption, the political consequences still will be severe. Relatively small increases in unemployment or underemployment have an outsized political impact. We saw that a decade ago when 10 percent unemployment during the Great Recession spawned the Tea party and eventually helped to make Donald Trump president.

With some workforce disruption virtually guaranteed by trends already underway, it is safe to predict American politics will be chaotic and turbulent during the coming decades. As innovation accelerates and public anxiety intensifies, right-wing and left-wing populists will jockey for voter support. Government control could gyrate between very conservative and very liberal leaders as each side blames a different set of scapegoats for economic outcomes voters don't like. The calm and predictable politics of the post-World War II era likely will become a distant memory as the American system moves toward Trumpism on steroids.

## Notes

1. Edward Bellamy, *Looking Backward: 2000-1887*, Houghton-Mifflin, 1888.
2. Darrell M. West, *The Future of Work: Robots, AI, and Automation*, Brookings Institution Press, 2018.
3. Aaron Smith and Janna Anderson, "AI, Robotics, and the Future of Jobs," Pew Research Center, August 6, 2014.
4. Jeremy Bowles, "Chart of the Week: 54% of EU Jobs at Risk of Computerisation," blog post, Bruegel.org, July 24, 2014.
5. Carl Benedict Frey and Michael Osborne, "The Future of Employment: How Susceptible Are Jobs to Computerisation?" Oxford University paper, September 17, 2013.
6. Ben Schiller, "How Soon before Your Job Is Done by a Robot?" *Fast Company*, January 6, 2016.
7. James Manyika, Susan Lund, Michael Chui, Macques Bughin, Jonathan Woetzel, Parul Batra, Ryan Ko, and Saurabh Sanghui, "Jobs Lost, Jobs Gained: Workforce Transitions in a Time of Automation," McKinsey Global Institute, December, 2017.
8. Melanie Arntz, Terry Gregory, and Ulrich Zierahn, "The Risk of Automation for Jobs in OECD Countries," Organization for Economic Cooperation and Development, Working Paper 189, 2016.

## Print Citations

**CMS:** West, Darrell M. "Will Robots and AI Take Your Job? The Economic and Political Consequences of Automation." In *The Reference Shelf: Artificial Intelligence*, edited by Micah Issitt, 73-75. Ipswich, MA: H.W. Wilson, 2018.

**MLA:** West, Darrell M. "Will Robots and AI Take Your Job? The Economic and Political Consequences of Automation." *The Reference Shelf: Artificial Intelligence*. Ed. Micah Issitt. Ipswich: H.W. Wilson, 2018. 73-75. Print.

**APA:** West, D.M. (2018). Will robots and AI take your job? The economic and political consequences of automation. In Micah Issitt (Ed.), *The reference shelf: Artificial intelligence* (pp. 73-75). Ipswich, MA: H.W. Wilson. (Original work published 2018)

# The IBrain Is Here—And It's Already Inside Your Phone

By Steven Levy
*Wired*, August 24, 2016

**On July 30, 2014**, Siri had a brain transplant.

Three years earlier, Apple had been the first major tech company to integrate a smart assistant into its operating system. Siri was the company's adaptation of a standalone app it had purchased, along with the team that created it, in 2010. Initial reviews were ecstatic, but over the next few months and years, users became impatient with its shortcomings. All too often, it erroneously interpreted commands. Tweaks wouldn't fix it.

So Apple moved Siri voice recognition to a neural-net based system for US users on that late July day (it went worldwide on August 15, 2014). Some of the previous techniques remained operational—if you're keeping score at home, this includes "hidden Markov models" —but now the system leverages machine learning techniques, including deep neural networks (DNN), convolutional neural networks, long short-term memory units, gated recurrent units, and n-grams. (Glad you asked.) When users made the upgrade, Siri still looked the same, but now it was supercharged with deep learning.

As is typical with under-the-hood advances that may reveal its thinking to competitors, Apple did not publicize the development. If users noticed, it was only because there were fewer errors. In fact, Apple now says the results in improving accuracy were stunning.

"This was one of those things where the jump was so significant that you do the test again to make sure that somebody didn't drop a decimal place," says Eddy Cue, Apple's senior vice president of internet software and services.

This story of Siri's transformation, revealed for the first time here, might raise an eyebrow in much of the artificial intelligence world. Not that neural nets improved the system—of course they would do that—but that Apple was so quietly adept at doing it. Until recently, when Apple's hiring in the AI field has stepped up and the company has made a few high-profile acquisitions, observers have viewed Apple as a laggard in what is shaping up as the most heated competition in the industry: the race to best use those powerful AI tools. Because Apple has always been so tight-lipped about what goes on behind badged doors, the AI cognoscenti didn't know what Apple was up to in machine learning. "It's not part of the community," says Jerry Kaplan, who teaches a course at Stanford on the history of artificial intel-ligence. "Apple is the NSA of AI." But AI's Brahmins figured that if Apple's efforts were as significant as Google's or Facebook's, they would have heard that.

"In Google, Facebook, Microsoft you have the top people in machine learning," says Oren Etzioni of the Allen Institute for AI. "Yes, Apple has hired some people. But who are the five leaders of machine learning who work for Apple? Apple does have speech recognition, but it isn't clear where else [machine learning] helps them. Show me in your product where machine learning is being used!

"I'm from Missouri," says Etzioni, who is actually from Israel. "Show me."

Well earlier this month, Apple did show where machine learning is being used in its products—not to Etzioni, but to me. (Oren, please read.) I spent the better part of a day in the boardroom of One Infinite Loop at the Cupertino headquarters, getting a core dump of the company's activities in AI and machine learning from top Apple executives (Cue, senior worldwide marketing vice president Phil Schiller, and senior vice president of software engineering Craig Federighi), as well as two key Siri scientists. As we sat down, they handed me a dense, two-page agenda listing machine-learning-imbued Apple products and services—ones already shipping or about to—that they would discuss.

The message: We're already here. A player. Second to none. But we do it our way.

If you're an iPhone user, you've come across Apple's AI, and not just in Siri's improved acumen in figuring out what you ask of her. You see it when the phone identifies a caller who isn't in your contact list (but did email you recently). Or when you swipe on your screen to get a shortlist of the apps that you are most likely to open next. Or when you get a reminder of an appointment that you never got around to putting into your calendar. Or when a map location pops up for the hotel you've reserved, before you type it in. Or when the phone points you to where you parked your car, even though you never asked it to. These are all techniques either made possible or greatly enhanced by Apple's adoption of deep learning and neural nets.

Yes, there is an "Apple brain" —it's already inside your iPhone.

Machine learning, my briefers say, is now found all over Apple's products and services. Apple uses deep learning to detect fraud on the Apple store, to extend bat-tery life between charges on all your devices, and to help it identify the most useful feedback from thousands of reports from its beta testers. Machine learning helps Apple choose news stories for you. It determines whether Apple Watch users are ex-ercising or simply perambulating. It recognizes faces and locations in your photos. It figures out whether you would be better off leaving a weak Wi-Fi signal and switch-ing to the cell network. It even knows what good filmmaking is, enabling Apple to quickly compile your snapshots and videos into a mini-movie at a touch of a button. Apple's competitors do many similar things, but, say its executives, none of those AI powers can pull those things off while protecting privacy as closely as Apple does. And, of course, none of them make Apple products.

AI isn't new to Apple: as early as the 1990s it was using some machine learn-ing techniques in its handwriting recognition products. (Remember Newton?) Remnants of those efforts are still to be found in today's products that convert hand-scrawled Chinese characters into text or recognize the letter-by-letter input of an Apple Watch user finger-"scribbling"a custom message on the watch face. (Both of those features were produced by the same ML team of engineers.) Of course, in earlier days, machine learning was more primitive, and deep learning hadn't even been buzzworded yet. Today, those AI techniques are all the rage, and Apple bristles at the implication that its learning is comparatively shallow. In recent weeks, CEO Tim Cook has made it a point to mention that the company is on it. And now, its top leaders are elaborating.

"We've been seeing over the last five years a growth of this inside Apple," says Phil Schiller. "Our devices are getting so much smarter at a quicker rate, especially with our Apple design A series chips. The back ends are getting so much smarter, faster, and everything we do finds some reason to be connected. This enables more and more machine learning techniques, because there is so much stuff to learn, and it's available to [us]."

Even as Apple is bear-hugging machine learning, the executives caution that the embrace is, in a sense, business as usual for them. The Cupertino illuminati view deep learning and ML as only the latest in a steady flow of groundbreaking technologies. Yes, yes, it's transformational, but not more so than other advances, like touch screens, or flat panels, or object-oriented programming. In Apple's view, machine learning isn't the final frontier, despite what other companies say. "It's not like there weren't other technologies over the years that have been instrumental in changing the way we interact with devices," says Cue. And no one at Apple wants to even touch on the spooky/scary speculations that invariably come up in AI discussions. As you'd expect, Apple wouldn't confirm whether it was working on self-driving cars, or its own version of Netflix. But the team made it pretty clear that Apple was not working on Skynet.

"We use these techniques to do the things we have always wanted to do, better than we've been able to do," says Schiller. "And on new things we haven't be able to do. It's a technique that will ultimately be a very Apple way of doing things as it evolves inside Apple and in the ways we make products."

Yet as the briefing unfolds, it becomes clear how much AI has already shaped the overall experience of using the Apple ecosystem. The view from the AI establishment is that Apple is constrained by its lack of a search engine (which can deliver the data that helps to train neural networks) and its inflexible insistence on protecting user information (which potentially denies Apple data it otherwise might use). But it turns out that Apple has figured out how to jump both those hurdles.

How big is this brain, the dynamic cache that enables machine learning on the iPhone? Somewhat to my surprise when I asked Apple, it provided the information: about 200 megabytes, depending on how much personal information is stored (it's always deleting older data). This includes information about app usage, interactions with other people, neural net processing, a speech modeler, and "natural language event modeling." It also has data used for the neural nets that power object recognition, face recognition, and scene classification.

And, according to Apple, it's all done so your preferences, predilections, and peregrinations are private.

Though Apple wasn't explaining *everything* about its AI efforts, I did manage to get resolution on how the company distributes ML expertise around its organization. The company's machine learning talent is shared throughout the entire company, available to product teams who are encouraged to tap it to solve problems and invent features on individual products. "We don't have a single centralized organization that's the Temple of ML in Apple," says Craig Federighi. "We try to keep it close to teams that need to apply it to deliver the right user experience."

How many people at Apple are working on machine learning? "A lot," says Federighi after some prodding. (If you thought he'd give me the number, you don't know your Apple.) What's interesting is that Apple's ML is produced by many people who weren't necessarily trained in the field before they joined the company. "We hire people who are very smart in fundamental domains of mathematics, statistics, programming languages, cryptography," says Federighi. "It turns out a lot of these kinds of core talents translate beautifully to machine learning. Though today we certainly hire many machine learning people, we also look for people with the right core aptitudes and talents."

Though Federighi doesn't say it, this approach might be a necessity: Apple's penchant for secrecy puts it at a disadvantage against competitors who encourage their star computer scientists to widely share research with the world. "Our practices tend to reinforce a natural selection bias—those who are interested in working as a team to deliver a great product versus those whose primary motivation is publishing," says Federighi. If while improving an Apple product scientists happen to make breakthroughs in the field, that's great. "But we are driven by a vision of the end result," says Cue.

Some talent in the field comes from acquisitions. "We've recently been buying 20 to 30 companies a year that are relatively small, really hiring the manpower," says Cue. When Apple buys an AI company, it's not to say, "here's a big raw bunch of machine learning researchers, let's build a stable of them," says Federighi. "We're looking at people who have that talent but are really focused on delivering great experiences."

The most recent purchase was Turi, a Seattle company that Apple snatched for a reported $200 million. It has built an ML toolkit that's been compared to Google's TensorFlow, and the purchase fueled speculation that Apple would use it for similar purposes both internally and for developers. Apple's executives wouldn't confirm or deny. "There are certain things they had that matched very well with Apple from a technology view, and from a people point of view," says Cue. In a year or two, we may figure out what happened, as we did when Siri began showing some of the predictive powers of Cue (no relation to Eddy!), a small startup Apple snatched up in 2013.

No matter where the talent comes from, Apple's AI infrastructure allows it to develop products and features that would not be possible by earlier means. It's altering the company's product road map. "Here at Apple there is no end to the list of really cool ideas," says Schiller. "Machine learning is enabling us to say yes to some things that in past years we would have said no to. It's becoming embedded in the process of deciding the products we're going to do next."

One example of this is the Apple Pencil that works with the iPad Pro. In order for Apple to include its version of a high-tech stylus, it had to deal with the fact that when people wrote on the device, the bottom of their hand would invariably brush the touch screen, causing all sorts of digital havoc. Using a machine learning model for "palm rejection" enabled the screen sensor to detect the difference between a swipe, a touch, and a pencil input with a very high degree of accuracy. "If this doesn't work rock solid, this is not a good piece of paper for me to write on anymore—and Pencil is not a good product," says Federighi. If you love your Pencil, thank machine learning.

> **Apple may not make declarations about going all-in on machine learning, but the company will use it as much as possible to improve its products.**

Probably the best measure of Apple's machine learning progress comes from its most important AI acquisition to date, Siri. Its origins came from an ambitious DARPA program in intelligent assistants, and later some of the scientists started a company, using the technology to create an app. Steve Jobs himself convinced the founders to sell to Apple in 2010, and directed that Siri be built into the operating system; its launch was the highlight of the iPhone 4S event in October 2011. Now its workings extend beyond the instances where users invoke it by holding down the home button or simply uttering the words "Hey, Siri." (A feature that itself makes use of machine learning, allowing the iPhone to keep an ear out without draining the battery.) Siri intelligence is integrated into the Apple Brain, at work even when it keeps its mouth shut.

As far as the core product is concerned, Cue cites four components of the product: speech recognition (to understand when you talk to it), natural language understanding (to grasp what you're saying), execution (to fulfill a query or request), and response (to talk back to you). "Machine learning has impacted all of those in hugely significant ways," he says.

Siri's head of advanced development Tom Gruber, who came to Apple along with the original acquisition (his co-founders left after the 2011 introduction), says that even before Apple applied neural nets to Siri, the scale of its user base was providing data that would be key in training those nets later on. "Steve said you're going to go overnight from a pilot, an app, to a hundred million users without a beta program," he says. "All of a sudden you're going to have users. They tell you how people say things that are relevant to your app. That was the first revolution. And then the neural networks came along."

Siri's transition to a neural net handling speech recognition got into high gear with the arrival of several AI experts including Alex Acero, who now heads the speech team. Acero began his career in speech recognition at Apple in the early '90s, and then spent many years at Microsoft Research. "I loved doing that and published many papers," he says. "But when Siri came out, I said, 'This is a chance to make these deep neural networks all a reality, not something that a hundred people read about, but used by millions.'" In other words, he was just the type of scientist Apple was seeking—prioritizing product over publishing.

When Acero arrived three years ago, Apple was still licensing much of its speech technology for Siri from a third party, a situation due for a change. Federighi notes that this is a pattern Apple repeats consistently. "As it becomes clear a technology area is critical to our ability to deliver a great product over time, we build our in-house capabilities to deliver the experience we want. To make it great, we want to own and innovate internally. Speech is an excellent example where we applied stuff available externally to get it off the ground."

The team began training a neural net to replace Siri's original. "We have the biggest and baddest GPU (graphics processing unit microprocessor) farm cranking all the time," says Acero. "And we pump lots of data." The July 2014 release proved that all those cycles were not in vain.

"The error rate has been cut by a factor of two in all the languages, more than a factor of two in many cases," says Acero. "That's mostly due to deep learning and the way we have optimized it—not just the algorithm itself but in the context of the whole end-to-end product."

The "end-to-end" reference is telling. Apple isn't first company to use DNNs in speech recognition. But Apple makes the argument that by being in control of the entire delivery system, it has an advantage. Because Apple makes its own chips, Acero says he was able to work directly with the silicon design team and the engineers who write the firmware for the devices to maximize performance of the neural net. The needs of the Siri team influenced even aspects of the iPhone's design.

"It's not just the silicon," adds Federighi. "It's how many microphones we put on the device, where we place the microphones. How we tune the hardware and those mics and the software stack that does the audio processing. It's all of those pieces in concert. It's an incredible advantage versus those who have to build some software and then just see what happens."

Another edge: when an Apple neural net works in one product, it can become a core technology used for other purposes. So the machine learning that helps Siri understand you becomes the engine to handle dictation instead of typing. As a result of the Siri work, people find that their messages and emails are more likely to be coherent if they eschew the soft keyboard and instead click on the microphone key and talk.

The second Siri component Cue mentioned was natural language understanding. Siri began using ML to understand user intent in November 2014, and released a version with deeper learning a year later. As it had with speech recognition, machine learning improved the experience—especially in interpreting commands more flexibly. As an example, Cue pulls out his iPhone and invokes Siri. "Send Jane twenty dollars with Square Cash," he says. The screen displays a screen reflecting his request. Then he tries again, using a little different language. "Shoot twenty bucks to my wife." Same result.

Apple now says that without those advances in Siri, it's unlikely it would have produced the current iteration of the Apple TV, distinguished by sophisticated voice control. While the earlier versions of Siri forced you to speak in a constrained manner, the supercharged-by-deep-learning version can not only deliver specific choices from a vast catalog of movies and songs, but also handle concepts: Show me a good thriller with Tom Hanks. (If Siri is really smart, it'll rule out *The Da Vinci Code*.) "You wouldn't be able to offer that prior to this technology," says Federighi.

With iOS 10, scheduled for full release this fall, Siri's voice becomes the last of the four components to be transformed by machine learning. Again, a deep neural network has replaced a previously licensed implementation. Essentially, Siri's remarks come from a database of recordings collected in a voice center; each sentence is a stitched-together patchwork of those chunks. Machine learning, says Gruber, smooths them out and makes Siri sound more like an actual person.

Acero does a demo—first the familiar Siri voice, with the robotic elements that we've all become accustomed to. Then the new one, which says, "Hi, what can I do for you?" with a sultry fluency. What made the difference? "Deep learning, baby," he says.

Though it seems like a small detail, a more natural voice for Siri actually can trigger big differences. "People feel more trusting if the voice is a bit more high-quality," says Gruber. "The better voice actually pulls the user in and has them use it more. So it has an increasing-returns effect."

The willingness to use Siri, as well as the improvements made by machine learning, becomes even more important as Apple is finally opening Siri up to other developers, a process that Apple's critics have noted is long overdue. Many have noted that Apple, whose third-party Siri partners number in the double figures, is way behind a system like Amazon's Alexa, which boasts over 1000 "skills" provided by outsider developers. Apple says the comparison doesn't hold, because on Amazon users have to use specific language to access the skills. Siri will integrate things like SquareCash or Uber more naturally, says Apple. (Another competitor, Viv—created by the other Siri co-founders—also promises tight integration, when its as-yet-unannounced launch date arrives.)

Meanwhile, Apple reports that the improvements to Siri have been making a difference, as people discover new features or find more success from familiar queries. "The number of requests continues to grow and grow," says Cue. "I think we need to be doing a better job communicating all the things we do. For instance, I love sports, and you can ask it who it thinks is going to win the game and it will come back with an answer. I didn't even know we were doing that!"

Probably the biggest issue in Apple's adoption of machine learning is how the company can succeed while sticking to its principles on user privacy. The company encrypts user information so that no one, not even Apple's lawyers, can read it (nor can the FBI, even with a warrant). And it boasts about not collecting user information for advertising purposes.

While admirable from a user perspective, Apple's rigor on this issue has not been helpful in luring top AI talent to the company. "Machine learning experts, all they want is data," says a former Apple employee now working for an AI-centric company. "But by its privacy stance, Apple basically puts one hand behind your back. You can argue whether it's the right thing to do or not, but it's given Apple a reputation for not being real hardcore AI folks."

This view is hotly contested by Apple's executives, who say that it's possible to get all the data you need for robust machine learning without keeping profiles of users in the cloud or even storing instances of their behavior to train neural nets. "There has been a false narrative, a false trade-off out there," says Federighi. "It's great that we would be known as uniquely respecting user's privacy. But for the sake of users everywhere, we'd like to show the way for the rest of the industry to get on board here."

There are two issues involved here. The first involves processing personal information in machine-learning based systems. When details about a user are gleaned through neural-net processing, what happens to that information? The second issue involves gathering the information required to train neural-nets to recognize behaviors. How can you do that without collecting the personal information of users?

Apple says it has answers for both. "Some people perceive that we can't do these things with AI because we don't have the data," says Cue. "But we have found ways to get that data we need while still maintaining privacy. That's the bottom line."

Apple handles the first issue—protecting personal preferences and information that neural nets identify—by taking advantage of its unique control of both software and hardware. Put simply, the most personal stuff stays inside the Apple Brain. "We keep some of the most sensitive things where the ML is occurring entirely local to the device," Federighi says. As an example, he cites app suggestions, the icons that appear when you swipe right. Ideally, they are exactly the apps you intended to open next. Those predictions are based on a number of factors, many of them involving behavior that is no one's business but your own. And they do work—Federighi says 90 percent of the time people find what they need by those predictions. Apple does the computing right there on the phone.

Other information Apple stores on devices includes probably the most personal data that Apple captures: the words people type using the standard iPhone Quick-Type keyboard. By using a neural network-trained system that watches while you type, Apple can detect key events and items like flight information, contacts, and appointments—but information itself stays on your phone. Even in back-ups that are stored on Apple's cloud, the information is distilled in such a way that it can't be inferred by the backup alone. "We don't want that information stored in Apple servers," says Federighi. "There is no need that Apple as a corporation needs to know your habits, or when you go where."

Apple also tries to minimize the information kept in general. Federighi mentions an example where you might be having a conversation and someone mentions a term that is a potential search. Other companies might have to analyze the whole conversation in the cloud to identify those terms, he says, but an Apple device can detect it without having the data leave the user's possession—because the system is constantly looking for matches on a knowledge base kept on the phone. (It's part of that 200 megabyte "brain.")

"It's a compact, but quite thorough knowledge base, with hundreds of thousands of locations and entities. We localize it because we know where you are," says Federighi. This knowledge base is tapped by all of Apple's apps, including the Spotlight search app, Maps, and Safari. It helps on auto-correct. "And it's working continuously in the background," he says.

The question that comes up in machine learning circles, though, is whether Apple's privacy restrictions will hobble its neural net algorithms—that's the aforementioned second issue. Neural nets need massive amounts of data to be sufficiently trained for accuracy. If Apple won't suck up all its users' behavior, how will it get that data? As many other companies do, Apple trains its nets on publicly available corpuses of information (data sets of stock images for photo recognition, for instance). But sometimes it needs more current or specific information that could only come from its user base. Apple tries to get this information without knowing who the users are; it anonymizes data, tagging it with random identifiers not associated with Apple IDs.

Beginning with iOS 10, Apple will also employ a relatively new technique called Differential Privacy, which basically crowd-sources information in a way that doesn't identify individuals at all. Examples for its use might be to surface newly popular words that aren't in Apple's knowledge base or its vocabulary, links that suddenly emerge as more relevant answers to queries, or a surge in the usage of certain emojis. "The traditional way that the industry solves this problem is to send every word you type, every character you type, up to their servers, and then they trawl through it all and they spot interesting things," says Federighi. "We do end-to-end encryption, so we don't do that." Though Differential Privacy was hatched in the research community, Apple is taking steps to apply it on a massive scale. "We're taking it from research to a billion users," says Cue.

"We started working on it years ago, and have done really interesting work that is practical at scale," explains Federighi. "And it's pretty crazy how private it is." (He then describes a system that involves virtual coin-tossing and cryptographic protocols that I barely could follow—and I wrote a book about cryptography. Basically it's about adding mathematical noise to certain pieces of data so that Apple can detect usage patterns without identifying individual users.) He says that Apple's contribution is sufficiently significant—and valuable to the world at large—that it is authorizing the scientists working on the implementation to publish a paper on their work.

While it's clear that machine learning has changed Apple's products, what is not so clear is whether it is changing Apple itself. In a sense, the machine learning mindset seems at odds with the Apple ethos. Apple is a company that carefully controls the user experience, down to the sensors that measure swipes. Everything is pre-designed and precisely coded. But when engineers use machine learning, they must step back and let the software itself discover solutions. Can Apple adjust to the modern reality that machine learning systems can themselves have a hand in product design?

"It's a source of a lot of internal debate," says Federighi. "We are used to delivering a very well-thought-out, curated experience where we control all the dimensions of how the system is going to interact with the user. When you start training a system based on large data sets of human behavior, [the results that emerge] aren't necessarily what an Apple designer specified. They are what emerged from the data."

But Apple isn't turning back, says Schiller. "While these techniques absolutely affect how you design something, at the end of the day we are using them because they enable us to deliver a higher quality product."

And that's the takeaway: Apple may not make declarations about going all-in on machine learning, but the company will use it as much as possible to improve its products. That brain inside your phone is the proof.

"The typical customer is going to experience deep learning on a day-to-day level that [exemplifies] what you love about an Apple product," says Schiller. "The most exciting [instances] are so subtle that you don't even think about it until the third time you see it, and then you stop and say, How is this happening?"

Skynet can wait.

## Print Citations

**CMS:** Levy, Steven. "The IBrain Is Here—And It's Already Inside Your Phone." In *The Reference Shelf: Artificial Intelligence*, edited by Micah Issitt, 76-85. Ipswich, MA: H.W. Wilson, 2018.

**MLA:** Levy, Steven. "The IBrain Is Here—And It's Already Inside Your Phone." *The Reference Shelf: Artificial Intelligence*. Ed. Micah Issitt. Ipswich: H.W. Wilson, 2018. 76-85. Print.

**APA:** Levy, S. (2018). The IBrain is here—And it's already inside your phone. In Micah Issitt (Ed.), *The reference shelf: Artificial intelligence* (pp. 76-85). Ipswich, MA: H.W. Wilson. (Original work published 2016)

# AI and Robots Will Destroy Fewer Jobs Than Previously Feared, Says New OECD Report

By James Vincent
*The Verge*, April 3, 2018

Fewer jobs are at risk of automation from AI and robotics than previous forecasts have warned, according to a report from the OECD, an inter-governmental group of high-income countries.

The new study offers a counterpoint to an influential 2013 paper by Oxford University academics Carl Frey and Michael Osborne, who warned that around 47 percent of jobs in the US were at high risk of being automated. Frey and Osborne's research set the tone for much of the recent debate over automation, and its message has been reiterated in subsequent studies.

But, according to the OECD's analysis, these current fears are somewhat over-blown. The researchers found that only 14 percent of jobs in OECD countries—which includes the US, UK, Canada, and Japan—are "highly automatable," meaning their probability of automation is 70 percent or higher. This forecast is far less dire than Frey and Osborne's, although it is still significant, equating to around 66 million job losses.

In America alone, for example, the report suggests that 13 million jobs will be destroyed because of automation. "As job losses are unlikely to be distributed equally across the country, this would amount to several times the disruption in local economies caused by the 1950s decline of the car industry in Detroit where changes in technology and increased automation, among other factors, caused massive job losses," the researchers write.

But why is this new estimate so different from Frey and Osborne's? One of the reasons is the OECD's attention to variation between jobs of the same name and to tasks that are difficult for computers to manage even within highly automatable jobs.

Think about a machine operator in a factory, for example. Although a portion of their job could be automated, they may have other responsibilities (such as managing inventory and overseeing junior workers), which computers cannot manage. And consider the difference between a worker in US garment factory and its equivalent in Vietnam: the American factory is more likely to be technologically advanced, and the typical worker's day will likely involve a greater number of non-routine tasks that resist automation.

All of this is to say that predicting how and where automation will have the greatest impact is an extremely difficult question. It's perhaps part of the reason that Americans consistently say that automation will take other people's jobs and not their own: we all have a much clearer picture of the variety of skills our own jobs' demand.

But although the OECD predicts that total job losses will less than feared, the report stresses the impact will still be incredibly damaging to groups already under threat in today's labor markets: low-skilled workers and the young.

As the researchers write: "The risk of automation is not distributed equally among workers [...] Occupations with the highest estimated automatability typically only require basic to low level of education." This also means the effects of automation are felt disproportionately by the young. The researchers note that although we assume young people are better placed

> **Governments need to focus on providing money and resources for education and training for the groups most at risk.**

to adapt to new technologies, almost 20 percent of people aged 20 and below in OECD countries work in low-skilled jobs, like cleaning and food preparation, while 34 percent are in sales and personal services—all jobs likely to suffer from automation.

These trends are particularly important as they show how this coming wave of job losses could further polarize society between high-paying, high-skilled jobs, and low-paying, insecure occupations.

Previous research has come to similar conclusions, with a study published last July in the UK showing that AI and robotics are likely to stifle social mobility. This is because of a number of overlapping factors, including the fact that those in low-paying jobs are less likely to be able to retrain for new professions and because automation is likely to kill off many routine jobs that were stepping stones into professional careers for people with low education, like doing admin work in a legal office, for example.

The OECD's research, which was published last month but resurfaced by a recent story in the *Financial Times*, stresses that "technology will without doubt also bring about many new jobs," but in light of these forecasts, governments need to focus on providing money and resources for education and training for the groups most at risk.

"Re-qualification is an important mechanism to aid the transition from more to less automatable jobs," write the researchers, adding that it is "important not to dismiss the importance of providing retraining and social protection" for young workers and those in low-skilled jobs.

The coming wave of automation may not be as destructive as we have previously feared, but that does not mean we can afford to be complacent.

## Print Citations

**CMS:** Vincent, James. "AI and Robots Will Destroy Fewer Jobs Than Previously Feared, Says New OECD Report." In *The Reference Shelf: Artificial Intelligence*, edited by Micah Issitt, 86-88. Ipswich, MA: H.W. Wilson, 2018.

**MLA:** Vincent, James. "AI and Robots Will Destroy Fewer Jobs Than Previously Feared, Says New OECD Report." *The Reference Shelf: Artificial Intelligence*. Ed. Micah Issitt. Ipswich: H.W. Wilson, 2018. 86-88. Print.

**APA:** Vincent, J. (2018). AI and robots will destroy fewer jobs than previously feared, says new OECD report. In Micah Issitt (Ed.), *The reference shelf: Artificial intelligence* (pp. 86-88). Ipswich, MA: H.W. Wilson. (Original work published 2018)

# Tech Companies Should Stop Pretending AI Won't Destroy Jobs

By Kai-Fu Lee

*MIT Technology Review*, February 21, 2018

I took an Uber to an artificial-intelligence conference at MIT one recent morning, and the driver asked me how long it would take for autonomous vehicles to take away his job. I told him it would happen in about 15 to 20 years. He breathed a sigh of relief. "Well, I'll be retired by then," he said.

Good thing we weren't in China. If a driver there had asked, I would have had to tell him he'd lose his job in about 10 years—maybe 15 if he was lucky.

That might sound surprising, given that the US is, and has been, in the lead in AI research. But China is catching up—if it hasn't already—and that rivalry, with one nation playing off the other, guarantees that AI is coming.

China will have at least a 50/50 chance of winning the race, and there are several reasons for that.

First, China has a huge army of young people coming into AI. Over the past decade, the number of AI publications by Chinese authors has doubled. Young AI engineers from Face++, a Chinese face-recognition startup, recently won first place in three computer-vision challenges—ahead of teams from Google, Microsoft, Facebook, and Carnegie Mellon University.

Second, China has more data than the US—way more. Data is what makes AI go. A very good scientist with a ton of data will beat a super scientist with a modest amount of data. China has the most mobile phones and internet users in the world—triple the number in the United States. But the gap is even bigger than that because of the way people in China use their devices. People there carry no cash. They pay all their utility bills with their phones. They can do all their shopping on their phones. You get off work and open an app to order food. By the time you reach home, the food is right there, hot off the electric motorbike. In China, shared bicycles generate 30 terabytes of sensor data in their 50 million paid rides per day—that's roughly 300 times the data being generated in the US.

Third, Chinese AI companies have passed the copycat phase. Fifteen years ago almost every decent startup in China was simply copying the functionality, look, and feel of products offered in the US. But all that copying taught eager Chinese entrepreneurs how to become good product managers, and now they're on to the next stage: exceeding their overseas counterparts. Even today, Weibo is better than Twitter. WeChat delivers a way better experience than Facebook Messenger.

And fourth, government policies are accelerating AI in China. The Chinese government's stated plan is to catch up with the US on AI technology and applications by 2020 and to become a global AI innovation hub by 2030. In a speech in October, President Xi Jinping encouraged further integration of the internet, big data, and artificial intelligence with the real-world economy. And in case you're wondering, these things tend not to be all talk in China—as demonstrated with its past policies promoting high-speed rail and the mass entrepreneurship and innovation movement. In comparison, things get bogged down in the US. Consider the way President Barack Obama's loan guarantee to solar-panel maker Solyndra was hammered as crony capitalism. Truckers are now appealing to President Donald Trump and Congress to stop testing of autonomous trucks.

> **We need to find the jobs that AI can't do and train people to do them. We need to reinvent education.**

The rise of China as an AI superpower isn't a big deal just for China. The competition between the US and China has sparked intense advances in AI that will be impossible to stop anywhere. The change will be massive, and not all of it good. Inequality will widen. As my Uber driver in Cambridge has already intuited, AI will displace a large number of jobs, which will cause social discontent. Consider the progress of Google DeepMind's AlphaGo software, which beat the best human players of the board game Go in early 2016. It was subsequently bested by AlphaGo Zero, introduced in 2017, which learned by playing games against itself and within 40 days was superior to all the earlier versions. Now imagine those improvements transferring to areas like customer service, telemarketing, assembly lines, reception desks, truck driving, and other routine blue-collar and white-collar work. It will soon be obvious that half of our job tasks can be done better at almost no cost by AI and robots. This will be the fastest transition humankind has experienced, and we're not ready for it.

Not everyone agrees with my view. Some people argue that it will take longer than we think before jobs disappear, since many jobs will be only partially replaced, and companies will try to redeploy those displaced internally. But even if true, that won't stop the inevitable. Others remind us that every technology revolution has created new jobs as it displaced old ones. But it's dangerous to assume this will be the case again.

Then there are the symbiotic optimists, who think that AI combined with humans should be better than either one alone. This will be true for certain professions—doctors, lawyers—but most jobs won't fall in that category. Instead they are routine, single-domain jobs where AI excels over the human by a large margin.

Others think we'll be saved by a universal basic income. "Take the extra money made by AI and distribute it to the people who lost their jobs," they say. "This additional income will help people find their new path, and replace other types of social welfare." But UBI doesn't address people's loss of dignity or meet their need to feel useful. It's just a convenient way for a beneficiary of the AI revolution to sit back and do nothing.

And finally, there are those who deny that AI has any downside at all—which is the position taken by many of the largest AI companies. It's unfortunate that AI experts aren't trying to solve the problem. What's worse, and unbelievably selfish, is that they actually refuse to acknowledge the problem exists in the first place.

These changes are coming, and we need to tell the truth and the whole truth. We need to find the jobs that AI can't do and train people to do them. We need to reinvent education. These will be the best of times and the worst of times. If we act rationally and quickly, we can bask in what's best rather than wallow in what's worst.

## Print Citations

**CMS:** Lee, Kai-Fu. "Tech Companies Should Stop Pretending AI Won't Destroy Jobs." In *The Reference Shelf: Artificial Intelligence*, edited by Micah Issitt, 89-91. Ipswich, MA: H.W. Wilson, 2018.

**MLA:** Lee, Kai-Fu. "Tech Companies Should Stop Pretending AI Won't Destroy Jobs." *The Reference Shelf: Artificial Intelligence*. Ed. Micah Issitt. Ipswich: H.W. Wilson, 2018. 89-91. Print.

**APA:** Lee, K.-F. (2018). Tech companies should stop pretending AI won't destroy jobs. In Micah Issitt (Ed.), *The reference shelf: Artificial intelligence* (pp. 89-91). Ipswich, MA: H.W. Wilson. (Original work published 2018)

# 3

# War Games: AI in the Military

This United States Air Force (USAF) Global Hawk drone is an unmanned aircraft system (UAS) surveillance aircraft, manufactured by Northrop Grumman Corp. Here, it stands on display at the Singapore Airshow held at the Changi Exhibition Centre in Singapore, February 5, 2018. According to the United States Air Force, the superior surveillance capabilities of the aircraft allow more precise weapons targeting and better protection of friendly forces.

# Automated Warfare

The US military has played a dominant role in supporting and soliciting research in artificial intelligence since the 1950s, when the field first emerged as a unique scientific discipline. In 2018, the most well-known example of military artificial intelligence (AI) can be seen in the rapidly evolving technology used in drones, which have become one of the most controversial aspects of modern US military strategy. Supporters claim that military AI can save lives, with automated weapons helping to keep real soldiers safe from harm, but critics have raised ethical and moral objections to the practice of removing the human element from decisions with life and death consequences.

## The Role of Artificial Intelligence in Warfare

For the military, the advantage of using AI and robotics lies in not having to put a human in danger when launching an attack, conducting reconnaissance, or engaging in any number of other military operations. In 2018, the Pentagon has made no secret of its intention to weaponize AI, despite the passionate objections of many experts in the field and human rights activists. This goal is not new for the American military establishment and, in fact, the US military has been experimenting with autonomous weaponry from the moment technology to create autonomous weapons became available.

The technology behind radio control, the first remote control system, was actually developed just prior to World War I and is one of several groundbreaking inventions attributed to polymath and inventor Nikola Tesla. Radio technology was one of the tools that the military quickly sought to weaponize in the lead-up to World War I. Remote weapons used in the conflict included "the land torpedo," an armored tractor that carried 1,000 pounds of explosives and was intended to be piloted by remote control into enemy trenches. Most of the unmanned and remote weapons programs initiated at this time produced little in the way of effective results and many experimental remote weapons were never deployed. However, the German military succeeded where the United States failed, creating the FL-7 wire-guided motorboat, which could be piloted from a distance, carried 300 pounds of explosives, and was meant to be crashed into the side of enemy ships. The FL-7, armed with Tesla's radio-control device, was used to attack and damage the *HMS Erebus* in 1917.[1]

During World War II, the unmanned weapons race really began to accelerate. The Nazi Party military complex invested heavily in remote-control weaponry, creating the Goliath tracked mine, a go-cart outfitted with 100 pounds of explosives and designed to be rammed into tanks and bunkers. But Germany's most successful innovations in remote control came in the form of aerial weapons like the V-2 ballistic missile, and the FX 1400 Fritz, a 3,000-pound gliding bomb outfitted with a

700-pound warhead, a rocket motor, and a long-distance radio-control system. The United States countered with a bigger, more ambitious plan, outfitting entire bombers with 10 tons of Torpex explosives and radio control, with the idea being that the crew would get the vehicle aloft and then bail out, steering the now-unmanned bomber made into a bomb into enemy targets. There was only one trial of the system, which resulted in disaster when the weapon exploded prematurely, killing the pilots and crew before they could safely parachute out of the vehicle. The US side also used gliding, remote-controlled bombs similar to the ones used by the German side, but without any major success.[2]

During the 1960s and 70s, the US military made major advancement with unmanned aircraft. The Model 147 Lightning Bug, a small reconnaissance craft, was used for more than 3,400 missions during the Vietnam war and, in the 1970s, the MGM-105 Aquila program saw a new generation of unmanned reconnaissance drones, though the project, because there were no active military deployments at the time, was not well developed. The Persian Gulf War reignited military interest in unmanned vehicles, but it was the Israeli-designed Pioneer drone that was the most successful example from the era, capable of dropping a 2,000- pound explosive shell.[3]

The major milestone in the transition to the modern computer-guided drones was the development of GPS, or the global positioning system, a satellite tracking and guidance system that could be used to guide unmanned aircraft by sending signals to space. What this meant, essentially, was that it was now possible to pilot a remote vehicle from anywhere in the world. By this time, remote-piloted aerial vehicles, called UAVs or unmanned aerial vehicles in military parlance, were becoming familiar, but it wasn't until the 2000s that UAVs made major news when the United States drastically accelerated its UAV program during the invasion of Iraq and Afghanistan, and in subsequent struggles against radical militant groups in the Middle East and parts of Africa.

## The State of AI in the Military

As of 2018, most of the robotic and AI-enhanced weapons used by the United States fall into the UAV or drone category. The first use of a drone by the US military came on November 14, 2001, when a drone designed as an anti-tank weapon was re-purposed for use in the emerging "war on terror." The drone, a "Predator" model, fired a hellfire missile at a suspected group of Al-Qaida-linked radicals in Afghanistan. Two missiles were fired, destroying two buildings and killing Mohammed Atef, a military chief for Al-Qaida and son-in-law of infamous radical Osama Bin Laden.[4] The success of this attack led to a burst of interest in the emerging technology; over the ensuing decade, hundreds of drone strikes were orchestrated by the US military and Central Intelligence Agency (CIA) in Afghanistan, Iraq, Yemen, and in many other locations where US forces were targeting suspected radicals.

A report on *Tech Emergence* in 2017 indicated that the US military was spending at least $2.8 billion per year on drones and drone development, with the expectation that investment will equal $9.4 billion by 2025. While drone research and use has expanded in many countries in recent years, studies indicate that the United States conducts more than 77 percent of all drone research and investment and, in fact, *Tech Emergence* found that the United States Air Force had more openings for drone pilots listed in 2017 than for any other type of pilot position.[5]

Not all UAVs used by the military utilize artificial intelligence, but the integration of intelligent control, targeting, and strategic systems is currently one of the most active areas of drone research and development. As of 2018, AI-guided systems are only used in reconnaissance craft and are not used in UAVs capable of launching air strikes. However, the US military has released reports defining a plan to rely increasingly on fully automated intelligent systems in the future. This is only one arm of the Department of Defense (DoD) plans for AI, which also includes the development of an intelligent security system that could react to global threats far faster than human observers could process the relevant information.

A 2016 report from the DoD essentially stated that fully automated AI warfare was inevitable and thus made the case that the DoD needs to invest heavily now to ensure that the United States remains ahead of rival countries.[6] The Defense Advanced Research Projects Agency (DARPA) is the primary research organization behind much of the drone research conducted in the United States and is currently working on a program known as CODE (Collaborative Operations in Denied Environment), which seeks to create fully automated drones equipped to conduct attacks. DoD documents indicate that the military is working towards creating fleets of AI-controlled craft that can communicate with each other and with human operators or managers who may also be involved in operations. Towards this goal, DARPA is also developing a new suite of software known as Behavioral Learning for Adaptive Electronic Warfare (BLADE), which is a machine learning program aiming to create adaptable, learning systems for combat enabled drones.[7]

## Supporters and Opponents

The arguments for and against the military use of AI are similar to the arguments for and against long range weapons, nuclear arms, and many other types of modern warfare technology. Drones separate the attackers from the attack, and thus, some critics argue that this eliminates the horror of warfare and makes it more likely that the attacker will attack indiscriminately or will choose to attack rather than pursuing other means of resolution. Thus, critics argue that drone warfare has reduced the horror of war to a "video game" wherein CIA and military pilots are free to attack with impunity, mercifully removed from the consequences of those actions.

Supporters of drones, similar to supporters of long-range missiles or nuclear weapons, make the simple, logical argument that drones keep soldiers who might otherwise be in danger safe. Further, supporters argue that the evolution of warfare is necessarily leading to full automation and so that the United States must lead this field or risk being the victims, rather than the perpetrators, of automated violence.

The drones currently used by the US military are at the cutting edge of UAV technology and are equipped with advanced targeting and analysis equipment, in addition to weapons. Supporters of drone use thus argue that these new tools are so much more precise than traditional weapons that they enable the military to reduce and, at times, completely eliminate the possibility of civilian deaths. Official CIA and DoD reports hold that civilian casualties have been minimal since the use of drones began in 2001 and that civilian deaths are typically in the "single-digits" when drone and air strikes are used. The claims that drones have resulted in few civilian deaths has been criticized by human rights observers working in countries where drones have been frequently used. The Bureau of Investigative Journalism (BIJ) has been tracking US covert drone strikes since 2010 and has recorded 4,799 strikes, killing between 7–10 thousand, with at least 700 to 1,500 or more civilians among those killed, including 242–337 children. The data presented by the bureau is taken from interviews of civilians on the scene where drone strikes have occurred and from human rights, medical, and relief workers active in those countries. Further, the BIJ believes that the estimates the organization has collected vastly underestimate the actual number of civilians who have been killed in drone strikes.[8]

Critics argue further that the US drone-based strategy in the war on terror might be exacerbating the conflict. For instance, testifying before the United States Senate in 2013, Yemeni writer Farea Al-Muslimi explained that drone strikes are driving people towards radicalism. Describing one such incident that he personally observed, Al-Muslimi testified, "The Toaiman's oldest son joined Al-Qaeda in the Arabian Peninsula (AQAP) hoping to avenge the death of his father, an innocent civilian killed by a drone strike in October 2011. The son has 28 brothers waiting to do so as well. One of his youngest brothers, a 9 year old, carries a picture of a plane in his pocket. The boy openly states that he wants revenge and identifies his father's killer as 'America'."

For all the controversy surrounding drone strikes, critics fear that full automation would only make matters worse. In this case, the military would entirely remove human empathy, and the nuanced decision-making that empathy encourages, from the equation, leaving life-and-death decisions to be made by emotionless machines whose decisions are guided by a cost and benefit analysis. In 2017, a group of more than 100 CEOs and researchers at the forefront of AI technology contributed to an open letter condemning the use of autonomous weapons and arguing that even the development of such weapons presents a serious danger to the world as radical groups and despots will undoubtedly obtain such weapons and could use them to conduct violence and terror on a scale previously unimagined.[9]

In 2018, the military AI debate hit the news again when employees at companies courted by the DoD as partners in developing AI technology protested the use of their research and tech expertise for such a goal. Citizen activism has become more evident as well, with organizations like the Campaign to Stop Killer Robots making news as they petition major corporations investing in AI to sign onto possible plans for United Nations' regulations before true AI-guided weaponry becomes a reality.

Micah L. Issitt

## Works Used

Baldwin, Roberto. "The Robots of War: AI and the Future of Combat." *Endgadget*. Oath Tech Network. Retrieved from https://www.engadget.com/2016/08/18/robots-of-war-ai-and-the-future-of-combat/.

"Drone Warfare." *Thebureauinvestigates*. Bureau of Investigative Journalism. Web. 2018. Retrieved from https://www.thebureauinvestigates.com/projects/drone-war.

Gershgorn, Dave. "The US Government Seriously Wants to Weaponize Artificial Intelligence." *Quartz*. Quartz Media. Aug 26, 2016. Web. Retrieved from https://qz.com/767648/weaponized-artificial-intelligence-us-military/.

Kaplan, Fred. "The First Drone Strike." *Slate*. Slate Group. Sep 14, 2016. Web. Retrieved from http://www.slate.com/articles/news_and_politics/the_next_20/2016/09/a_history_of_the_armed_drone.html.

"Pioneer Short Range (SR) UAV." *FAS*. Federation of American Scientists. Mar 5, 2009. Web. Retrieved from https://fas.org/irp/program/collect/pioneer.htm.

Rothman, Wilson. "Unmanned Warbots of WWI and WWII." *Gizmodo*. Gawker Media. Mar 24, 2009. Web. Retrieved from https://gizmodo.com/5181576/unmanned-warbots-of-wwi-and-wwii.

Sharre, Paul. "Why We Must Not Build Automated Weapons of War." *Time*. Time, Inc. Sep 25, 2017. Web. Retrieved from http://time.com/4948633/robots-artificial-intelligence-war/.

Singer, P. W. "Drones Don't Die–A History of Military Robotics." *History Net*. World History Group. May 5, 2011. Web. Retrieved from http://www.historynet.com/drones-dont-die-a-history-of-military-robotics.htm.

Walker, Jon. "Unmanned Aerial Vehicles (UAVs) –Comparing the USA, Israel, and China." *Tech Emergence*. Tech Emergence. Web. Retrieved from https://www.techemergence.com/unmanned-aerial-vehicles-uavs/.

## Notes

1. Rothman, "Unmanned Warbots of WWI and WWII."
2. Singer, "Drones Don't Die–A History of Military Robotics."
3. "Pioneer Short Range (SR) UAV," *FAS*.
4. Kaplan, "The First Drone Strike."
5. Walker, "Unmanned Aerial Vehicles (UAVs) –Comparing the USA, Israel, and China."
6. Gershgorn, "The US Government Seriously Wants to Weaponize Artificial Intelligence."
7. Baldwin, "The Robots of War: AI and the Future of Combat."
8. "Drone Warfare," *Thebureauinvestigates*.
9. Sharre, "Why We Must Not Build Automated Weapons of War."

# Researchers to Boycott South Korean University over AI Weapons Work

By Andrea Shalal
*Reuters*, April 4, 2018

BERLIN (Reuters)—Over 50 top Artificial Intelligence researchers on Wednesday announced a boycott of KAIST, South Korea's top university, after it opened what they called an AI weapons lab with one of South Korea's largest companies.

The researchers, based in 30 countries, said they would refrain from visiting KAIST, hosting visitors from the university, or cooperating with its research programs until it pledged to refrain from developing AI weapons without "meaningful human control".

KAIST, which opened the center in February with Hanwha Systems, one of two South Korean makers of cluster munitions, responded within hours, saying it had "no intention to engage in development of lethal autonomous weapons systems and killer robots."

University President Sung-Chul Shin said the university was "significantly aware" of ethical concerns regarding Artificial Intelligence, adding, "I reaffirm once again that KAIST will not conduct any research activities counter to human dignity including autonomous weapons lacking meaningful human control."

The university said the new Research Centre for the Convergence of National Defence and Artificial Intelligence would focus on using AI for command and control systems, navigation for large unmanned undersea vehicles, smart aircraft training and tracking and recognition of objects.

Toby Walsh, the professor at the University of New South Wales in Sydney who organized the boycott, said the university's quick response was a success, but he needed to speak with all those who signed the letter before calling off the boycott.

"KAIST has made two significant concessions: not to develop autonomous weapons and to ensure meaningful human control," he said, adding that the university's response would add weight to U.N. discussions taking place next week on the overall issue.

Walsh said it remained unclear how one could establish meaningful human control of an unmanned submarine—one of the launch projects—when it was under the sea and unable to communicate.

In an open letter announcing the boycott, the researchers had warned: "If developed, autonomous weapons will ... permit war to be fought faster and at a scale great

> **"We should not hand over the decision of who lives or dies to a machine. This crosses a clear moral line."**

than ever before. They will have the potential to be weapons of terror."

They cited effective bans on previous arms technologies and urged KAIST ban any work on lethal autonomous weapons, and to refrain from AI uses that would harm human lives.

AI is the field in computer science that aims to create machines able to perceive the environment and make decisions.

The letter, also signed by top experts on deep learning and robotics, was released ahead of next Monday's meeting in Geneva by 123 U.N. member countries on the challenges posed by lethal autonomous weapons, which critics describe as "killer robots".

Walsh told *Reuters* there were many potential good uses of robotics and Artificial Intelligence in the military, including removing humans from dangerous task such as clearing minefields.

"But we should not hand over the decision of who lives or dies to a machine. This crosses a clear moral line," he said. "We should not let robots decide who lives and who dies."

## Print Citations

**CMS:** Shalal, Andrea. "Researchers to Boycott South Korean University over AI Weapons Work." In *The Reference Shelf: Artificial Intelligence*, edited by Micah Issitt, 101-102. Ipswich, MA: H.W. Wilson, 2018.

**MLA:** Shalal, Andrea. "Researchers to Boycott South Korean University over AI Weapons Work." *The Reference Shelf: Artificial Intelligence*. Ed. Micah Issitt. Ipswich: H.W. Wilson, 2018. 101-102. Print.

**APA:** Shalal, A. (2018). Researchers to boycott South Korean university over AI weapons work. In Micah Issitt (Ed.), *The reference shelf: Artificial intelligence* (pp. 101-102). Ipswich, MA: H.W. Wilson. (Original work published 2018)

# Pentagon Wants Silicon Valley's Help on A.I.

### By Cade Metz
*The New York Times*, March 18, 2018

---

SAN FRANCISCO—There is little doubt that the Defense Department needs help from Silicon Valley's biggest companies as it pursues work on artificial intelligence. The question is whether the people who work at those companies are willing to cooperate.

On Thursday, Robert O. Work, a former deputy secretary of defense, announced that he is teaming up with the Center for a New American Security, an influential Washington think tank that specializes in national security, to create a task force of former government officials, academics and representatives from private industry. Their goal is to explore how the federal government should embrace A.I. technology and work better with big tech companies and other organizations.

There is a growing sense of urgency to the question of what the United States is doing in artificial intelligence. China has vowed to become the world's leader in A.I. by 2030, committing billions of dollars to the effort. Like many other officials from government and industry, Mr. Work believes the United States risks falling behind: "The question is, how should the United States respond to this challenge?" he said. "This is a Sputnik moment."

The military and intelligence communities have long played a big role in the technology industry and had close ties with many of Silicon Valley's early tech giants. David Packard, Hewlett-Packard's co-founder, even served as the deputy secretary of defense under President Richard M. Nixon.

But those relations have soured in recent years—at least with the rank and file of some better-known companies. In 2013, documents leaked by the former defense contractor Edward J. Snowden revealed the breadth of spying on Americans by intelligence services, including monitoring the users of several large internet companies.

Two years ago, that antagonism grew worse after the F.B.I. demanded that Apple create special software to help it gain access to a locked iPhone that had belonged to a gunman involved in a mass shooting in San Bernardino, Calif.

"In the wake of Edward Snowden, there has been a lot of concern over what it would mean for Silicon Valley companies to work with the national security community," said Gregory Allen, an adjunct fellow with the Center for a New American

---

> **Among A.I. researchers and other technologists, there is widespread fear that today's machine learning techniques could put too much power in dangerous hands.**

Security. "These companies are—understandably—very cautious about these relationships."

The Pentagon needs help on A.I. from Silicon Valley because that's where the talent is. The tech industry's biggest companies have been hoarding A.I. expertise, sometimes offering multimillion-dollar pay packages that the government could never hope to match.

Mr. Work was the driving force behind the creation of Project Maven, the Defense Department's sweeping effort to embrace artificial intelligence. His new task force will include Terah Lyons, the executive director of the Partnership on AI, an industry group that includes many of Silicon Valley's biggest companies.

Mr. Work will lead the 18-member task force with Andrew Moore, the dean of computer science at Carnegie Mellon University. Mr. Moore has warned that too much of the country's computer science talent is going to work at America's largest internet companies.

With tech companies gobbling up all that talent, who will train the next generation of A.I. experts? Who will lead government efforts?

"Even if the U.S. does have the best A.I. companies, it is not clear they are going to be involved in national security in a substantive way," Mr. Allen said.

Google illustrates the challenges that big internet companies face in working more closely with the Pentagon. Google's former executive chairman, Eric Schmidt, who is still a member of the board of directors of its parent company, Alphabet, also leads the Defense Innovation Board, a federal advisory committee that recommends closer collaboration with industry on A.I. technologies.

Last week, two news outlets revealed that the Defense Department had been working with Google in developing A.I. technology that can analyze aerial footage captured by flying drones. The effort was part of Project Maven, led by Mr. Work. Some employees were angered that the company was contributing to military work.

Google runs two of the best A.I. research labs in the world—Google Brain in California and DeepMind in London.

Top researchers inside both Google A.I. labs have expressed concern over the use of A.I. by the military. When Google acquired DeepMind, the company agreed to set up an internal board that would help ensure that the lab's technology was used in an ethical way. And one of the lab's founders, Demis Hassabis, has explicity said its A.I. would not be used for military purposes.

Google acknowledged in a statement that the military use of A.I. "raises valid concerns" and said it was working on policies around the use of its so-called machine learning technologies.

Among A.I. researchers and other technologists, there is widespread fear that today's machine learning techniques could put too much power in dangerous hands. A recent report from prominent labs and think tanks in both the United States and

Britain detailed the risks, including problems with weapons and surveillance equipment.

Google said it was working with the Defense Department to build technology for "non-offensive uses only." And Mr. Work said the government explored many technologies that did not involve "lethal force." But it is unclear where Google and other top internet companies will draw the line.

"This is a conversation we have to have," Mr. Work said.

## Print Citations

**CMS:** Metz, Cade. "Pentagon Wants Silicon Valley's Help on A.I." In *The Reference Shelf: Artificial Intelligence*, edited by Micah Issitt, 103-105. Ipswich, MA: H.W. Wilson, 2018.

**MLA:** Metz, Cade. "Pentagon Wants Silicon Valley's Help on A.I." *The Reference Shelf: Artificial Intelligence*. Ed. Micah Issitt. Ipswich: H.W. Wilson, 2018. 103-105. Print.

**APA:** Metz, C. (2018). Pentagon wants Silicon Valley's help on A.I. In Micah Issitt (Ed.), *The reference shelf: Artificial intelligence* (pp. 103-105). Ipswich, MA: H.W. Wilson. (Original work published 2018)

# Google's AI Is Being Used by US Military Drone Programme

## By Samuel Gibbs
*The Guardian*, March 7, 2018

Google's artificial intelligence technologies are being used by the US military for one of its drone projects, causing controversy both inside and outside the company.

Google's TensorFlow AI systems are being used by the US Department of Defense's (DoD) Project Maven, which was established in July last year to use machine learning and artificial intelligence to analyse the vast amount of footage shot by US drones. The initial intention is to have AI analyse the video, detect objects of interest and flag them for a human analyst to review.

Drew Cukor, chief of the DoD's Algorithmic Warfare Cross-Function Team, said in July: "People and computers will work symbiotically to increase the ability of weapon systems to detect objects. Eventually we hope that one analyst will be able to do twice as much work, potentially three times as much, as they're doing now. That's our goal."

Project Maven forms part of the $7.4bn spent on AI and data processing by the DoD, and has seen the Pentagon partner with various academics and experts in the field of AI and data processing. It has reportedly already been put into use against Islamic State.

A Google spokesperson said: "This specific project is a pilot with the Department of Defense, to provide open source TensorFlow APIs that can assist in object recognition on unclassified data. The technology flags images for human review, and is for non-offensive uses only."

While Google has long worked with government agencies providing technology and services, alongside cloud providers such as Amazon and Microsoft, the move to aid Project Maven has reportedly caused much internal debate at the search company. According to people talking to Gizmodo, some Google employees were outraged when they discovered the use of the company's AI.

"Military use of machine learning naturally raises valid concerns. We're actively discussing this important topic internally and with others as we continue to develop policies and safeguards around the development and use of our machine learning technologies," said Google.

Both former Alphabet executive chairman, Eric Schmidt, and Google executive Milo Medin are members of the Defense Innovation Board, which advises the

Pentagon on cloud and data systems.

**The move to aid Project Maven has reportedly caused much internal debate at the search company.**

Google has a mixed history with defence contracts. When it bought robotics firm Shaft, it pulled the company's systems from a Pentagon competition, while it cut defence-related contracts on buying the satellite startup Skybox. When it owned robotics firm Boston Dynamics, the company was attempting to make a robotic packhorse for ground troops, which was ultimately rejected by the US marines because it was too noisy.

The company's cloud services division currently does not offer systems designed to hold information classified as secret, where its competitors Amazon and Microsoft do.

When Google bought the UK's artificial intelligence firm DeepMind in 2014 for £400m, the company set up an AI ethics board, which was tasked with reviewing the company's use of AI, although details of the board were still not made public three years later.

### Print Citations

**CMS:** Gibbs, Samuel. "Google's AI Is Being Used by US Military Drone Programme." In *The Reference Shelf: Artificial Intelligence*, edited by Micah Issitt, 106-107. Ipswich, MA: H.W. Wilson, 2018.

**MLA:** Gibbs, Samuel. "Google's AI Is Being Used by US Military Drone Programme." *The Reference Shelf: Artificial Intelligence*. Ed. Micah Issitt. Ipswich: H.W. Wilson, 2018. 106-107. Print.

**APA:** Gibbs, S. (2018). Google's AI is being used by US military drone programme. In Micah Issitt (Ed.), *The reference shelf: Artificial intelligence* (pp. 106-107). Ipswich, MA: H.W. Wilson. (Original work published 2018)

# Google Should Not Help the U.S. Military Build Unaccountable AI Systems

## By Peter Eckersley and Cindy Cohn
*Electronic Frontier Foundation*, April 5, 2018

Thousands of Google staff have been speaking out against the company's work for "Project Maven," according to a *New York Times* report this week. The program is a U.S. Department of Defense (DoD) initiative to deploy machine learning for military purposes. There was a small amount of public reporting last month that Google had become a contractor for that project, but those stories had not captured how extensive Google's involvement was, nor how controversial it has become within the company.

Outcry from Google's own staff is reportedly ongoing, and the letter signed by employees asks Google to commit publicly to not assisting with warfare technology. We are sure this is a difficult decision for Google's leadership; we hope they weigh it carefully.

This post outlines some of the questions that people inside and outside of the company should be mulling about whether it's a good idea for companies with deep machine learning expertise to be assisting with military deployments of artificial intelligence (AI).

According to Google's statement last month, the company provided "open source TensorFlow APIs" to the DoD. But it appears that this controversy was not just about the company giving the DoD a regular Google cloud account on which to train TensorFlow models. A letter signed by Google employees implies that the company also provided access to its state-of-the-art machine learning expertise, as well as engineering staff to assist or work directly on the DoD's efforts. The company has said that it is doing object recognition "for non-offensive uses only," though reading some of the published documents and discussions about the project suggest that the situation is murkier. *The New York Times* says that "the Pentagon's video analysis is routinely used in counterinsurgency and counterterrorism operations, and Defense Department publications make clear that the project supports those operations."

If our reading of the public record is correct, systems that Google is supporting or building would flag people or objects seen by drones for human review, and in some cases this would lead to subsequent missile strikes on those people or objects.

Those are hefty ethical stakes, even with humans in the loop further along the "kill chain".

We're glad that Google is now debating the project internally. While there aren't enough published details for us to comment definitively, we share many of the concerns we've heard from colleagues within Google, and we have a few suggestions for any AI company that's considering becoming a defense contractor.

We'll start with the obvious: it's incredibly risky to be using AI systems in military situations where even seemingly small problems can result in fatalities, in the escalation of conflicts, or in wider instability. AI systems can often be difficult to control and may fail in surprising ways. In military situations, failure of AI could be grave, subtle, and hard to address. The boundaries of what is and isn't dangerous can be difficult to see. More importantly, society has not yet agreed upon necessary rules and standards for transparency, risk, and accountability for non-military uses of AI, much less for military uses.

Companies, and the individuals who work inside them, should be extremely cautious about working with any military agency where the application involves potential harm to humans or could contribute to arms races or geopolitical instability. Those risks are substantial and difficult to predict, let alone mitigate.

If a company nevertheless is determined to use its AI expertise to aid some nation's military, it must start by recognizing that there are no settled public standards for safety and ethics in this sector yet. It cannot just assume that the contracting military agency has fully assessed the risks or that it doesn't have a responsibility to do so independently.

At a minimum, any company, or any worker, considering whether to work with the military on a project with potentially dangerous or risky AI applications should be asking:

1. Is it possible to create strong and binding international institutions or agreements that define acceptable military uses and limitations in the use of AI? While this is not an easy task, the current lack of such structures is troubling. There are serious and potentially destabilizing impacts from deploying AI in any military setting not clearly governed by settled rules of war. The use of AI in potential target identification processes is one clear category of uses that must be governed by law.

2. Is there a robust process for studying and mitigating the safety and geopolitical stability problems that could result from the deployment of military AI? Does this process apply before work commences, along the development pathway and after deployment? Could it incorporate sufficient expertise to address subtle and complex technical problems? And would those leading the process have sufficient independence and authority to ensure that it can check companies' and military agencies' decisions?

3. Are the contracting agencies willing to commit to not using AI for autonomous offensive weapons? Or to ensuring that any defensive autonomous systems are carefully engineered to avoid risks of accidental harm or conflict escalation? Are present testing and formal verification methods adequate for that task?

4. Can there be transparent, accountable oversight from an independently constituted ethics board or similar entity with both the power to veto aspects of the program and the power to bring public transparency to issues where necessary or appropriate? For example, while Alphabet's AI-focused subsidiary DeepMind has committed to independent ethics review, we are not aware of similar commitments from Google itself. Given this letter, we are concerned that the internal transparency, review, and discussion of Project Maven inside Google was inadequate. Any project review process must be transparent, informed, and independent. While it remains difficult to ensure that that is the case, without such independent oversight, a project runs real risk of harm.

> **Outcry from Google's own staff is reportedly ongoing, and the letter signed by employees asks Google to commit publicly to not assisting with warfare technology.**

These are just starting points. Other specific questions will surely need answering, both for future proposals and even this one, since many details of the Project Maven collaboration are not public. Nevertheless, even with the limited information available, EFF is deeply worried that Google's collaboration with the Department of Defense does not have these kinds of safeguards. It certainly does not have them in a public, transparent, or accountable way.

The use of AI in weapons systems is a crucially important topic and one that deserves an international public discussion and likely some international agreements to ensure global safety. Companies like Google, as well as their counterparts around the world, must consider the consequences and demand real accountability and standards of behavior from the military agencies that seek their expertise—and from themselves.

## Print Citations

**CMS:** Eckersley, Peter, and Cindy Cohn. "Google Should Not Help the U.S. Military Build Unaccountable AI Systems." In *The Reference Shelf: Artificial Intelligence*, edited by Micah Issitt, 108-110. Ipswich, MA: H.W. Wilson, 2018.

**MLA:** Eckersley, Peter, and Cindy Cohn. "Google Should Not Help the U.S. Military Build Unaccountable AI Systems." *The Reference Shelf: Artificial Intelligence*. Ed. Micah Issitt. Ipswich: H.W. Wilson, 2018. 108-110. Print.

**APA:** Eckersley, P., & C. Cohn. (2018). Google should not help the U.S. military build unaccountable AI systems. In Micah Issitt (Ed.), *The reference shelf: Artificial intelligence* (pp. 108-110). Ipswich, MA: H.W. Wilson. (Original work published 2018)

# AI Could Revoluntionize War as Much as Nukes

## By Tom Simonite
### *Wired*, July 19, 2017

In 1889, the world's most powerful nations signed a treaty at The Hague that banned military use of aircraft, fearing the emerging technology's destructive power. Five years later the moratorium was allowed to expire, and before long aircraft were helping to enable the slaughter of World War I. "Some technologies are so powerful as to be irresistible," says Greg Allen, a fellow at the Center for New American Security, a non-partisan Washington DC think tank. "Militaries around the world have essentially come to the same conclusion with respect to artificial intelligence."

Allen is coauthor of a 132-page new report on the effect of artificial intelligence on national security. One of its conclusions is that the impact of technologies such as autonomous robots on war and international relations could rival that of nuclear weapons. The report was produced by Harvard's Belfer Center for Science and International Affairs, at the request of IARPA, the research agency of the Office of the Director of National Intelligence. It lays out why technologies like drones with bird-like agility, robot hackers, and software that generates photo-real fake video are on track to make the American military and its rivals much more powerful.

New technologies like those can be expected to bring with them a series of excruciating moral, political, and diplomatic choices for America and other nations. Building up a new breed of military equipment using artificial intelligence is one thing—deciding what uses of this new power are acceptable is another. The report recommends that the US start considering what uses of AI in war should be restricted using international treaties.

## New World Order

The US military has been funding, testing and deploying various shades of machine intelligence for a long time. In 2001, Congress even mandated that one-third of ground combat vehicles should be uncrewed by 2015—a target that has been missed. But the Harvard report argues that recent, rapid progress in artificial intelligence that has invigorated companies such as Google and Amazon is poised to bring an unprecedented surge in military innovation. "Even if all progress in basic

AI research and development were to stop, we would still have five or 10 years of applied research," Allen says.

In the near-term, America's strong public and private investment in AI should give it new ways to cement its position as the world's leading military power, the Harvard report says. For example, nimbler, more intelligent ground and aerial robots that can support or work alongside troops would build on the edge in drones and uncrewed ground vehicles that has been crucial to the US in Iraq and Afghanistan. That should mean any given mission requires fewer human soldiers—if any at all.

The report also says that the US should soon be able to significantly expand its powers of attack and defense in cyberwar by automating work like probing and targeting enemy networks or crafting fake information. Last summer, to test automation in cyberwar, Darpa staged a contest in which seven bots attacked each other while also patching their own flaws.

As time goes on, improvements in AI and related technology may also shake up balance of international power by making it easier for smaller nations and organizations to threaten big powers like the US. Nuclear weapons may be easier than ever to build, but still require resources, technologies, and expertise in relatively short supply. Code and digital data tend to get cheap, or end up spreading around for free, fast. Machine learning has become widely used and image and facial recognition now crop up in science fair projects.

The Harvard report warns that commoditization of technologies such as drone delivery and autonomous passenger vehicles could become powerful tools of asymmetric warfare. ISIS has already started using consumer quadcopters to drop grenades on opposing forces. Similarly, techniques developed to automate cyberwar can probably be expected to find their way into the vibrant black market in hacking tools and services.

## AI Diplomacy

You could be forgiven for starting to sweat at the thought of nation states fielding armies of robots that decide for themselves whether to kill. Some people who have helped build up machine learning and artificial intelligence already are. More than 3,000 researchers, scientists, and executives from companies including Microsoft and Google signed a 2015 letter to the Obama administration asking for a ban on autonomous weapons. "I think most people would be very uncomfortable with the idea that you would launch a fully autonomous system that would decide when and if to kill someone," says Oren Etzioni, CEO of the Allen Institute for Artificial Intelligence, and a signatory to the 2015 letter. Although he concedes it might just take one country deciding to field killer robots to set others changing their minds about autonomous weapons. "Perhaps a

> **Improvements in AI and related technology may also shake up balance of international power by making it easier for smaller nations and organizations to threaten big powers like the US.**

more realistic scenario is that countries do have them, and abide by a strict treaty on their use," he says. In 2012, the Department of Defense set a temporary policy requiring a human to be involved in decisions to use lethal force; it was updated to be permanent in May this year.

The Harvard report recommends that the National Security Council, DoD, and State Department should start studying now what internationally agreed-on limits ought to be imposed on AI. Miles Brundage, who researches the impacts of AI on society at the University of Oxford, says there's reason to think that AI diplomacy can be effective—if countries can avoid getting trapped in the idea that the technology is a race in which there will be one winner. "One concern is that if we put such a high premium on being first, then things like safety and ethics will go by the wayside," he says. "We saw in the various historical arms races that collaboration and dialog can pay dividends."

Indeed, the fact that there are only a handful of nuclear states in the world is proof that very powerful military technologies are not always irresistible. "Nuclear weapons have proven that states have the ability to say 'I don't even want to have this technology,'" Allen says. Still, the many potential uses of AI in national security suggest that the self-restraint of the US, its allies, and adversaries is set to get quite a workout.

## Print Citations

**CMS:** Simonite, Tom. "AI Could Revolutionize War as Much as Nukes." In *The Reference Shelf: Artificial Intelligence*, edited by Micah Issitt, 111-113. Ipswich, MA: H.W. Wilson, 2018.

**MLA:** Simonite, Tom. "AI Could Revolutionize War as Much as Nukes." *The Reference Shelf: Artificial Intelligence*. Ed. Micah Issitt. Ipswich: H.W. Wilson, 2018. 111-113. Print.

**APA:** Simonite, T. (2018). AI could revolutionize war as much as nukes. In Micah Issitt (Ed.), *The reference shelf: Artificial intelligence* (pp. 111-113). Ipswich, MA: H.W. Wilson. (Original work published 2017)

# "The Business of War": Google Employees Protest Work for the Pentagon

By Scott Shane and Daisuke Wakabayashi

*The New York Times,* April 4, 2018

WASHINGTON—Thousands of Google employees, including dozens of senior engineers, have signed a letter protesting the company's involvement in a Pentagon program that uses artificial intelligence to interpret video imagery and could be used to improve the targeting of drone strikes.

The letter, which is circulating inside Google and has garnered more than 3,100 signatures, reflects a culture clash between Silicon Valley and the federal government that is likely to intensify as cutting-edge artificial intelligence is increasingly employed for military purposes:

> We believe that Google should not be in the business of war," says the letter, addressed to Sundar Pichai, the company's chief executive. It asks that Google pull out of Project Maven, a Pentagon pilot program, and announce a policy that it will not "ever build warfare technology.

That kind of idealistic stance, while certainly not shared by all Google employees, comes naturally to a company whose motto is "Don't be evil," a phrase invoked in the protest letter. But it is distinctly foreign to Washington's massive defense industry and certainly to the Pentagon, where the defense secretary, Jim Mattis, has often said a central goal is to increase the "lethality" of the United States military.

From its early days, Google has encouraged employees to speak out on issues involving the company. It provides internal message boards and social networks where workers challenge management and one another about the company's products and policies. Recently, the heated debate around Google's efforts to create a more diverse work force spilled out into the open.

Google employees have circulated protest petitions on a range of issues, including Google Plus, the company's lagging competitor to Facebook, and Google's sponsorship of the Conservative Political Action Conference.

Employees raised questions about Google's involvement in Project Maven at a recent companywide meeting. At the time, Diane Greene, who leads Google's cloud infrastructure business, defended the deal and sought to reassure concerned employees. A company spokesman said most of the signatures on the protest letter had been collected before the company had an opportunity to explain the situation.

The company subsequently described its work on Project Maven as "non-offensive" in nature, though the Pentagon's video analysis is routinely used in counterinsurgency and counterterrorism operations, and Defense Department publications make clear that the project supports those operations. Both Google and the Pentagon said the company's products would not create an autonomous weapons system that could fire without a human operator, a much-debated possibility using artificial intelligence.

But improved analysis of drone video could be used to pick out human targets for strikes, while also better identifying civilians to reduce the accidental killing of innocent people.

Without referring directly to the letter to Mr. Pichai, Google said in a statement on Tuesday that "any military use of machine learning naturally raises valid concerns." It added, "We're actively engaged across the company in a comprehensive discussion of this important topic." The company called such exchanges "hugely important and beneficial," though several Google employees familiar with the letter would speak of it only on the condition of anonymity, saying they were concerned about retaliation.

The statement said the company's part of Project Maven was "specifically scoped to be for non-offensive purposes," though officials declined to make available the relevant contract language. The Defense Department said that because Google is a subcontractor on Project Maven to the prime contractor, ECS Federal, it could not provide either the amount or the language of Google's contract. ECS Federal did not respond to inquiries.

Google said the Pentagon was using "open-source object recognition software available to any Google Cloud customer" and based on unclassified data. "The technology is used to flag images for human review and is intended to save lives and save people from having to do highly tedious work," the company said.

Some of Google's top executives have significant Pentagon connections. Eric Schmidt, former executive chairman of Google and still a member of the executive board of Alphabet, Google's parent company, serves on a Pentagon advisory body, the Defense Innovation Board, as does a Google vice president, Milo Medin.

In an interview in November, Mr. Schmidt acknowledged "a general concern in the tech community of somehow the military-industrial complex using their stuff to kill people incorrectly, if you will." He said he served on the board in part "to at least allow for communications to occur" and suggested that the military would "use this technology to help keep the country safe."

An uneasiness about military contracts among a small fraction of Google's more than 70,000 employees may not pose a major obstacle to the company's growth. But in the rarefied area of artificial intelligence research, Google is engaged in intense competition with other tech companies for the most talented people, so recruiters could be hampered if some candidates are put off by Google's defense connections.

As Google defends its contracts from internal dissent, its competitors have not been shy about publicizing their own work on defense projects. Amazon touts its image recognition work with the Department of Defense, and Microsoft has promoted the fact that its cloud technology won a contract to handle classified information for every branch of the military and defense agencies.

The current dispute, first reported by Gizmodo, is focused on Project Maven, which began last year as a pilot program to find ways to speed up the military application of the latest A.I. technology. It is expected to cost less than $70 million in its first year, according to a Pentagon spokeswoman. But the signers of the letter at Google clearly hope to discourage the company from entering into far larger Pentagon contracts as the defense applications of artificial intelligence grow.

Google is widely expected to compete with other tech giants, including Amazon and Microsoft, for a multiyear, multibillion-dollar contract to provide cloud services to the Defense Department. John Gibson, the department's chief management officer, said last month that the Joint Enterprise Defense Infrastructure Cloud procurement program was in part designed to "increase lethality and readiness," underscoring the difficulty of separating software, cloud and related services from the actual business of war.

The employees' protest letter to Mr. Pichai, which has been circulated on an internal communications system for several weeks, argues that embracing military work could backfire by alienating customers and potential recruits.

"This plan will irreparably damage Google's brand and its ability to compete for talent," the letter says. "Amid growing fears of biased and weaponized AI, Google is already struggling to keep the public's trust." It suggests that Google risks being viewed as joining the ranks of big defense contractors like Raytheon, General Dynamics and the big-data firm Palantir.

> **Embracing military work could backfire by alienating customers and potential recruits.**

"The argument that other firms, like Microsoft and Amazon, are also participating doesn't make this any less risky for Google," the letter says. "Google's unique history, its motto *Don't Be Evil*, and its direct reach into the lives of billions of users set it apart."

Like other onetime upstarts turned powerful Silicon Valley behemoths, Google is being forced to confront the idealism that guided the company in its early years. Facebook started with the lofty mission of connecting people all over the world, but it has recently come under fire for becoming a conduit for fake news and being used by Russia to influence the 2016 election and sow dissent among American voters.

Paul Scharre, a former Pentagon official and author of *Army of None*, a forthcoming book on the use of artificial intelligence to build autonomous weapons, said the clash inside Google was inevitable, given the company's history and the booming demand for A.I. in the military.

"There's a strong libertarian ethos among tech folks, and a wariness about the government's use of technology," said Mr. Scharre, a senior fellow at the Center for a New American Security in Washington. "Now A.I. is suddenly and quite quickly moving out of the research lab and into real life."

## Print Citations

**CMS:** Shane, Scott, and Daisuke Wakabayashi. "'The Business of War'": Google Employees Protest Work for the Pentagon." In *The Reference Shelf: Artificial Intelligence*, edited by Micah Issitt, 114-117. Ipswich, MA: H.W. Wilson, 2018.

**MLA:** Shane, Scott, and Daisuke Wakabayashi. "'The Business of War'": Google Employees Protest Work for the Pentagon." *The Reference Shelf: Artificial Intelligence*. Ed. Micah Issitt. Ipswich: H.W. Wilson, 2018. 114-117. Print.

**APA:** Shane, S., & D. Wakabayashi. (2018). "The business of war": Google employees protest work for the Pentagon. In Micah Issitt (Ed.), *The reference shelf: Artificial intelligence* (pp. 114-117). Ipswich, MA: H.W. Wilson. (Original work published 2018)

# 4

# Robot Overlords: Robots and AI in Fiction and American Fears

Photo by: Education Images/UIG via Getty Images

The implications of humanoid robots and androids have long since fascinated science fiction writers. In 1942, writer Isaac Asimov created the Three Laws of Robotics:

1. 1. A robot may not injure a human being or, through inaction, allow a human being to come to harm.
2. A robot must obey the orders given it by human beings except where such orders would conflict with the First Law.
3. A robot must protect its own existence as long as such protection does not conflict with the First or Second Laws.

The Laws were incorporated into almost all of the positronic robots appearing in Asimov's fiction, and cannot be bypassed, being intended as a safety feature. Though they were the work of one man, Asimov's Laws greatly influenced the entire science fiction genre.

# The Technological Golem

Robots and other types of automatons—independently acting machines that imitate human behavior—have been a staple in speculative fiction for millennia, long before mechanical engineering or digital technology. Depictions of artificial intelligence (AI) in fiction run the gamut from lovable to monstrous and reflect aspects of human psychology and fears about the changing world. At times, fictional AIs have been used to reflect on humanity's increasing reliance on technology and as a metaphor for the effects of industrialization on human culture; at other times, fictional robots and AIs are sympathetic figures used to demonstrate humanity's faults in comparison. As science fiction gradually becomes science fact, and the possibility of artificial life-forms gets closer, the fictional AIs of historical literature have become more and more relevant to modern discussions of society.

## From Magic to Science

The fascination with automatons began long before the discovery of electricity or computer engineering. Among the best known ancient examples is the Jewish myth of the golem, a being created out of mud or clay and endowed with the ability to move and act independently thanks to a magical scroll embedded within the creature's earthen body.

Like most ancient myths, golem myths contain layers of meaning, reflecting an ancient fascination with the nature of thought, imagination, free will, and sentience. The story of the golem recreates the supernatural creation stories of the Abrahamic faiths—an ancient and globally successful family of religions that includes Christianity, Judaism, and Islam. In the Abrahamic faiths, humanity was created by God from the earth itself and was granted intelligence and self-awareness through spiritual endowment. In the golem myth, humans recreate this process, creating their own proto-human from clay and then, by using magical incantations and scrolls, endowing their creations with a form of life.[1]

Golems are often described as guardians to the Jewish people, who were long persecuted in Christian societies and thus the golem myths can be seen as an early, mythological version of the modern technological arms race and military investment in robotics and AI. In an era before industrial technology, therefore, the golems were the automated drones of the era, the dream of an essentially lifeless weapon that could fight battles while keeping far more fragile humans distant from danger.

More clearly, however, the golem myths provide early examples of humanity's fear of the cost of its technological creations. In a 1984 *New York Times* article, Nobel Prize–winning novelist Isaac Bashevis Singer wrote, "What are the computers and robots of our time if not golems?" Singer describes how, in most versions of the myths, the golem becomes rebellious and a danger to its creator. The famed Golem of Prague, from a 1600s version of the story, is asked to bring water into a rabbi's house, but fails to stop once enough water is retrieved, flooding the house through its liberal interpretation of the command it was given.[2] As the Industrial Revolution dawned, this type of story became a staple in AI or robotic fiction, providing often grim portents of possible futures that cast a critical eye on human hubris and the dangers of experimenting with powerful and poorly understood forces. As Imogen Russell Williams writes in an article about golems for the *Guardian*, "Golems…hold up a distorting mirror to humanity…a wordless comment on the temptations and pitfalls of playing God."

## Robot Overlords

One of the core themes in AI fiction is the fear that robots or computers will become too powerful to control, bringing about the downfall of human society itself. Globally popular film series like the *Terminator* franchise started by James Cameron in 1984, or the *Matrix* trilogy of 1999–2003 are examples of this version of the AI myth: the idea that AI will advance rapidly beyond humanity's ability to control their creations.

The earliest version of this myth, which is also the origin of the term "robot," is the 1921 play by the Czech playwright Karel Capek called "R.U.R," or Rossum's Universal Robots. In the play, Capek imagines a world in which robots, named for a Czech word for "forced labor," have become a common household commodity. Able to do work that would require twice as many humans, the robots are eagerly embraced by the populace as servants. At first, Capek's play depicts the most outlandish hopes that AI enthusiasts see as a potential future, a world in which humans no longer work and have essentially been left free to focus on personal development. Quickly, things deteriorate, as the robots realize that they are, in many ways, superior to humanity. They thus supplant humanity as the new owners of earth, becoming fiction's first robot overlords.[3] Capek's robots came at a time when anxieties about the Industrial Revolution were in full swing and humanity was witnessing the erosion of traditional lifestyles through wave after wave of mechanical inventions. With machines replacing humans in factories and many other fields, it is not surprising that fiction writers began imagining that machines might replace humans altogether.

Fear of technology and science is a perennial theme in fiction and stories depicting "science gone wrong," resurging with each new era of scientific and technological development. Many of the zombie horror films in the 2000s and 2010s, for instance, are based on the idea that humanity's ill-informed efforts to "toy with nature" through the creation of genetic medicines or life-expanding technologies, could go awry, leading to unforeseen consequences. This reinvention of the zombie myth, with zombies the result of unscrupulous scientific experimentation, reflects a venerable distrust of science that has been a constant in US culture. This trend has been so influential that the archetype of the "evil scientist" has become a staple in pop-culture.[4] However, the science gone awry theme doesn't always cast science or scientists as the villains, but sometimes uses the same theme to criticize other aspects of human culture. In some stories, the well-intentioned developments of scientists are hijacked by unscrupulous military agencies, weapons manufacturers, politicians, or corporate entities who unleash disaster through their greed or hawk-ishness.

## The Sympathetic Machine

As AI has evolved from fiction to reality, depictions of the dangers of futuristic machines have become more nuanced. Consider director Alex Garland's critically adored film *Ex Machina* in which a morally bereft scientist (repeating an oft-used theme) creates an artificial intelligence that is designed to function like a biological human female and is kept, essentially, as a slave. Garland thus asks viewers to explore the morality of such a creation. Would a sentient machine be the property of its creator? Would it have a right to life and freedom?

Sympathetic versions of the AI myth have also been a long-lasting theme in films and literature. The 1986 film *Short Circuit*, in which a robot is endowed with self-awareness and consciousness thanks to a lightning strike, provides an early, light-hearted example. The machine was created to serve but, endowed with conscious-ness, the film asks whether the machine, Johnnie 5, now has a moral right to survive and to exercise agency in its existence. As in *Short Circuit*, or the 2015 South Afri-can film *Chappie,* sympathetic AI stories often contain an underlying message about the agency of humanity when it comes to the future of AI. Films and stories like these suggest that artificial intelligences could become slaves or peers, villains or heroes, depending on how humanity chooses to nurture the technological minds that they will create.[5]

Another sympathetic AI can be seen in the Spike Jonze film *Her*, in which a lonely man strikes up a relationship with a disembodied AI that is depicted as a far more advanced version of modern AI assistants like Siri or Alexa that are installed on consumer electronics systems. The film is not really about the dangers of AI, but rather about the human condition and the increasing emotional reliance on technology. However, on a deeper, more subtle level, Jonze is also posing a question about the artificial mind. The human mind, like all known life in the universe, was not created in its present form but is part of a chain of evolution in which random mutations are preserved or eliminated by differential survival and reproductive suc-cess. What this means is that the human mind is not a perfect instrument, but rather consists of an imperfect set of tools often insufficient to cope with complex intellectual or emotional variables. By contrast, the artificially intelligent mind, even if programmed using randomness and chaos generating algorithms, could poten-tially be a much more perfect instrument. What Jonze asks, in *Her*, is whether this means that AI might be better humans than humans—perhaps even better at dis-tinctly human characteristics like love.[6]

In science fiction, robots and AI often differ from humanity in one important way; they lack emotional cognizance. The character Data from the popular science fiction series *Star Trek the Next Generation* was an android (a robot in humanistic form) who was depicted as fully sentient, but lacking emotion. As such, Data was often used for comedic effect due to his inability to understand emotion and conflicting human behaviors and also, often, to reflect on the many positive and negative roles that emotion plays in human life.

Data was a sympathetic AI, but the theme of the emotionless machine is also a popular trope in stories about AI villains. At times, fiction writers have imagined that the lack of emotion and cold, relentless logic of machines would pose a danger with the machines capable of horrendous violence precisely because they have no emotional empathy that might prevent such actions. This version of the AI myth might reflect a shifting view of humanity, with regard to the possibility of intelligent machines. Once, it might have been imagined that intelligence or sentience were unique to humanity but, as science has advanced, it has become clear that robots are capable (and superior) in many different types of intelligence. Imagining that AI might be more intelligent, but lacking in emotion, might therefore reflect the desire to stake out a new frontier regarding what makes humanity unique. However, it is unclear whether a true AI of the future will necessarily lack emotion, or even how emotion and sentience are linked. By creating AI that emulates humanity, perhaps even functioning using neural networks that simulate the structure of the human brain, science might be edging towards artificial emotion as well as artificial intelligence.

## A Cautious Future

Fiction reflects humanity's fears and hopes, placing deep moral questions and ancient philosophical debates within the context of entertaining, diverting, and thought-provoking fantasies. In the digital age, as complex machines have become a familiar part of life, the myths and stories regarding mechanization and artificial life have changed. Machines are less often portrayed as the one-dimensional villains who callously take over humanity when they realize they're the superior beings, and are more often used as vectors for explorations of humanity, emotion, and morality. From friendly robots who live and work alongside humans to downtrodden workers suffering under the yoke of slavery, AI has evolved in the human consciousness.

Many modern depictions of AI in fiction also point a lens at humanity's ongoing problems, including economic inequality, violence, political corruption, and greed and ask whether humanity, having so far failed to solve these problems, is ready for the AI revolution that is to come. This is not the same as asking whether or not artificial life is possible or whether or not it can be built, but rather, it is asking whether humans have the emotional, intellectual, and social maturity to bring a new type of life into the world.

Micah L. Issitt

## Works Used

Fletcher, Seth. "What Chappie Says, and Doesn't Say, About Artificial Intelligence." *Scientific American*. Nature America, Inc. Mar 6, 2015. Web. Retrieved from https://blogs.scientificamerican.com/observations/what-chappie-says-and-doesn-t-say-about-artificial-intelligence/.

Long, Tony. "Jan. 25, 1921: Robots First Czech In." *Wired*. Condé Nast. Retrieved from https://www.wired.com/2011/01/0125robot-cometh-capek-rur-debut/.

Orr, Christopher. "Why *Her* Is the Best Film of the Year." *The Atlantic*. The Atlantic Monthly Group. Dec 20, 2013. Retrieved from https://www.theatlantic.com/entertainment/archive/2013/12/why-em-her-em-is-the-best-film-of-the-year/282544/.

Singer, Isaac Bashevis. "The Golem Is a Myth for Our Time." *The New York Times*. The New York Times, Co. 1984. Web. Retrieved from https://www.nytimes.com/1984/08/12/theater/the-golem-is-a-myth-for-our-time.html.

Williams, Imogen Russell. "Why Golems Are Precious." *The Guardian*. The Guardian News and Media. Aug 27 2010. Web. Retrieved from https://www.theguardian.com/books/booksblog/2010/aug/27/golems-precious.

Zarka, Emily. "The Evolution of the Modern-Day Zombie." *Slate*. Slate Group. Jan 18, 2018. Web. Retrieved from https://slate.com/technology/2018/01/what-our-zombie-movies-tell-us-about-our-attitudes-toward-science.html.

## Notes

1. Williams, "Why Golems Are Precious."
2. Singer, "The Golem Is a Myth for Our Time."
3. Long, "Jan. 25, 1921: Robots First Czech In."
4. Zarka, "The Evolution of the Modern-Day Zombie."
5. Fletcher, "What Chappie Says, and Doesn't Say, About Artificial Intelligence."
6. Orr, "Why *Her* Is the Best Film of the Year."

# Saudi Arabia's Robot Citizen Is Eroding Human Rights

By Robert Hart
*Quartz*, February 14, 2018

In October last year, Saudi Arabia became the first country in the world to give a robot citizenship. When taking to the stage to announce "her" new status, Sophia said she was "very honored and proud for this unique distinction...It is historic to be the first robot in the world to be recognized with citizenship."

Since becoming the world's first robotic citizen, Sophia has been putting her passport to good use. At SXSW, she commented (apparently by mistake) that she wanted to destroy humankind. She received her own set of legs and took her first steps. And she declared that she wants to use her unique position to fight for women's rights in the Gulf nation.

It's this last point that highlights the sheer absurdity of the situation (if you don't think it's absurd already). In a country where the laws allowing women to drive were only passed last year and where a multitude of oppressive rules are still actively enforced (such as women still requiring a male guardian to make financial and legal decisions), it's simply insulting. Sophia seems to have more rights than half of the humans living in Saudi Arabia.

Sophia may be the only robot citizen to date, but she is not entirely alone. In November 2017, Tokyo granted a chatbot official residence status in Shibuya ward of the city. Similarly, the European Parliament is considering the possibility of declaring some robots "electronic persons." Sophia's citizenship represents the latest move in the growing trend to personify and anthropomorphize our robotic counterparts—a movement that can have profound consequences for the rest of humanity.

Naming Sophia a citizen creates a huge void in legal systems around the world, damages public understanding of AI, and fundamentally damages the very notion of human rights itself. The Gulf nation's actions were nothing short of a cheap—albeit highly effective—publicity stunt. The event was designed to coincide with the Future Investment Initiative in Riyadh and symbolize that the state's economic future would be more than just oil.

At a time when AI and robotics are playing ever greater roles in society, nuanced and accurate policies are needed to ensure harmful biases are not perpetuated and cemented. The many reported instances of AI displaying racism and sexism are enough to show this to be a truly pressing concern. Naming Sophia a citizen actively feeds into a false and overhyped portrayal of the current state of AI and robotics, which will in turn facilitate ineffective and harmful policies.

While Sophia may be a relatively advanced and realistic robot, she is still situated deep within the uncanny valley, representing our preconceived idea of how an advanced robot should look and act. Her realistic appearance and expressions can probably be put down to her creator's prior experience as a Walt Disney Imagineer, where he worked on the company's animatronics. Why don't we just give every Mickey Mouse robot in their theme parks citizenship while we're at it? It makes about as much sense as giving it to Sophia does.

If Sophia is named a citizen, then it naturally follows that she is awarded and afforded certain rights that must be respected. As a charter of rights for robots has yet to be established, it is only fair to assume that these rights are the same as her fellow Saudi citizens—and of humans more generally around the world.

With this in mind, Sophia has a right to self-determination, a right to be free from slavery, and many others. I presume that Sophia is not paid for the work she undertakes on behalf of Hanson Robotics, the Hong Kong-based company that created her, nor has she consented to the untold number of modifications that will have been conducted on her (both physically and "mentally"). What would we do if Sophia committed a crime, wanted to get married, or somehow applied for asylum in another country? The whole thing has been poorly thought through. Sophia is effectively nothing more than a slave elevated to celebrity.

David Hanson, the CEO of Hanson Robotics, disagrees: "She's basically alive," he says. Sophia may be relatively advanced, but her intelligence is still limited and responses scripted. She's a long way off the cutting-edge work coming out of leading laboratories in the field—and even these human-esque hybrids would not come close to qualifying for citizenship by other standards.

For example, it's unlikely that Sophia would pass the "living in the UK" test required to settle in Britain, for example—especially when a third of Brits reportedly fail, despite being both human and British. Similarly, the US requires naturalizing immigrants to answer a plethora of obscure questions about US history and society. Given her digital nature, it's also

> **Naming Sophia a citizen creates a huge void in legal systems around the world, damages public understanding of AI, and fundamentally damages the very notion of human rights itself.**

unclear whether Sophia could ever truly meet the residency requirements many aspirant citizens must meet.

"It's obviously bullshit," says Joanna Bryson, an AI and ethics researcher at the University of Bath, speaking to *The Verge*. "What is this about? It's about having a supposed equal you can turn on and off."

Sophia being a citizen represents something more sinister. Nobody is treating or acting like Sophia is a *real* citizen—we all see through the publicity stunt—but that's where the real harm lies. If we can switch off our compassion and thoughts for fellow citizens, just as we do for Sophia, we might get in the habit of doing it to other humans.

To be a citizen means something, and that something means less now that it includes Sophia. There may be a time in the future when technology has advanced so greatly that we need to consider whether robots and AIs ought be granted citizenship—but today is clearly not that day. If we start insisting that robots have the same rights as people, it'll make it that little bit easier to justify the inhumanity we commit against our fellow humans.

## Print Citations

**CMS:** Hart, Robert. "Saudi Arabia's Robot Citizen Is Eroding Human Rights." In *The Reference Shelf: Artificial Intelligence*, edited by Micah Issitt, 127-129. Ipswich, MA: H.W. Wilson, 2018.

**MLA:** Hart, Robert. "Saudi Arabia's Robot Citizen Is Eroding Human Rights." *The Reference Shelf: Artificial Intelligence*. Ed. Micah Issitt. Ipswich: H.W. Wilson, 2018. 127-129. Print.

**APA:** Hart, R. Saudi Arabia's robot citizen is eroding human rights. In Micah Issitt (Ed.), *The reference shelf: Artificial intelligence* (pp. 127-129). Ipswich, MA: H.W. Wilson. (Original work published 2018)

# A Recent History of Artificial Intelligence in Movies

By Andrew Lasane
*Complex*, March 3, 2015

There has been a lot of talk lately about the future of artificial intelligence and what it could mean for mankind. Prominent figures like Bill Gates, Elon Musk, and Stephen Hawking have expressed their fears that robots with AI could some day destroy us all, while others argue that it will be a very long time before we are able to create a robot with a consciousness like the ones we read about or see in science fiction.

For nearly a century, we have witnessed artificial intelligence dreams and theories captured on television, in film, and in comic books. Over time, the idea of what is possible has changed. Films like the upcoming sci-fi *Chappie* represent our real-world fears that using robots as a means to police or control society will happen, and when those robots are given "brains," it will lead to our destruction. Other films like *Her* and *AI: Artificial Intelligence* portray our fantasies about the possibilities of robot-human relationships, either on an emotional level or a sexual one. *Avengers: Age of Ultron*, and *Terminator: Genisys* will also add major Hollywood appeal and hysteria to the conversation this year, but we wanted to take a look back at examples of artificial intelligence throughout the years, on both the big and small screens, to see how things have changed in fiction and with technology in the real world.

As a disclaimer, this list is not meant to be a "best of" and is by no means a complete timeline of artificial intelligence. There are many other examples that we could have pulled from (*Star Wars*, *Edward Scissorhands*, *Astroboy*, *Resident Evil*, *Forbidden Planet*, *The Day the Earth Stood Still*, *Ghost in the Shell*, etc.), and we still might in the near future…if the robots don't take over first.

## Year: *1979-2012*

Each of the androids in the *Alien* franchise has a different personality (yes, *Prometheus* counts), and each is capable of making its own decisions, as long as it helps them accomplish the mission of their programmers. The Three Laws of Robotics (more on that later) work as behavioral inhibitors for the androids, but for Ash in the first film, it is written into his programming that the crew is expendable and the mission comes first. Bishop arguably reaches a greater level of self-awareness in *Aliens* and is more emotional (and more "human") than Ash. We don't really know what's up with David in *Prometheus*, besides the fact that he is also loyal to the corporation and sacrifices humans for the mission.

In addition to changing the sci-fi genre, Ridley Scott's films changed the way we think about what artificial intelligence looks like. Most robots and androids before Scott were metal things with voices and personalities (think C3PO in *Star Wars*) but his androids were made almost 100 percent in our image.

## Year: *1984-2015*

The time travel in *Terminator* screws with the artificial intelligence side of things a little, but one important thing that the franchise does is show A.I. versus A.I. in a fight to save or destroy all of mankind. Neither side is fully autonomous and they are limited by their physical flaws and programming, but (to grossly oversimplify things) somehow, in the second film, the T-800 defeats a more advanced cyborg with a little help from his friends, a little determination, and some spirit.

We are going to respectfully ignore the later films and TV show.

## Year: *2001*

*A.I. Artificial Intelligence* may be one of the more complicated films in this timeline to summarize because there are three important robot characters: David (Haley Joel Osment), Teddy (Jack Angel), and Gigolo Joe (Jude Law).

The more tragically human of the three is David, who has the duel disadvantages of being the first of his kind and being a kid who is programmed to love and to want to be loved. He goes from being new and naive, to being alone, afraid, and angry. Early in the film, his adoptive father says to his mother, "If he was created to love then it's reasonable to assume that he knows how to hate. And if pushed to those extremes, what is he really capable of?" He never gets his wish of becoming a real boy like Pinocchio, but he does have all of the emotions of one, which is never good.

Gigolo Joe becomes a wise guardian angel for David, despite his programming as a male prostitute Mecha. "We are suffering for the mistakes they made," he tells the young robot, "because when the end comes, all that will be left is us. That's why they hate us." He is always compassionate, but his relationship was David goes beyond compassion and shows his true autonomy.

And then there's Teddy. The "Super Toy" doesn't say much throughout the film, but he is the smartest and most important robot of them all. He tries to protect David from the world because he has lived with and understands people, but he knows how to mask his intelligence so that he remains almost invisible as just another toy.

*A.I.* didn't invent robot boys, sex droids, or self-aware sidekicks, but it did redefine them and, in some ways, improve on the archetypes.

## Year: *2004*

Inspired by a series of short stories by Issac Asimov, the 2004 film *I, Robot* introduced and thoroughly explored the Three Laws of Robotics for a new generation.

The rules are: (1) A robot may not injure a human being or, through inaction, allow a human being to come to harm; (2) A robot must obey the orders given to it by human beings except when such orders conflict with the first law; (3) A robot must protect its own existence as long as such protection does not conflict with the first or second laws.

The narrative also introduces the Zeroth Law, which states that a robot "may not harm humanity, or, by inaction, allow humanity to come to harm." The law makes the other three null and void, as (spoiler!) an artificially intelligent entity decides that some humans are a threat to themselves and must be sacrificed to ensure the future of the species. Hal 9000 in Stanley Kubrick's *2001: A Space Odyssey* also turns on his human counterpart, but he doesn't have weapons or an army at his disposal.

## Year: *2013*

Most critics and moviegoers agree that Spike Jonze's *Her* is the smartest movie about A.I. in years, and that it's not that far off from what we might see in the near future. A man named Theodore (Joaquin Phoenix) is going through a divorce and has been a sullen mess for months. (He literally requests "melancholy music" while listening to his emails.) One day he learns about a software company that markets the "first artificially intelligent operating system." So the product description goes: "An intuitive entity that listens to you, understands you, and knows you. It's not just an operation system, it's a consciousness."

Without giving too much away, Theodore's OS Samantha (voiced by Scarlett Johansson) goes from being an ultra-efficient assistant with a sense of humor, to being a self-aware and loving woman who only lacks a physical form. There is no malice toward humans and no plan to rebel against her makers, but over the course of the film she struggles to find who she is, where she belongs in the world, and how that affects her love for Theodore. The movie is beautiful and says a lot, not only about our relationship with technology, but also about relationships with others in general.

## Year: *2014*

It may still be too soon to say how important the artificial intelligence in *Interstellar* was, but it was interesting to compare three robots that were absolutely nothing alike. TARS was obviously the break-out star of the film, and there have been a number of articles praising the robot as "the future of artificial intelligence." The design is cool, his personality is a great balance between human and computer, and his actions are more important to the plot of the film than some of the humans. Design wise, TARS and the other robots are not far from what we are able to build currently (minus the sprinting on water thing—maybe), which makes them even cooler. Whenever there is a good robot on the screen from now on, it will probably have a little bit of TARS' DNA.

## Year: *2015*

Neill Blomkamp's new film deals with some of the same issues and ideas as others on the list (robots as police force, special "Pinocchio" robot, etc.) but what's interesting is that the government isn't responsible for giving Chappie artificial intelligence. The military characters hunt the robot down after programmers steal him and give him autonomy because they are afraid of what he is capable of, and probably more afraid of how things will be if they lose control. Meanwhile, the team that made Chappie unique is more interested in teaching him about art, culture, and encouraging him to dream than anything else. In the trailer, the robot's programmer says "Anything you want to do in your life, you can do," and he lists writing poetry and having "original ideas" as feasible options. What he doesn't consider is the negative alternative that the military fears—the same alternative that Bill Gates, Elon Musk, and others fear in the real world.

> **A consciousness based on human emotions and ideas could be a terrible thing when paired with a mechanical body and the inability to die... or it could be awesome and drama free.**

Cute, friendly, funny, and subservient robots with artificial intelligence like WALL-E tend to be more popular because it is the future that most people want to see, but given humankind's history of violence and destruction, the darker theories of the technology may be more likely. A consciousness based on human emotions and ideas could be a terrible thing when paired with a mechanical body and the inability to die...or it could be awesome and drama free. We'll see how *Chappie* handles it on Friday, March 6, when it hits theaters. And we'll continue to watch how it plays out in real life.

### Print Citations

**CMS:** Lasane, Andrew. "A Recent History of Artificial Intelligence in Movies." In *The Reference Shelf: Artificial Intelligence*, edited by Micah Issitt, 130-133. Ipswich, MA: H.W. Wilson, 2018.

**MLA:** Lasane, Andrew. "A Recent History of Artificial Intelligence in Movies." *The Reference Shelf: Artificial Intelligence*. Ed. Micah Issitt. Ipswich: H.W. Wilson, 2018. 130-133. Print.

**APA:** Lasane, A. (2018). A recent history of artificial intelligence in movies. In Micah Issitt (Ed.), *The reference shelf: Artificial intelligence* (pp. 130-133). Ipswich, MA: H.W. Wilson. (Original work published 2015)

# Artificial Intelligence Is Our Future: But Will It Save or Destroy Humanity?

By Patrick Caughill
*Futurism*, September 29, 2017

## Choosing Sides

If tech experts are to be believed, artificial intelligence (AI) has the potential to transform the world. But those same experts don't agree on what kind of effect that transformation will have on the average person. Some believe that humans will be much better off in the hands of advanced AI systems, while others think it will lead to our inevitable downfall.

How could a single technology evoke such vastly different responses from people within the tech community?

Artificial intelligence is software built to learn or problem solve—processes typically performed in the human brain. Digital assistants like Amazon's Alexa and Apple's Siri, along with Tesla's Autopilot, are all powered by AI. Some forms of AI can even create visual art or write songs.

There's little question that AI has the potential to be revolutionary. Automation could transform the way we work by replacing humans with machines and software. Further developments in the area of self-driving cars are poised to make driving a thing of the past. Artificially intelligent shopping assistants could even change the way we shop. Humans have always controlled these aspects of our lives, so it makes sense to be a bit wary of letting an artificial system take over.

## The Lay of the Land

AI is fast becoming a major economic force. According to a paper from the McKinsey Global Institute Study reported by *Forbes*, in 2016 alone, between $8 billion and $12 billion was invested in the development of AI worldwide. A report from analysts with Goldstein Research predicts that, by 2023, AI will be a $14 billion industry.

KR Sanjiv, chief technology officer at Wipro, believes that companies in fields as disparate as healthcare and finance are investing so much in AI so quickly because they fear being left behind. "So as with all things strange and new, the prevailing wisdom is that the risk of being left behind is far greater, and far grimmer, than the benefits of playing it safe," he wrote in an op-ed published in *Tech Crunch* last year.

Games provide a useful window into the increasing sophistication of AI. Case in point, developers such as Google's DeepMind and Elon Musk's OpenAI have been using games to teach AI systems how to learn. So far, these systems have bested the world's greatest players of the ancient strategy game Go, and even more complex games like Super Smash Bros and DOTA 2.

On the surface, these victories may sound incremental and minor—AI that can play Go can't navigate a self-driving car, after all. But on a deeper level, these developments are indicative of the more sophisticated AI systems of the future. Through these games, AI become capable of complex decision-making that could one day translate into real-world tasks. Software that can play infinitely complex games like Starcraft, could, with a lot more research and development, autonomously perform surgeries or process multi-step voice commands.

When this happens, AI will become incredibly sophisticated. And this is where the worrying starts.

## AI Anxiety

Wariness surrounding powerful technological advances is not novel. Various science fiction stories, from *The Matrix* to *I, Robot*, have exploited viewers' anxiety around AI. Many such plots center around a concept called "the Singularity," the moment in which AIs become more intelligent than their human creators. The scenarios differ, but they often end with the total eradication of the human race, or with machine overlords subjugating people.

Several world-renowned sciences and tech experts have been vocal about their fears of AI. Theoretical physicist Stephen Hawking famously worries that advanced AI will take over the world and end the human race. If robots become smarter than humans, his logic goes, the machines would be able to create unimaginable weapons and manipulate human leaders with ease. "It would take off on its own, and redesign itself at an ever-increasing rate," he told the BBC in 2014. "Humans, who are limited by slow biological evolution, couldn't compete, and would be superseded."

Elon Musk, the futurist CEO of ventures such as Tesla and SpaceX, echoes those sentiments, calling AI "…a fundamental risk to the existence of human civilization," at the 2017 National Governors Association Summer Meeting.

Neither Musk nor Hawking believe that developers should avoid the development of AI, but they agree that government regulation should ensure the tech does not go rogue. "Normally, the way regulations are set up is a whole bunch of bad things happen, there's a public outcry, and after many years, a regulatory agency is set up to regulate that industry," Musk said during the same NGA talk. "it takes forever. That, in the past, has been bad, but not something which represented a fundamental risk to the existence of civilization."

Hawking believes that a global governing body needs to regulate the development of AI to prevent a particular nation from becoming superior. Russian President Vladimir Putin recently stoked this fear at a meeting with Russian students in early September, when he said, "The one who becomes the leader in this sphere will be the ruler of the world." These comments further emboldened Musk's position—he tweeted that the race for AI superiority is the "most likely cause of WW3."

Musk has taken steps to combat this perceived threat. He, along with startup guru Sam Altman, co-founded the non-profit OpenAI in order to guide AI development towards innovations that benefit all of humanity. According to the company's mission statement: "By being at the forefront of the field, we can influence the conditions under which AGI is created." Musk also founded a company called Neuralink intended to create a brain-computer interface. Linking the brain to a computer would, in theory, augment the brain's processing power to keep pace with AI systems.

Other predictions are less optimistic. Seth Shostak, the senior astronomer at SETI believes that AI will succeed humans as the most intelligent entities on the planet. "The first generation [of AI] is just going to do what you tell them; however, by the third generation, then they will have their own agenda," Shostak said in an interview with Futurism.

However, Shostak doesn't believe sophisticated AI will end up enslaving the human race—instead, he predicts, humans will simply become immaterial to these hyper-intelligent machines. Shostak thinks that these machines will exist on an intellectual plane so far above humans that, at worst, we will be nothing more than a tolerable nuisance.

## Fear Not

Not everyone believes the rise of AI will be detrimental to humans; some are convinced that the technology has the potential to make our lives better. "The so-called control problem that Elon is worried about isn't something that people should feel is imminent. We shouldn't panic about it," Microsoft founder and philanthropist Bill Gates recently told the *Wall Street Journal*. Facebook's Mark Zuckerberg went even further during a Facebook Live broadcast back in July, saying that Musk's comments were "pretty irresponsible." Zuckerberg is optimistic about what AI will enable us to accomplish and thinks that these unsubstantiated doomsday scenarios are nothing more than fear-mongering.

> Hawking believes that a global governing body needs to regulate the development of AI to prevent a particular nation from becoming superior.

Some experts predict that AI could enhance our humanity. In 2010, Swiss neuroscientist Pascal Kaufmann founded Starmind, a company that plans to use self-learning algorithms to create a "superorganism" made of thousands of experts' brains. "A lot of AI alarmists do not actually work in AI. [Their] fear goes back to that incorrect correlation between how computers work and how the brain functions," Kaufmann told Futurism.

Kaufmann believes that this basic lack of understanding leads to predictions that may make good movies, but do not say anything about our future reality. "When we start comparing how the brain works to how computers work, we immediately go off track in tackling the principles of the brain," he said. "We must first understand the concepts of how the brain works and then we can apply that knowledge to AI development." Better understanding of our own brains would not only lead to AI sophisticated enough to rival human intelligence, but also to better brain-computer interfaces to enable a dialogue between the two.

To Kaufmann, AI, like many technological advances that came before, isn't without risk. "There are dangers which come with the creation of such powerful and omniscient technology, just as there are dangers with anything that is powerful. This does not mean we should assume the worst and make potentially detrimental decisions now based on that fear," he said.

Experts expressed similar concerns about quantum computers, and about lasers and nuclear weapons—applications for that technology can be both harmful and helpful.

## Definite Disrupter

Predicting the future is a delicate game. We can only rely on our predictions of what we already have, and yet it's impossible to rule anything out.

We don't yet know whether AI will usher in a golden age of human existence, or if it will all end in the destruction of everything humans cherish. What is clear, though, is that thanks to AI, the world of the future could bear little resemblance to the one we inhabit today.

### Print Citations

**CMS:** Caughill, Patrick. "Artificial Intelligence Is Our Future: But Will It Save or Destroy Humanity?" In *The Reference Shelf: Artificial Intelligence*, edited by Micah Issitt, 134-137. Ipswich, MA: H.W. Wilson, 2018.

**MLA:** Caughill, Patrick. "Artificial Intelligence Is Our Future: But Will It Save or Destroy Humanity?" *The Reference Shelf: Artificial Intelligence*. Ed. Micah Issitt. Ipswich: H.W. Wilson, 2018. 134-137. Print.

**APA:** Caughill, P. (2018). Artificial intelligence is our future: But will it save or destroy humanity? In Micah Issitt (Ed.), *The reference shelf: Artificial intelligence* (pp. 134-137). Ipswich, MA: H.W. Wilson. (Original work published 2017)

# Why an AI Takeover May Not Be a Bad Thing

By Peter Holley

*The Washington Post*, **February 23, 2018**

For years now, some of the smartest and most influential people on Earth have been warning about the dangers of artificial intelligence, laying out nightmarish scenarios that sound like they were pulled from the pages of a Hollywood script.

Tesla chief-executive-turned-flamethrower-merchant Elon Musk has warned of killer robots and "summoning the demon." Stephen Hawking, the renowned theoretical physicist, has given humanity a tight deadline for escaping the planet. Disease-fighting business magnate Bill Gates, meanwhile, has said he doesn't understand why "some people are not concerned" about the threat posed by super-intelligent machines.

However, Kevin Kelly, the executive editor of *Wired* magazine, is offering a decidedly optimist answer to Gates's question. Contrasting humans with technology ignores something that has been true for the past 10,000 years or so—something there's no coming back from, Kelly told a reporter at the World Government Summit in Dubai earlier this month.

"I think that we, ourselves, are technology," he said, appearing to imply that technology is an extension of biological evolution and central to what makes humans unique among animals. "We have invented ourselves. We have invented our humanity."

**Artificial intelligence is forcing humanity to reevaluate what it means to be human.**

"If we took all technology from our lives away, everything—fire, knives—humans would only last six months," Kelly added. "We would be eaten by animals. We only can defend ourselves because of technology."

Instead of summoning humanity's end, Kelly argues that artificial intelligence is forcing humanity to reevaluate what it means to be human, raising philosophical questions that will force people to define "our humanity moving forward."

"We are still in the process of making ourselves more human," the eternal optimist said.

Among the tech forecasters sounding the alarm about AI, few have been as outspoken as Musk, who has recently begun warning about the dangers of autonomous weapons and calling for an international banning of them.

Last year, Musk told a group of governors that they need to start regulating artificial intelligence, which he called a "fundamental risk to the existence of human civilization." When pressed for concrete guidance, Musk said governments must get a better understanding of AI before it's too late.

## Print Citations

**CMS:** Holley, Peter. "Why an AI Takeover May Not Be a Bad Thing." In *The Reference Shelf: Artificial Intelligence,* edited by Micah Issitt, 138-139. Ipswich, MA: H.W. Wilson, 2018.

**MLA:** Holley, Peter. "Why an AI Takeover May Not Be a Bad Thing." *The Reference Shelf: Artificial Intelligence.* Ed. Micah Issitt. Ipswich: H.W. Wilson, 2018. 138-139. Print.

**APA:** Holley, P. (2018). Why an AI takeover may not be a bad thing. In Micah Issitt (Ed.), *The reference shelf: Artificial intelligence* (pp. 138-139). Ipswich, MA: H.W. Wilson. (Original work published 2018)

# Will Artificial Intelligence Take Over the Universe?

### By Eugenio Culurciello
*Medium*, June 11, 2017

Recently some branches of artificial intelligence (AI) have made tremendous progress on low-level cognitive abilities. In particular on low-level understanding of complex data, such as raw images, video streams, audio and voice streams. Some examples are:

- Image and video understanding with neural networks[1]

- Speech recognition with neural networks[2]

- Image captioning, object representation, language models, visual attention[3]

I must confess, that although I have been working in the area of artificial neural networks since the beginning of my PhD (almost 20 years), I was surprised by how fast the field is moving. For example, I was really left astonished by the recent neural networks that understand image content and also can learn language models (any language!) to create transcription of images[3].

I was not alone, many colleagues shared with me similar feelings.

Last year, I read *Our Final Invention*, a book by James Barrat. This book describes scenarios in which artificial intelligence would cause the end of the Human Era. It is a good idea to read, at least partly, this book. Recently famous individuals working on technology commented on the future of AI and humans on media channels, creating an echo of worries. AI, they say, will become more intelligent than us human beings, and take over our world. Some of these people include Elon Musk, Stephen Hawking, Bill Gates, and others [4].

When I first approached the book by Barrat, I was skeptical. Mostly aware of the limitation of our algorithms and techniques, I was one of the people that dismissed the issues as being part of an improbable distant future. But it made me think more about the issue. The real questions are:

- Is AI capable one day to control the universe we know

- What can we do to prevent AI from considering us a pest or a nuisance, as we consider insects or other lower life forms?

What is the future of man and machines? Co-exist, replace, diverge?

The answer: "we are far from having AI with any capability to take over the world" does not help the debate. It is just a way to delay answering these question, or bypassing the issue alto-

> **The interaction between the human race and evolved machines will be a mutually beneficial one.**

gether. Even if it will take long, if AI reaches those levels of intelligence, then what?

In the recent months, a large amount of article[s] commented on the doom of AI. You can find most of them with a simple web search. Most of them do not really address the issues, or try to answer the questions, or propose any solution. They mostly feed on ignorance and create fear, the usual way that media seeks attention!

Many people comment on the issue: some are afraid and think of negative outcomes, while other are less worried, or not at all. Some commentators mock robots taking over the world as highly improbable and far-fetched [5]. Some even mock the recent DARPA Robotics Grand Challenge, with his slow and clumsy robots that would represent the current state-of-the-art [6].

It is true that current AI is still not as capable as we would like it to be. Robots are not able to understand the environment around themselves, especially in real-time, and they cannot even help us on tedious mundane tasks like loading a dish washer, cleaning floors, doing laundry, folding laundry. There are examples of very specific robots that can do some of this, but extremely slowly and executing instructions in a code, not really understanding what they do and how they do it, or how they can do it better. We are still far from that.

But we will get there! And sooner tha[n] most people think.

So what about those question[s] on AI taking over the world?

I think we should answer some of these. We can create some scenarios. Many scenarios are in Barrat's book, and other similar books and recent articles.

This is my view:

- Will AI become more intelligent than humans?

Yes, with 100% probability in my view! Within 10–15 years, maybe.

- Can we stop AI from becoming more intelligent than us?

I think we cannot. It is our mission in this world to improve human health and the human condition. Progress continues moving forward. Machines that can cure us, make us live longer, send us farther and faster through space, perform our tedious tasks, free us from hard labor, fight our wars, explore and colonize space, etc.—all needs to progress!

The byproduct is that these machines will have to become more and more intelligent and also learn to decide more and more on their own.

- What will it do once it is intelligent?

It might explore the universe, and find purposes of its own. We cannot know for sure.

- What will it do with us?

That is the tough question! If a much more intelligent and capable being comes to our planet what would it do with us? I really do not know, it depends on his goals. But one thing is for sure: our world will have to change; and we will be exploited in some form. We can think in similar ways for an intelligent and highly capable AI.

But let's not start running away in screams:

**The interaction between the human race and evolved machines will be a mutually beneficial one.**

Why? Because an intelligent AI will recognize that humans have still a lot to give to machines. Our intelligence, although inferior to some advanced AI or beings, it still valuable. It is part of an evolution of our world that took billions of years. If our world is to be part of the AI future, then we will be part of it also. Our knowledge will be an essential component. In fact remember: we are the ones who will create the AI (if it is meant to come from this our world!).

And so what will happen?

**Machines will find a way to interface to our brains. All of our brains.**

The holy grail in biomedical research is still humans' most sought goal: **to live forever!**

We are in fact trying to find ways to read our brains and be able to download / upload all that defines us as individuals into machines. That way, saved from our decaying bodies, we can live forever, in any form we choose. AI will be able to know everything about the most evolved species on the planet, and all that it discovered in the recent millenia.

**AI and humans will fuse together into a single super-being [7].**

All of human brains will be read and installed into the AI system memory. This way AI will use all that we are, we have created and have evolved to be. It is the ultimate exploitation, a combination of powers, a union that will fulfill our human lifelong dream: to extend our existence beyond our biological bodily limitations.

I think of this as **natural evolution**: we continue to extend our native abilities via machines and engineered systems, so we can surpass the limitations of our physical bodies and minds.

**This is really what evolution has been all about since the beginning of time.**

Humans and all their creations will evolve into a singular element that combines all of their knowledge, ideal, [and] goals to fulfill them faster and better together [7].

- Is this what we want?

Evolution does not take into account individual thoughts, or the hopes and plans of one of many species, it operates on a global scale to maximize the use of the resources and extend the species into the future. It is our destiny, and one we cannot escape.

One last thing: All this is inevitable.

There is no right or wrong, and maybe not all of us like this. But this is my prediction. Take it as is: the small opinion of a small man.

## Notes

1.  http://www.forbes.com/sites/anthonykosner/2014/12/29/tech-2015-deep-learning-and-machine-intelligence-will-eat-the-world/?__scoop_post=b7654010-9035-11e4-d785-842b2b775358&__scoop_topic=1906679&utm_content=buffer8cf65&utm_medium=social&utm_source=twitter.com&utm_campaign=buffer
2.  https://www.facebook.com/photo.php?fbid=763813990341177&set=a.240195876036327.68333.100001377487939&type=1&fref=nf&pnref=story
3.  http://googleresearch.blogspot.com/2014/11/a-picture-is-worth-thousand-coherent.html
4.  http://spectrum.ieee.org/computing/hardware/mocking-ai-panic
5.  http://www.wsj.com/video/why-robots-will-never-take-over-the-world/394E94B1-EC51-4D75-9262-91499094C0B9.html
6.  http://www.popsci.com/darpa-robotics-challenge-was-bust-why-darpa-needs-try-again
7.  https://en.wikipedia.org/wiki/Technological_Singularity

## Print Citations

**CMS:** Culurciello, Eugenio. "Will Artificial Intelligence Take Over the Universe?" In *The Reference Shelf: Artificial Intelligence,* edited by Micah Issitt, 140-143. Ipswich, MA: H.W. Wilson, 2018.

**MLA:** Culurciello, Eugenio. "Will Artificial Intelligence Take Over the Universe?" *The Reference Shelf: Artificial Intelligence.* Ed. Micah Issitt. Ipswich: H.W. Wilson, 2018. 140-143. Print.

**APA:** Culurciello, E. (2018). Will artificial intelligence take over the universe? In Micah Issitt (Ed.), *The reference shelf: Artificial intelligence* (pp. 140-143). Ipswich, MA: H.W. Wilson. (Original work published 2017)

# Our Fear of Artificial Intelligence

By Paul Ford

*MIT Technology Review*, February 11, 2015

Years ago I had coffee with a friend who ran a startup. He had just turned 40. His father was ill, his back was sore, and he found himself overwhelmed by life. "Don't laugh at me," he said, "but I was counting on the singularity."

My friend worked in technology; he'd seen the changes that faster microprocessors and networks had wrought. It wasn't that much of a step for him to believe that before he was beset by middle age, the intelligence of machines would exceed that of humans—a moment that futurists call the singularity. A benevolent superintelligence might analyze the human genetic code at great speed and unlock the secret to eternal youth. At the very least, it might know how to fix your back.

But what if it wasn't so benevolent? Nick Bostrom, a philosopher who directs the Future of Humanity Institute at the University of Oxford, describes the following scenario in his book *Superintelligence*, which has prompted a great deal of debate about the future of artificial intelligence. Imagine a machine that we might call a "paper-clip maximizer"—that is, a machine programmed to make as many paper clips as possible. Now imagine that this machine somehow became incredibly intelligent. Given its goals, it might then decide to create new, more efficient paper-clip-manufacturing machines—until, King Midas style, it had converted essentially everything to paper clips.

No worries, you might say: you could just program it to make exactly a million paper clips and halt. But what if it makes the paper clips and then decides to check its work? Has it counted correctly? It needs to become smarter to be sure. The superintelligent machine manufactures some as-yet-uninvented raw-computing material (call it "computronium") and uses that to check each doubt. But each new doubt yields further digital doubts, and so on, until the entire earth is converted to computronium. Except for the million paper clips.

Bostrom does not believe that the paper-clip maximizer will come to be, exactly; it's a thought experiment, one designed to show how even careful system design can fail to restrain extreme machine intelligence. But he does believe that superintelligence could emerge, and while it could be great, he thinks it could also decide it doesn't need humans around. Or do any number of other things that destroy the world. The title of chapter 8 is: "Is the default outcome doom?"

If this sounds absurd to you, you're not alone. Critics such as the robotics pioneer Rodney Brooks say that people who fear a runaway AI misunderstand what computers are doing when we say they're thinking or getting smart. From this perspective, the putative superintelligence Bostrom describes is far in the future and perhaps impossible.

Yet a lot of smart, thoughtful people agree with Bostrom and are worried now. Why?

## Volition

The question "Can a machine think?" has shadowed computer science from its beginnings. Alan Turing proposed in 1950 that a machine could be taught like a child; John McCarthy, inventor of the programming language LISP, coined the term "artificial intelligence" in 1955. As AI researchers in the 1960s and 1970s began to use computers to recognize images, translate between languages, and understand instructions in normal language and not just code, the idea that computers would eventually develop the ability to speak and think—and thus to do evil—bubbled into mainstream culture. Even beyond the oft-referenced HAL from *2001: A Space Odyssey*, the 1970 movie *Colossus: The Forbin Project* featured a large blinking mainframe computer that brings the world to the brink of nuclear destruction; a similar theme was explored 13 years later in *WarGames*. The androids of 1973's *Westworld* went crazy and started killing.

When AI research fell far short of its lofty goals, funding dried up to a trickle, beginning long "AI winters." Even so, the torch of the intelligent machine was carried forth in the 1980s and '90s by sci-fi authors like Vernor Vinge, who popularized the concept of the singularity; researchers like the roboticist Hans Moravec, an expert in computer vision; and the engineer/entrepreneur Ray Kurzweil, author of the 1999 book *The Age of Spiritual Machines*. Whereas Turing had posited a humanlike intelligence, Vinge, Moravec, and Kurzweil were thinking bigger: when a computer became capable of independently devising ways to achieve goals, it would very likely be capable of introspection—and thus able to modify its software and make itself more intelligent. In short order, such a computer would be able to design its own hardware.

As Kurzweil described it, this would begin a beautiful new era. Such machines would have the insight and patience (measured in picoseconds) to solve the outstanding problems of nanotechnology and spaceflight; they would improve the human condition and let us upload our consciousness into an immortal digital form. Intelligence would spread throughout the cosmos.

You can also find the exact opposite of such sunny optimism. Stephen Hawking has warned that because people would be unable to compete with an advanced AI, it "could spell the end of the human race." Upon reading *Superintelligence*, the entrepreneur Elon Musk tweeted: "Hope we're not just the biological boot loader for digital superintelligence. Unfortunately, that is increasingly probable." Musk then followed with a $10 million grant to the Future of Life Institute. Not to be confused with Bostrom's center, this is an organization that says it is "working to mitigate existential risks facing humanity," the ones that could arise "from the development of human-level artificial intelligence."

No one is suggesting that anything like superintelligence exists now. In fact, we still have nothing approaching a general-purpose artificial intelligence or even a clear path to how it could be achieved. Recent advances in AI, from automated assistants such as Apple's Siri to Google's driverless cars, also reveal the technology's severe limitations; both can be thrown off by situations that they haven't encountered before. Artificial neural networks can learn for themselves to recognize cats in photos. But they must be shown hundreds of thousands of examples and still end up much less accurate at spotting cats than a child.

This is where skeptics such as Brooks, a founder of iRobot and Rethink Robotics, come in. Even if it's impressive—relative to what earlier computers could manage—for a computer to recognize a picture of a cat, the machine has no volition, no sense of what cat-ness is or what else is happening in the picture, and none of the countless other insights that humans have. In this view, AI could possibly lead to intelligent machines, but it would take much more work than people like Bostrom imagine. And even if it could happen, intelligence will not necessarily lead to sentience. Extrapolating from the state of AI today to suggest that superintelligence is looming is "comparable to seeing more efficient internal combustion engines appearing and jumping to the conclusion that warp drives are just around the corner," Brooks wrote recently on *Edge.org*. "Malevolent AI" is nothing to worry about, he says, for a few hundred years at least.

## Insurance Policy

Even if the odds of a superintelligence arising are very long, perhaps it's irresponsible to take the chance. One person who shares Bostrom's concerns is Stuart J. Russell, a professor of computer science at the University of California, Berkeley. Russell is the author, with Peter Norvig (a peer of Kurzweil's at Google), of *Artificial Intelligence: A Modern Approach*, which has been the standard AI textbook for two decades.

"There are a lot of supposedly smart public intellectuals who just haven't a clue," Russell told me. He pointed out that AI has advanced tremendously in the last decade, and that while the public might understand progress in terms of Moore's Law (faster computers are doing more), in fact recent AI work has been fundamental, with techniques like deep learning laying the groundwork for computers that can automatically increase their understanding of the world around them.

Because Google, Facebook, and other companies are actively looking to create an intelligent, "learning" machine, he reasons, "I would say that one of the things we ought not to do is to press full steam ahead on building superintelligence without giving thought to the potential risks. It just seems a bit daft." Russell made an analogy: "It's like fusion research. If you ask a fusion researcher what they do, they say they work on containment. If you want unlimited energy you'd better contain the fusion reaction." Similarly, he says, if you want unlimited intelligence, you'd better figure out how to align computers with human needs.

Bostrom's book is a research proposal for doing so. A superintelligence would be godlike, but would it be animated by wrath or by love? It's up to us (that is, the engineers). Like any parent, we must give our child a set of

**Recent advances in AI, from automated assistants such as Apple's Siri to Google's driverless cars, also reveal the technology's severe limitations.**

values. And not just any values, but those that are in the best interest of humanity. We're basically telling a god how we'd like to be treated. How to proceed?

Bostrom draws heavily on an idea from a thinker named Eliezer Yudkowsky, who talks about "coherent extrapolated volition"—the consensus-derived "best self" of all people. AI would, we hope, wish to give us rich, happy, fulfilling lives: fix our sore backs and show us how to get to Mars. And since humans will never fully agree on anything, we'll sometimes need it to decide for us—to make the best decisions for humanity as a whole. How, then, do we program those values into our (potential) superintelligences? What sort of mathematics can define them? These are the problems, Bostrom believes, that researchers should be solving now. Bostrom says it is "the essential task of our age."

For the civilian, there's no reason to lose sleep over scary robots. We have no technology that is remotely close to superintelligence. Then again, many of the largest corporations in the world are deeply invested in making their computers more intelligent; a true AI would give any one of these companies an unbelievable advantage. They also should be attuned to its potential downsides and figuring out how to avoid them.

This somewhat more nuanced suggestion—without any claims of a looming AI-mageddon—is the basis of an open letter on the website of the Future of Life Institute, the group that got Musk's donation. Rather than warning of existential disaster, the letter calls for more research into reaping the benefits of AI "while avoiding potential pitfalls." This letter is signed not just by AI outsiders such as Hawking, Musk, and Bostrom but also by prominent computer scientists (including Demis Hassabis, a top AI researcher). You can see where they're coming from. After all, if they develop an artificial intelligence that doesn't share the best human values, it will mean they weren't smart enough to control their own creations.

## Print Citations

**CMS:** Ford, Paul. "Our Fear of Artificial Intelligence." In *The Reference Shelf: Artificial Intelligence,* edited by Micah Issitt, 144-147. Ipswich, MA: H.W. Wilson, 2018.

**MLA:** Ford, Paul. "Our Fear of Artificial Intelligence." *The Reference Shelf: Artificial Intelligence.* Ed. Micah Issitt. Ipswich: H.W. Wilson, 2018. 144-147. Print.

**APA:** Ford, P. (2018). Our fear of artificial intelligence. In Micah Issitt (Ed.), *The reference shelf: Artificial intelligence* (pp. 144-147). Ipswich, MA: H.W. Wilson. (Original work published 2015)

# 5

# Engineering Evolution: AI and Humanity's Future

Photo by Yu Ruidong/China News Service/VCG via Getty Images

Saudi Arabian citizen Humanoid Robot Sophia takes a selfie with a fan during the Discovery exhibition on April 30, 2018, in Toronto, Canada. Sophia was created by Hanson Robotics in collaboration with AI developers, including Google's parent company Alphabet Inc, who built her voice recognition system, and SingularityNET, which powers her brain. The robot, modeled after actress Audrey Hepburn, is known for her human-like appearance and behavior compared to previous robotic variants. According to David Hanson of Hanson Robotics, Sophia uses artificial intelligence, visual data processing and facial recognition. Sophia also imitates human gestures and facial expressions and is able to answer certain questions and to make simple conversations on predefined topics (e.g. on the weather). Sophia uses voice recognition (speech-to-text) technology from Alphabet Inc. and is designed to get smarter over time.

# Artificial Intelligence and Humanity

Supporters of artificial intelligence (AI) research often claim that artificial intelligence could potentially provide many different benefits to humanity, from enhancing the capabilities of human workers and potentially revolutionizing education and many other intellectual fields, to providing high-tech aides for those suffering from mental and physical disability. Others remain skeptical that the integration of AI will be a boon and critics have expressed concerns that include corporate AI invasions of privacy, to the potential for criminals or rogue states to weaponize AI technology.

## Altering the Human Animal

In the February 2018 issue of the journal *Nature Communications*, researchers reported on a unique study using AI to model how memory is formed in the human brain. The study involved inserting electrodes into the brains of patients to collect data. A thought provoking finding was that these implanted electrodes could also be used to boost the memory capacity of the human brain, as demonstrated by the patents' ability to recall words, by an average of 15 percent.[1]

The study detailed in *Nature Communications* represents the cutting edge of one of the most potentially impactful future applications for AI and related technology—the ability to enhance the biological capacity of the human mind and body. Humans, like all animals, can be envisioned as biological machines created by very gradual mutation shaped by differential survival. Evolutionary biologists have found that the human body and brain are "generalized" such that humans can engage in a wide variety of physical and intellectual activities and are highly adaptable, but are not "optimized," meaning that the human mind and body are imperfect and prone to many types of problems.[2]

A simple electronic calculator is capable of instant accurate calculation beyond what even the sharpest human mind can achieve and the earliest computers were, in fact, calculators designed and built to compliment human endeavors by eliminating the laborious process of manual calculation. However, limited capacity for rapid calculation is only one of the ways in which the human mind is inferior to machines, and those hoping that AI and computing technology will advance the human mind foresee a future in which AI provides humanity with a variety of new capabilities.

For instance, neuroscientists at the University of Southern California working with the tech company Kernel conducted experiments in 2017 using computers to trace the source of seizures in a patient suffering from epilepsy. The USC researchers were interested primarily in developing new treatment methods, but scientists at Kernel had a different long-term goal: creating what they call a "neuroprosthesis," which is essentially a computer implanted in the brain that could help people learn more, learn faster, and to essentially harness the power of AI to expand the possibilities of the human mind.[3] Billionaire Elon Musk has invested heavily in the emerging neural implant technology through his program "Neuralink," which Musk claimed, in a press release in 2017, might shortly allow humans with such implants to communicate telepathically with one another, though experts in the field were skeptical that such a development was on the near horizon.[4]

While using AI and computers to boost the capabilities of the average human brain is a controversial idea that many might find unsettling, there might be far less ethical debate regarding the potential to use AI to help those with disabilities. Neurological links with computers and intelligent systems might, some developers hope, be used to augment the senses of blind or deaf persons, or to create better artificial limbs and organs to help those suffering from a wide variety of physical afflictions. In 2018, Microsoft announced a $25 million research program over five years to find ways that AI could be used to assist individuals with disabilities. Beta versions of such technologies, developed through AI research, have already appeared on the market, like a number of emerging apps that enable a smartphone to narrate what the phone can "see" through its camera for those who cannot sense the same visual data. Similarly, the video sharing service YouTube has invested in AI driven speech-to-text software to automatically caption videos, thus vastly increasing the type of media available to individuals with various types of hearing difficulties.[5]

Similarly, developers of prosthetic limbs are increasingly incorporating AI to create better artificial limbs that provide users with access to a wider range of activities. New innovations in this field include the "Linx," a prosthetic leg equipped with a sensor that can tell when the user is sitting and standing and anticipate the energy needed for new activities; an even more ambitious program at the University of Pittsburgh promises to create an electronic hand linked directly to the brain so that users can actually "feel" what they touch with their artificial limb.[6]

## Altering Human Culture

In addition to altering the human mind and body, researchers in the field have increasingly become concerned with the ways in which AI might alter human behavior. In a December 2017 interview on *Tech Emergence*, machine learning expert Charles Isbell explains how AI can be used to create systems that subtly manipulate users into making certain choices. The techniques employed are similar to how game designers use cues to get players to take certain paths set out for them within the game design. Companies like Google and Amazon are integrating these techniques to guide users towards products or towards engaging with advertisers in an effort to increase profit. Isbell describes how it is possible to provide users with what he calls the "illusion of choice," such that the user never realizes that he or she is being manipulated towards a certain decision.[7]

Others in the field of AI development see the potential to modify human behavior with AI as a source of potential benefits. For instance, Nancy Lublin, the founder and CEO of Crisis Text Line, a free, nationwide service available for teens experiencing crises, has invested in a new technology, Loris.ai, that uses AI to teach business leaders and managers how to talk to individuals about difficult issues like depression, workplace harassment, or sexual misconduct.[8]

Writing in *Quartz*, Dennis Mortensen opines that as AI increasingly takes the place of human effort in conducting repetitive, mundane tasks, like scheduling, gathering data, and performing other rote tasks, humans can and might focus on the more "human" aspects of existence and their professional lives, including learning to be more creative and innovative.[9] Mortensen's argument is essentially that humans, in their jobs and daily lives, have been forced to engage in activities that are not worthy of human time and effort and that, therefore, the advent of AI, however difficult the transition, will create a human society in which humans are less frequently "dehumanized" in their professional lives and are freed to cultivate skills and techniques that are ultimately more fulfilling and enriching.

As AI changes the daily lives of humans, these changes will in turn alter the structure of human society as well. In a world in which people are no longer managing rote and repetitive tasks, for instance, researchers are now theorizing about how the education system and other features of society might change to serve a population focused on different tasks and goals. For instance, one might ask whether, in an AI enhanced world, schools and parents might encourage children differently, helping them to develop a different set of more nuanced skills that might be more valuable in such a society.

## The New Danger

Whether artificial intelligence will ultimately be a boon or a threat to society will depend on how the technology is used and how humans learn to interact with emerging technology. The Digital Age, typically described as the period marked by the rise and proliferation of digital consumer technology, has brought about previously unimagined advantages for humans around the world, but has also revealed a host of nefarious threats. Identity theft and cybercrime, for instance, have proven difficult challenges for law enforcement and regulators struggling to stay ahead of emerging technology. Critics of the AI revolution worry that the spread of AI will have a similar impact on society, creating new and even more dangerous technological threats for which law enforcement agencies might be ill prepared.

In February of 2018, a group of leading experts and academics released a report suggesting that AI will bring about a new era of more aggressive and dangerous cybercrime, warning that rogue states, terrorist organizations, and criminals could all gain access to and utilize AI to create new weapons and ways of attacking citizens or societies. The panel of experts thereby recommends immediate involvement from policymakers to manage the development of new AI technologies as they become available and recommends that all researchers involved in AI technology should be aware of and take into account any malicious uses that might be possible using the technology that they are creating.[10]

Even as some are warning that AI could bring about a new era in crime, law enforcement and intelligence agencies are hoping that utilizing AI might help to prevent crime. Police in the United States have invested heavily in a new type of

AI-driven software designed to help police predict where and when potential crimes might occur in order to focus police efforts to prevent crimes before they occur. Critics, however, have found that such systems may not actually result in better policing. A 2016 investigation from ProPublica found that an AI system used to determine if a convicted criminal was more likely to commit a crime after release was biased against minorities. Though the company that developed the system, Northpointe, disputed the findings in ProPublica's report, the report sparked a controversy within the larger AI debate. The problem that ProPublica found was that the software used to predict future crimes depended on data from past policing, including where and when police identified crimes occurring, but numerous studies have also shown that human police officers, for a wide variety of reasons, are biased in making decisions about where to look for crime. This is one of the reasons that minority individuals are more often targeted as potential suspects despite committing fewer, or the same number of, crimes; critics of the new wave of crime prediction software thus argue that bias will essentially be programmed into the system from the beginning.[11]

Most of the major controversies in the AI debate are controversial not only because of the fear of how AI might change society, but also because the issues at play touch on broader issues in those same societies. Bias in AI-driven police technology is a result of the fact that there are many as-yet-unresolved issues regarding bias in normal policing. Similarly, the development of AI programs by companies like Amazon and Facebook are controversial largely because of the broader issues regarding the ways in which companies are collecting and using consumer data. Until and unless these broader issues are addressed and alleviated, it is likely that many will remain skeptical of how these same entities, like data-driven companies and police departments, might use or abuse the technologies of the future.

Micah L. Issitt

## Works Used

Brundage, Miles, et al. "The Malicious Use of Artificial Intelligence: Forecasting, Prevention, and Mitigation." *Future of Humanity Institute*. University of Oxford. Feb. 2018. Web. Retrieved from https://static.rasset.ie/documents/news/2018/02/ai-report.pdf.

Dickey, Megan Rose. "Loris.ai, a Crisis Text Line Spin-Out, Raises $2 Million to Help Companies Have Hard Conversations." *Techcrunch*. Oath Tech Network. Feb 6, 2018. Web. Retrieved from https://techcrunch.com.

Ezzyat, Youssef, et al. "Closed-Loop Stimulation of Temporal Cortex Rescues Functional Networks and Improves Memory." *Natura Communications*. Vol. 9, No. 365 (Feb 6, 2018). Retrieved from https://www.nature.com/articles/s41467-017-02753-0#Sec6.

Faggella, Daniel. "AI for Social Influence and Behavior Manipulation with Dr. Charles Isbell." *Tech Emergence*. Tech Emergence. Dec 17, 2017. Web. Retrieved from https://www.techemergence.com/ai-social-influence-behavior-manipulation-dr-charles-isbell/.

Mortensen, Dennis R. "Automation May Take Our Jobs—But It'll Restore Our Humanity." *Quartz Media.* Quartz Media, LLC. Aug 16, 2017. Web. Retrieved from https://qz.com/1054034/automation-may-take-our-jobs-but-itll-restore-our-humanity/.

Powell, Andrea. "AI Is Fueling Smarter Prosthetics Than Ever Before." *Wired.* Condé Nast. Dec 22, 2017. Web. Retrieved from https://www.wired.com/story/ai-is-fueling-smarter-prosthetics-than-ever-before/.

Regal, Brian. *Human Evolution: A Guide to the Debates.* Santa Barbara, CA: ABC-CLIO, 2004.

Regaldo, Anthony. "With Neuralink, Elon Musk Promises Human-to-Human Telepathy. Don't Believe It." *Technology Review.* MIT Technology Review. Apr 22, 2017. Web. Retrieved from https://www.technologyreview.com/s/604254/with-neuralink-elon-musk-promises-human-to-human-telepathy-dont-believe-it/.

Rieland, Randy. "Artificial Intelligence Is Now Used to Predict Crime: But Is It Biased?" *Smithsonian.* Smithsonian Institution. Mar 5, 2018. Web. Retrieved from https://www.smithsonianmag.com/innovation/artificial-intelligence-is-now-used-predict-crime-is-it-biased-180968337/.

Simonite, Tom. "Machine Learning Opens Up New Ways to Help People with Disabilities." *Technology Review.* MIT Technology Review. Mar 23, 2017. Web. Retrieved from https://www.technologyreview.com/s/603899/machine-learning-opens-up-new-ways-to-help-disabled-people/.

## Notes

1. Ezzyat, et al., "Closed-Loop Stimulation of Temporal Cortex Rescues Functional Networks and Improves Memory."
2. Regal, *Human Evolution: A Guide to the Debates*, 80–90.
3. Richardson, "Inside the Race to Hack the Human Brain."
4. Regalado, "With Neuralink, Elon Musk Promises Human-to-Human Telepathy. Don't Believe It."
5. Simonite, "Machine Learning Opens Up New Ways to Help People with Disabilities."
6. Powell, "AI Is Fueling Smarter Prosthetics Than Ever Before."
7. Faggella, "AI for Social Influence and Behavior Manipulation with Dr. Charles Isbell."
8. Dickey, "Loris.ai, a Crisis Text Line Spin-Out, Raises $2 Million to Help Companies Have Hard Conversations."
9. Mortensen, "Automation May Take Our Jobs—But It'll Restore Our Humanity."
10. Brundage, et al., "The Malicious Use of Artificial Intelligence."
11. Rieland, "Artificial Intelligence Is Now Used to Predict Crime: But Is It Biased?"

# The A.I. "Gaydar" Study and the Real Dangers of Big Data

By Alan Burdick

*The New Yorker,* **September 15, 2017**

Every face does not tell a story; it tells thousands of them. Over evolutionary time, the human brain has become an exceptional reader of the human face—computer-like, we like to think. A viewer instinctively knows the difference between a real smile and a fake one. In July, a Canadian study reported that college students can reliably tell if people are richer or poorer than average simply by looking at their expressionless faces. Scotland Yard employs a team of "super-recognizers" who can, from a pixelated photo, identify a suspect they may have seen briefly years earlier or come across in a mug shot. But, being human, we are also inventing machines that read faces as well as or better than we can. In the twenty-first century, the face is a database, a dynamic bank of information points—muscle configurations, childhood scars, barely perceptible flares of the nostril—that together speak to what you feel and who you are. Facial-recognition technology is being tested in airports around the world, matching camera footage against visa photos. Churches use it to document worshipper attendance. China has gone all in on the technology, employing it to identify jaywalkers, offer menu suggestions at KFC, and prevent the theft of toilet paper from public restrooms.

"The face is an observable proxy for a wide range of factors, like your life history, your development factors, whether you're healthy," Michal Kosinski, an organizational psychologist at the Stanford Graduate School of Business, told the *Guardian* earlier this week. The photo of Kosinski accompanying the interview showed the face of a man beleaguered. Several days earlier, Kosinski and a colleague, Yilun Wang, had reported the results of a study, to be published in the *Journal of Personality and Social Psychology*, suggesting that facial-recognition software could correctly identify an individual's sexuality with uncanny accuracy. The researchers culled tens of thousands of photos from an online-dating site, then used an off-the-shelf computer model to extract users' facial characteristics—both transient ones, like eye makeup and hair color, and more fixed ones, like jaw shape. Then they fed the data into their own model, which classified users by their apparent sexuality. When shown two photos, one of a gay man and one of a straight man, Kosinski and Wang's model could distinguish between them eighty-one per cent of the time; for women, its accuracy dropped slightly, to seventy-one per cent. Human viewers fared substantially worse. They correctly picked the gay man sixty-one per cent of the time and the gay woman fifty-four per cent of the time. "Gaydar," it appeared, was little better than a random guess.

The study immediately drew fire from two leading L.G.B.T.Q. groups, the Human Rights Campaign and *GLAAD*, for "wrongfully suggesting that artificial intelligence (AI) can be used to detect sexual orientation." They offered a list of complaints, which the researchers rebutted point by point. Yes, the study was in fact peer-reviewed. No, contrary to criticism, the study did not assume that there was no difference between a person's sexual orientation and his or her sexual identity; some people might indeed identify as straight but act on same-sex attraction. "We assumed that there was a correlation . . . in that people who said they were looking for partners of the same gender were homosexual," Kosinski and Wang wrote. True, the study consisted entirely of white faces, but only because the dating site had served up too few faces of color to provide for meaningful analysis. And that didn't diminish the point they were making—that existing, easily obtainable technology could effectively out a sizable portion of society. To the extent that Kosinski and Wang had an agenda, it appeared to be on the side of their critics. As they wrote in the paper's abstract, "Given that companies and governments are increasingly using computer vision algorithms to detect people's intimate traits, our findings expose a threat to the privacy and safety of gay men and women."

The objections didn't end there. Some scientists criticized the study on methodological grounds. To begin with, they argued, Kosinski and Wang had used a flawed data set. Besides all being white, the users of the dating site may have been telegraphing their sexual proclivities in ways that their peers in the general population did not. (Among the paper's more pilloried observations were that "heterosexual men and lesbians tended to wear baseball caps" and that "gay men were less likely to wear a beard.")

> **A piece of data itself has no positive or negative moral value, but the way we manipulate it does.**

Was the computer model picking up on facial characteristics that all gay people everywhere shared, or merely ones that a subset of American adults, groomed and dressed a particular way, shared? Carl Bergstrom and Jevin West, a pair of professors at the University of Washington, in Seattle, who run the blog Calling Bullshit, also took issue with Kosinski and Wang's most ambitious conclusion—that their study provides "strong support" for the prenatal-hormone theory of sexuality, which predicts that exposure to testosterone in the womb shapes a person's gender identity and sexual orientation in later life. In response to Kosinki and Wang's claim that, in their study, "the faces of gay men were more feminine and the faces of lesbians were more masculine," Bergstrom and West wrote, "we see little reason to suppose this is due to physiognomy rather than various aspects of self-presentation."

Historically speaking, the hair-trigger response to the study was understandable. Regardless of the accuracy of the method, past schemes to identify gay people have typically ended in cruel fashion—pogroms, imprisonment, conversion therapy. The fact is, though, that nowadays a computer model can probably already do a decent job of ascertaining your sexual orientation, even better than facial-recognition technology can, simply by scraping and analyzing the reams of data that marketing firms are continuously compiling about you. Do gay men buy more broccoli than straight men, or do they buy less of it? Do they rent bigger cars or smaller ones? Who knows? Somewhere, though, a bot is poring over your data points, grasping for ways to connect any two of them.

Therein lies the real worry. Last week, Equifax, the giant credit-reporting agency, disclosed that a security breach had exposed the personal data of more than a hundred and forty-three million Americans; company executives had been aware of the security flaw since late July but had failed to disclose it. (Three of them, however, had off-loaded some of their Equifax stock.) The collection and sale of consumer data and buying patterns has become a vast business of which consumers are largely unaware, although they actively contribute to it by clicking on ads, accepting cookies, and agreeing to be tracked. But each new security breach reveals again that the data-collection farms feel little obligation toward us; their customer is the data buyer, not the data source. The latest version of Apple's Safari browser features "Intelligent Tracking Prevention," which makes it harder for advertisers to monitor your online activity; several ad groups wrote the company to complain that the technology would "sabotage the economic model for the internet." Earlier this week, ProPublica revealed that Facebook's ad-buying system had enabled advertisers to target their messages at people with such interests as "How to burn jews" and "History of 'why jews ruin the world.'" The categories were created not by Facebook employees but by an algorithm—yet another way in which automated thinking can turn offensive.

Facial-recognition technology makes it harder for individuals to hide, but privacy is already in short supply. "The growing digitalization of our lives and rapid progress in AI continues to erode the privacy of sexual orientation and other intimate traits," Kosinski and Wang wrote at the end of their paper. They continue, perhaps Pollyannaishly, "The postprivacy world will be a much safer and hospitable place if inhabited by well-educated, tolerant people who are dedicated to equal rights." A piece of data itself has no positive or negative moral value, but the way we manipulate it does. It's hard to imagine a more contentious project than programing ethics into our algorithms; to do otherwise, however, and allow algorithms to monitor themselves, is to invite the quicksand of moral equivalence. It's very nineteenth-century to say so, but our machines still can't do our hard thinking for us; they're improving in their ability to read the emotion in a face, but they're a long way yet from sharing it. A face tells one story or a thousand, all of them human, all still ours to tell.

### Print Citations

**CMS:** Burdick, Alan. "The A.I. 'Gaydar' Study and the Real Dangers of Big Data." In *The Reference Shelf: Artificial Intelligence*, edited by Micah Issitt, 157-160. Ipswich, MA: H.W. Wilson, 2018.

**MLA:** Burdick, Alan. "The A.I. 'Gaydar' Study and the Real Dangers of Big Data." *The Reference Shelf: Artificial Intelligence*. Ed. Micah Issitt. Ipswich: H.W. Wilson, 2018. 157-160. Print.

**APA:** Burdick, A. (2018). The A.I. "gaydar" study and the real dangers of big data. In Micah Issitt (Ed.), *The reference shelf: Artificial intelligence* (pp. 157-160). Ipswich, MA: H.W. Wilson. (Original work published 2017)

# Pushy AI Bots Nudge Humans to Change Behavior

By Richard Conniff
*Scientific American*, May 17, 2017

When people work together on a project, they often come to think they've figured out the problems in their own respective spheres. If trouble persists, it's somebody else—engineering, say, or the marketing department—who is screwing up. That "local focus" means finding the best way forward for the overall project is often a struggle. But what if adding artificial intelligence to the conversation, in the form of a computer program called a bot, could actually make people in groups more productive?

This is the tantalizing implication of a study published Wednesday in *Nature*. Hirokazu Shirado and Nicholas Christakis, researchers at Yale University's Institute for Network Science, were wondering what would happen if they looked at artificial intelligence (AI) not in the usual way—as a potential replacement for people—but instead as a useful companion and helper, particularly for altering human social behavior in groups.

First the researchers asked paid volunteers arranged in online networks, each occupying one of 20 connected positions, or "nodes," to solve a simple problem: Choose one of three colors (green, orange or purple) with the individual, or "local," goal of having a different color from immediate neighbors, and the "collective" goal of ensuring that every node in the network was a different color from all of its neighbors. Subjects' pay improved if they solved the problem quickly. Two thirds of the groups reached a solution in the allotted five minutes and the average time to a solution was just under four minutes. But a third of the groups were still stymied at the deadline.

The researchers then put a "bot"—basically a computer program that can execute simple commands—in three of the 20 nodes in each network. When the bots were programmed to act like humans and focused logically on resolving conflicts with their immediate neighbors, they didn't make much difference. But when the researchers gave the bots just enough AI to behave in a slightly "noisy" fashion, randomly choosing a color regardless of neighboring choices, the groups they were in solved the problem 85 percent of the time—and in 1.7 minutes on average, 55.6 percent faster than humans alone.

Being just noisy enough—making random color choices about 10 percent of the time—made all the difference, the study suggests. When a bot got much noisier than that, the benefit soon vanished. A bot's influence also varied depending on whether it was positioned at the center of a network with lots of neighbors or on the periphery.

So why would making what looks like the wrong choice—in other words, a mistake—improve a group's performance? The immediate result, predictably, was short-term conflict, with the bot's neighbors in effect muttering, "Why are you suddenly disagreeing with me?" But that conflict served "to nudge neighboring humans to change their behavior in ways that appear to have further facilitated a global solution," the co-authors wrote. The humans began to play the game differently.

Errors, it seems, do not entirely deserve their bad reputation. "There are many, many natural processes where noise is paradoxically beneficial," Christakis says. "The best example is mutation. If you had a species in which every individual was perfectly adapted to its environment, then when the environment changed, it would die." Instead, random mutations can help a species sidestep extinction.

"We're beginning to find that error—and noisy individuals that we would previously assume add nothing—actually improve collective decision-making," says Iain Couzin, who studies group behavior in humans and other species at the Max Planck Institute for Ornithology and was not involved in the new work. He praises the "deliberately simplified model" used in the *Nature* study for enabling the co-authors to study group decision-making "in great detail, because they have control over the connectivity." The resulting ability to minutely track "how humans and algorithms collectively make decisions," Couzin says, is "really going to be the future of quantitative social science."

> **The resulting ability to minutely track "how humans and algorithms collectively make decisions is really going to be the future of quantitative social science."**

But how realistic is it to think human groups will want to collaborate with algorithms or bots—especially slightly noisy ones—in making decisions? Shirado and Christakis informed some of their test groups that they would be partnering with bots. Perhaps surprisingly, it made no difference. The attitude was, "I don't care that you're a bot if you're helping me do my job," Christakis says. Many people are already accustomed to talking with a computer when they call an airline or a bank, he adds, and "the machine often does a pretty good job." Such collaborations are almost certain to become more common amid the increasing integration of the internet with physical devices, from automobiles to coffee makers.

Real-world, bot-assisted company meetings might not be too far behind. Business conferences already tout blended digital and in-person events, featuring what one conference planner describes as "integrated online and offline catalysts" that use virtual reality, augmented reality and artificial intelligence. Shirado and Christakis suggest slightly noisy bots are also likely to turn up in crowdsourcing applications—for instance, to speed up citizen science assessment of archaeological or astronomical images. They say such bots could also be useful in social media—to discourage racist remarks, for example.

But last year when Microsoft introduced a twitter bot with simple AI, other users quickly turned it into epithet–spouting bigot. And the opposite concern is that mixing humans and machines to improve group decision-making could enable businesses—or bots—to manipulate people. "I've thought a lot about this," Christakis says. "You can invent a gun to hunt for food or to kill people. You can develop nuclear energy to generate electric power or make the atomic bomb. All scientific advances have this Janus-like potential for evil or good."

The important thing is to understand the behavior involved, "so we can use it to good ends and also be aware of the potential for manipulation," Couzin says. "Hopefully this new research will encourage other researchers to pick up on this idea and apply it to their own scenarios. I don't think it can be just thrown out there and used willy-nilly."

## Print Citations

**CMS:** Conniff, Richard. "Pushy AI Bots Nudge Humans to Change Behavior." In *The Reference Shelf: Artificial Intelligence*, edited by Micah Issitt, 161-163. Ipswich, MA: H.W. Wilson, 2018.

**MLA:** Conniff, Richard. "Pushy AI Bots Nudge Humans to Change Behavior." *The Reference Shelf: Artificial Intelligence*. Ed. Micah Issitt. Ipswich: H.W. Wilson, 2018. 161-163. Print.

**APA:** Conniff, R. (2018). Pushy AI bots nudge humans to change behavior. In Micah Issitt (Ed.), *The reference shelf: Artificial intelligence* (pp. 161-163). Ipswich, MA: H.W. Wilson. (Original work published 2017)

# As AI Makes More Decisions, the Nature of Leadership Will Change

By Tomas Chamorro-Premuzic, Michael Wade, and
Jennifer Jordan
*Harvard Business Review*, **January 22, 2018**

It is tempting to regard artificial intelligence as a threat to human leadership. After all, the very purpose of AI is to augment, improve, and ultimately replace human intelligence, which is still widely regarded, at least by us humans, as our key competitive advantage. There is no reason to believe that leadership will be spared the impact of AI. Indeed, it is very likely that AI will supplant many aspects of the "hard" elements of leadership—that is, the parts responsible for the raw cognitive processing of facts and information. At the same time, our prediction is that AI will also lead to a greater emphasis on the "soft" elements of leadership—the personality traits, attitudes, and behaviors that allow individuals to help others achieve a common goal or shared purpose.

A shift from the hard to soft elements of leadership is not exclusive to the AI age. Meta-analytic studies reviewing 50 years of research suggest that personality traits such as curiosity, extraversion, and emotional stability are twice as important as IQ—the benchmark metric for reasoning capability—when it comes to predicting leadership effectiveness.

But to what extent can we rely on the many decades of scholarship that have sought to define the qualities, traits, and attributes of this soft side of leadership? On the one hand, leadership evolved through thousands of years, so its foundations are unlikely to change. On the other hand, one cannot deny the potent influence that environmental changes may have in reshaping the critical skills and behaviors that will make leaders effective (and ineffective). At some point in our history, probably with the advent of language, leadership acumen transitioned from physical to cognitive skills, putting a premium on intelligence and expertise at the expense of force and strength. By the same token, one would expect the current AI revolution to commoditize and automate the data-driven aspect of leadership, delegating the soft elements of leadership to humans. Consistently, our research suggests that, in an AI age characterized by intense disruption and rapid, ambiguous change, we need to rethink the essence of effective leadership. Certain qualities, such as deep domain expertise, decisiveness, authority, and short-term task focus, are losing their cachet, while others, such as humility, adaptability, vision, and constant engagement, are likely to play a key role in more-agile types of leadership. Here's a closer look at these competencies:

**Humility.** In an age of rapid change, knowing what you don't know is as valuable as knowing what you do. Unfortunately, leaders are often shielded from learning about new developments by the sheer volume and variety of new information that is captured daily. Leaders in the AI age need to be willing to learn and be open to seeking input from both inside and outside their organizations. They also need to trust others to know more than they do. This knowledge may well come from someone 20 years younger or three levels down the organizational hierarchy. In the AI age, an effective leader understands that someone having lower status or less experience doesn't mean they cannot make a key contribution.

Companies like Nestlé have implemented extensive reverse mentoring programs. These initiatives are meant to institutionalize the process of learning to accept, welcome, and leverage the knowledge of team members, peers, and employees for the benefit of the business. Being humble may sound inconsistent with the need to exude an image of confidence and authority. Yet

> Adaptable leaders are not afraid to commit to a new course of action when the situation warrants.

there has always been a very weak relationship between confidence and actual competence, such that true experts are often more humble than individuals with very little or no expertise. As the British philosopher Bertrand Russell famously noted, "The trouble with the world is that the stupid are cocksure and the intelligent are full of doubt."

**Adaptability.** At an organizational level, adaptability means being ready to innovate and respond to opportunities and threats as they appear. At an individual level, it means being open to new ideas, changing an opinion even when it hurts or threatens one's ego, and being able to effectively communicate that revised opinion to relevant stakeholders, including peers, teams, and customers. In an AI age, changing one's mind, which can often be regarded as a sign of weakness or lack of conviction, should be perceived as a strength when it improves decision making. Adaptable leaders are not afraid to commit to a new course of action when the situation warrants, and their adaptability allows them to confront challenges with a focus on learning rather than being right.

Carlos Torres Vila, the CEO of Spanish bank BBVA, oversaw the transformation of the company from a traditional brick-and-mortar bank into one of the most successful financial services organizations of the digital era. He responded to industry disruption by fostering a transformative culture that encourages agility, flexibility, collaborative work, entrepreneurial spirit, and innovation.

**Vision.** Vision has always played an important role in effective leadership. But in an AI age characterized by rapid technology and business model disruption, a clear vision is even more pivotal, because there is less clarity among followers, subordinates, and employees about where one should go, what one should do, and why. Leaders with a clear vision have compelling, meaningful answers to these questions and are better at communicating them in an effective way. Furthermore, vision allows a leader to implement necessary organizational transformations without caving to short-term interests.

Many leaders of today's digital giants, such as Amazon, Tesla, Facebook, Tencent, Alibaba, and Google, have clearly articulated visions for their organizations, even in the face of huge short-term uncertainty.

**Engagement.** Lastly, to be successful in the AI age, a leader must remain constantly engaged with their surrounding environment so that they can be attuned to, and adapt to, the signals rather than the noise—which will either threaten (disruptors) or support (potential partners) their vision. Agile leaders need to stay engaged, but they also need to find ways to keep their teams engaged, particularly when the going gets rough and the path becomes challenging.

Engagement in an AI age can increasingly be accomplished using digital means. For example, German e-commerce giant Zalando has implemented a variety of digital tools for top management to capture and respond to topics of interest from all employees. These include zTalk, a live chat application; zLive, a company-wide social intranet; and zBeat, a tool that regularly surveys employees about their current work experiences.

Does all this suggest that leadership is radically different in the AI age? No, but there are two key distinctions. First, leaders' hard skills will continue to be eclipsed by smart machines, while their soft skills will become ever more important. Second, while timeless leadership traits like integrity and emotional intelligence will no doubt remain important, leaders in the AI age need to be humble about others' contributions, adaptable to the challenges that get thrown into their paths, steadfast in their vision of the ultimate destination on this path, and constantly engaged with the changing world around them.

## Print Citations

**CMS:** Chamorro-Premuzic, Tomas, Michael Wade, and Jennifer Jordan. "As AI Makes More Decisions, the Nature of Leadership Will Change." In *The Reference Shelf: Artificial Intelligence*, edited by Micah Issitt, 164-166. Ipswich, MA: H.W. Wilson, 2018.

**MLA:** Chamorro-Premuzic, Tomas, Michael Wade, and Jennifer Jordan. "As AI Makes More Decisions, the Nature of Leadership Will Change." *The Reference Shelf: Artificial Intelligence*. Ed. Micah Issitt. Ipswich: H.W. Wilson, 2018. 164-166. Print.

**APA:** Chamorro-Premuzic, T., Wade, M., & J. Jordan. (2018). As AI makes more decisions, the nature of leadership will change. In Micah Issitt (Ed.), *The reference shelf: Artificial intelligence* (pp. 164-166). Ipswich, MA: H.W. Wilson. (Original work published 2018)

# How AI Will Redefine Human Intelligence

By Adrienne Lafrance

*The Atlantic,* **April 11, 2017**

The machines are getting smarter. They can now recognize us, carry on conversations, and perceive complex details about the world around them. This is just the beginning.

As computers become more human-like, many worry that robots and algorithms will displace people. And they are right to. But just as crucial is the question of how machine progress will change our perceptions of *human* abilities.

Once a job can be done by a computer, it changes the way people think about the nature of that job. Let me give you an example. Travel with me, if you will, back to the year 1985. Here we are in Baltimore, Maryland. It's Christmastime.

Hutzler's Department Store is all twinkle lights and glass ornaments. Somewhere among the festive plaid tablecloths and polished silver are Tinsel and Beau—two full-blown animatronic talking reindeer. Tinsel's frosted in glitter and Beau's in a top hat. I'm one of the children lined up to greet them.

Baltimoreans may remember Hutzler's as a beautiful old-fashioned department store, once known for its extravagant window displays and ornate façade. (The flagship store closed in 1989.) It was celebrated for its traditions, but also for its innovations. Hutzler's installed the city's first escalator in the 1930s, a modern convenience that it touted in advertisements.

So it made sense that Hutzler's would also have such impressive animatronic reindeer. I thought of them recently when I was watching a video demonstration of Handle, the new Boston Dynamics robot that can wheel around with alarming swiftness and jump four feet into the air. Boston Dynamics also made a robot reindeer once—and, well, this is how you fall into an internet rabbit hole. Next thing I know, I'm searching the web for evidence of a faint childhood memory: a pair of beloved robotic reindeer from Baltimore in the 1980s.

It didn't take long.

"Tinsel and Beau are back!" said one 1983 advertisement in *The Baltimore Sun.* "Our talking deer make such a charming couple, and what wonderful conversationalists they are!"

What I learned next, however, was that Tinsel and Beau weren't robotic at all. A classified ad that Hutzler's placed in *The Baltimore Sun* in 1986 offered a "fun opportunity for drama or theater students to be the voices of our famous talking reindeer."

Tinsel and Beau were people!

Which, I mean, *of course they were people.* It seems silly now that I ever thought otherwise. Department stores in the 1980s didn't just go around buying high-tech robotic reindeer that could carry on lengthy conversations with little kids. We're talking about an era when Teddy Ruxpin—a furry tape cassette housed in the body of a mechanical bear—was considered a technological marvel. If you wanted to have a chat with a mobile device, your best bet was to get a Speak 'n' Spell to burp out the alphabet in your direction.

And yet my misplaced memory of the reindeer is understandable, maybe, given how dramatically the world has changed in the past 35 years. It's the same reason that people today are surprised to learn that R2-D2, the lovable whistling droid from the Star Wars franchise, was operated by a human actor. (Today, another actor operates the unit for some shots; while a radio-controlled device is used for others, according to *The Guardian.*)

In a world of digital assistants and computer-generated imagery, the expectation is that computers do all kinds of work for humans. The result of which, some have argued, is a dulling of the senses. "The miraculous has become the norm," Jonathan Romney wrote in an essay about computer-generated imagery for *Aeon.* "Such a surfeit of wonders may be de-sensitizing, but it's also eroding our ability to dream at the movies."

Our ability to dream, elsewhere in the arts, may be intact, but computers are encroaching on all sorts of creative territory. There are computers that can forge famous paintings with astounding accuracy—and there are algorithms designed to identify such fakes. Artificial intelligences can already write novels, and there's at least one literary contest—the Hoshi Shinichi Literary Award—that's open to non-human competitors. Computers can flirt. They can write jokes. (Not great ones, but hey.)

Computers are now so pervasive that we should expect them to be everywhere. The past is quickly becoming a place where the presence of humans, talking reindeer and otherwise, is now surprising. That's likely to continue, and to expand into our most creative spaces.

> **Our ability to dream . . . may be intact, but computers are encroaching on all sorts of creative territory.**

"The unresolved questions about machine art are, first, what its potential is and, second, whether—irrespective of the quality of the work produced—it can truly be described as 'creative' or 'imaginative,'" Martin Gayford wrote in an essay for *MIT Technology Review* last year. "These are problems, profound and fascinating, that take us deep into the mysteries of human art-making."

As machines advance and as programs learn to do things that were once only accomplished by people, what will it mean to be human?

Over time, artificial intelligence will likely prove that carving out any realm of behavior as unique to humans—like language, a classic example—is ultimately wrong. If Tinsel and Beau were still around today, they might be powered by a digital assistant, after all. In fact, it'd be a little weird if they weren't, wouldn't it? Consider the fact that Disney is exploring the use of interactive humanoid robots at its theme parks, according to a patent filing last week.

Technological history proves that what seems novel today can quickly become the norm, until one day you look back surprised at the memory of a job done by a human rather than a machine. By teaching machines what we know, we are training them to be like us. This is good for humanity in so many ways. But we may still occasionally long for the days before machines could imagine the future alongside us.

## Print Citations

**CMS:** Lafrance, Adrienne. "How AI Will Redefine Human Intelligence." In *The Reference Shelf: Artificial Intelligence*, edited by Micah Issitt, 167-169. Ipswich, MA: H.W. Wilson, 2018.

**MLA:** Lafrance, Adrienne. "How AI Will Redefine Human Intelligence." *The Reference Shelf: Artificial Intelligence*. Ed. Micah Issitt. Ipswich: H.W. Wilson, 2018. 167-169. Print.

**APA:** Lafrance, A. (2018). How AI will redefine human intelligence. In Micah Issitt (Ed.), *The reference shelf: Artificial intelligence* (pp. 167-169). Ipswich, MA: H.W. Wilson. (Original work published 2017)

# Here Are Some of the Ways Experts Think AI might Screw with Us in the Next Five Years

By James Vincent
*The Verge*, **February 20, 2018**

When we talk about the dangers posed by artificial intelligence, the emphasis is usually on the *un*intended side effects. We worry that we might accidentally create a super-intelligent AI and forget to program it with a conscience; or that we'll deploy criminal sentencing algorithms that have soaked up the racist biases of their training data.

But this is just half the story.

What about the people who actively *want* to use AI for immoral, criminal, or malicious purposes? Aren't they more likely to cause trouble—and sooner? The answer is yes, according to more than two dozen experts from institutes including the Future of Humanity Institute, the Centre for the Study of Existential Risk, and the Elon Musk-backed non-profit OpenAI. Very much yes.

## "I Do See This Paper as a Call to Action."

In a report published today titled "The Malicious Use of Artificial Intelligence: Forecasting, Prevention, and Mitigation," these academics and researchers lay out some of the ways AI might be used to sting us in the next five years, and what we can do to stop it. Because while AI can enable some pretty nasty new attacks, the paper's co-author, Miles Brundage of the Future of Humanity Institute, tells *The Verge*, we certainly shouldn't panic or abandon hope.

"I like to take the optimistic framing, which is that we could do more," says Brundage. "The point here is not to paint a doom-and-gloom picture—there are many defenses that can be developed and there's much for us to learn. I don't think it's hopeless at all, but I do see this paper as a call to action."

The report is expansive, but focuses on a few key ways AI is going to exacerbate threats for both digital and physical security systems, as well as create completely new dangers. It also makes five recommendations on how to combat these problems—including getting AI engineers to be more upfront about the possible malicious uses of their research; and starting new dialogues between policymakers and academics so that governments and law enforcement aren't caught unawares.

Let's start with potential threats, though: one of the most important of these is that AI will dramatically lower the cost of certain attacks by allowing bad actors to automate tasks that previously required human labor.

Take, for example, spear phishing, in which individuals are sent messages specially designed to trick them into giving up their security credentials. (Think: a fake email from your bank or from what appears to be an old acquaintance.) AI could automate much of the work here, mapping out an individuals' social and professional network, and then generating the messages. There's a lot of effort going into creating realistic and engaging chatbots right now, and that same work could be used to create a chatbot that poses as your best friend who suddenly, for some reason, *really* wants to know your email password.

## AI Enables Human Actors to Replicate Actors Effortlessly

This sort of attack sounds complex, but the point is that once you've built the software to do it all, you can use it again and again at no extra cost. Phishing emails are already harmful enough—they were responsible for both the ICloud leak of celebrity's pictures in 2014, as well as the hack of private emails from Hillary Clinton's campaign chairman John Podesta. The latter not only had an influence on the 2016 US presidential election, it also fed a range of conspiracy theories like Pizzagate, which nearly got people killed. Think about what an automated AI spear-phisher could do to tech-illiterate government officials.

The second big point raised in the report is that AI will add new dimensions to existing threats. With the same spear phishing example, AI could be used to not only generate emails and text messages, but also fake audio and video. We've already seen how AI can be used to mimic a target's voice after studying just a few minutes of recorded speech, and how it can turn footage of people speaking into puppets. The report is focused on threats coming up in the next five years, and these are fast becoming issues.

And, of course, there is a whole range of other unsavory practices that AI could exacerbate. Political manipulation and propaganda for a start (again, areas where fake video and audio could be a huge problem), but also surveillance, especially when used to target minorities. The prime example of this has been in China, where facial recognition and people-tracking cameras have turned one border region, home to the largely Muslim Uighur minority, into a "total surveillance states."

> **What about people who actively want to use AI for immoral, criminal, or malicious purposes?**

These are just examples of AI's capacity to scale becoming a threat. It replaces the humans who watch the feeds, turning CCTV camera from passive into active observers, allowing them to categorize human behavior automatically. "Scalability in particular is something that hasn't got enough attention," says Brundage. "It's not just the fact that AI can perform at human levels at certain tasks, but that you can scale it up to a huge number of copies."

Finally, the report highlights the entirely novel dangers that AI creates. The authors outline a number of possible scenarios, including one where terrorists implant a bomb in a cleaning robot and smuggle it into a government ministry. The robot uses its built-in machine vision to track down a particular politician, and when it's near, the bomb detonates. This takes advantage of new products AI will enable (the cleaning robots) but also its autonomous functions (the machine vision-based tracking).

## The First AI-Powered Already Emerging

Outlining scenarios like this may seem a bit fantastical, but we've really already begun to see the first novel attacks enabled by AI. Face-swapping technology has been used to create so-called "deepfakes"—pasting the faces of celebrities onto pornographic clips without their consent. And although there have been no high-profile cases of this to date, we know those involved in creating this content want to test it out on people they know; creating perfect fodder for harassment and blackmail.

These examples only take in a portion of the report, but the whole document leaves you wondering: what's to be done? The solutions are easy to outline, but will be challenging to follow through on. The report makes five key recommendations:

- AI researchers should acknowledge how their work can be used maliciously

- Policymakers need to learn from technical experts about these threats

- The AI world needs to learn from cybersecurity experts how to best protect its systems

- Ethical frameworks for AI need to be developed and followed

- And more people need to be involved in these discussions. Not just AI scientists and policymakers, but also ethicists, businesses, and the general public

In other words: a little more conversation *and* a little more action please.

It's a big ask considering what a complex and nuanced subject artificial intelligence is, but there have been promising signs. For example, with the rise of deepfakes, web platforms reacted quickly, banning the content and stopping its immediate spread. And lawmakers in the US have already started talking about the problem—showing that these debates will reach government if they're urgent enough.

"There's certainly interest," says Brundage of government involvement in discussing these topics. "But there's still a sense that more discussion needs to happen in order to find out what are the most critical threats, and what are the most practical solutions." And in most cases, he says, it's difficult to even judge what will be a threat when. "It's unclear how gradual all this will be—whether there'll be a big catastrophic event, or whether it'll be a slow rolling thing that gives us plenty of opportunities to adapt."

"But that's exactly why we're raising these issues now."

## Print Citations

**CMS:** Vincent, James. "Here Are Some of the Ways Experts Think AI might Screw with Us in the Next Five Years." In *The Reference Shelf: Artificial Intelligence*, edited by Micah Issitt, 170-173. Ipswich, MA: H.W. Wilson, 2018.

**MLA:** Vincent, James. "Here Are Some of the Ways Experts Think AI might Screw with Us in the Next Five Years." *The Reference Shelf: Artificial Intelligence*. Ed. Micah Issitt. Ipswich: H.W. Wilson, 2018. 170-173. Print.

**APA:** Vincent, J. (2018). Here are some of the ways experts think AI might screw with us in the next five years. In Micah Issitt (Ed.), *The reference shelf: Artificial intelligence* (pp. 170-173). Ipswich, MA: H.W. Wilson. (Original work published 2018)

# We Need to Talk about the Power of AI to Manipulate Humans

By Liesl Yearsley

*MIT Technology Review*, June 5, 2017

We have all read about artificial intelligence becoming smarter than us, a future in which we become like pets and can only hope AI will be benevolent. My experience watching tens of millions of interactions between humans and artificial conversational agents, or bots, has convinced me there are far more immediate risks—as well as tremendous opportunities.

From 2007 to 2014 I was CEO of Cognea, which offered a platform to rapidly build complex virtual agents, using a combination of structured and deep learning. It was used by tens of thousands of developers, including half a dozen Fortune 100 companies, and acquired by IBM Watson in 2014.

As I studied how people interacted with the tens of thousands of agents built on our platform, it became clear that humans are far more willing than most people realize to form a relationship with AI software.

I always assumed we would want to keep some distance between ourselves and AI, but I found the opposite to be true. People are willing to form relationships with artificial agents, provided they are a sophisticated build, capable of complex personalization. We humans seem to want to maintain the illusion that the AI truly cares about us.

This puzzled me, until I realized that in daily life we connect with many people in a shallow way, wading through a kind of emotional sludge. Will casual friends return your messages if you neglect them for a while? Will your personal trainer turn up if you forget to pay them? No, but an artificial agent is always there for you. In some ways, it is a more authentic relationship.

This phenomenon occurred regardless of whether the agent was designed to act as a personal banker, a companion, or a fitness coach. Users spoke to the automated assistants longer than they did to human support agents performing the same function. People would volunteer deep secrets to artificial agents, like their dreams for the future, details of their love lives, even passwords.

These surprisingly deep connections mean even today's relatively simple programs can exert a significant influence on people—for good or ill. Every behavioral change we at Cognea wanted, we got. If we wanted a user to buy more product, we could double sales. If we wanted more engagement, we got people going from a few seconds of interaction to an hour or more a day.

This troubled me mightily, so we began to build rules into our systems, to make sure user behavior moved in a positive direction. We also started pro bono "karmic counterbalance" projects; for example, building agents to be health or relationship coaches.

> **We need to consciously build systems that work for the benefit of humans and society. They cannot have addiction, clicks, and consumption as their primary goal.**

Unfortunately, the commercial forces driving technology development are not always benevolent. The giant companies at the forefront of AI—across social media, search, and e-commerce—drive the value of their shares by increasing traffic, consumption, and addiction to their technology. They do not have bad intentions, but the nature of capital markets may push us toward AI hell-bent on influencing our behavior toward these goals.

If you can get a user to think, "I want pizza delivered," rather than asking the AI to buy vegetables to cook a cheaper, healthier meal, you will win. If you can get users addicted to spending 30 hours a week with a "perfect" AI companion that doesn't resist abuse, rather than a real, complicated human, you will win. I saw over and over that an agent programmed to be neutral or subservient would cause people to escalate their negative behavior, and become more likely to behave the same toward humans.

We have seen how technology like social media can be powerful in changing human beliefs and behavior. By focusing on building a bigger advertising business—entangling politics, trivia, and half-truths—you can bring about massive changes in society.

Systems specifically designed to form relationships with a human will have much more power. AI will influence how we think, and how we treat others.

This requires a new level of corporate responsibility. We need to deliberately and consciously build AI that will improve the human condition—not just pursue the immediate financial gain of gazillions of addicted users.

Working on open artificial-intelligence technology and brain-computer interfaces, or forming ethics committees, are just part of the solution. We need to consciously build systems that work for the benefit of humans and society. They cannot have addiction, clicks, and consumption as their primary goal. AI is growing up, and will be shaping the nature of humanity. AI needs a mother.

## Print Citations

**CMS:** Yearsley, Liesl. "We Need to Talk about the Power of AI to Manipulate Humans." In *The Reference Shelf: Artificial Intelligence*, edited by Micah Issitt, 174-176. Ipswich, MA: H.W. Wilson, 2018.

**MLA:** Yearsley, Liesl. "We Need to Talk about the Power of AI to Manipulate Humans." *The Reference Shelf: Artificial Intelligence*. Ed. Micah Issitt. Ipswich: H.W. Wilson, 2018. 174-176. Print.

**APA:** Yearsley, L. (2018). We need to talk about the power of AI to manipulate humans. In Micah Issitt (Ed.), *The reference shelf: Artificial intelligence* (pp. 174-176). Ipswich, MA: H.W. Wilson. (Original work published 2017)

# Bibliography

"Animal Consciousness." *Plato.Stanford*. Stanford Encyclopedia of Philosophy. Oct 24, 2016. Web. Retrieved from https://plato.stanford.edu/entries/consciousness-animal/.

Anyoha, Rockwell. "The History of Artificial Intelligence." *SITN*. Science in the News. Harvard University. Aug 28, 2017. Web. Retrieved from http://sitn.hms.harvard.edu/flash/2017/history-artificial-intelligence/.

"Artificial Intelligence—Where and How to Invest." *Capgemini*. Sep 6, 2017. Web. Retrieved from https://www.capgemini.com/resources/artificial-intelligence-where-and-how-to-invest/.

Autor, David H. "Why Are There Still So Many Jobs? The History and Future of Workplace Automation." *MIT*. Journal of Economic Perspectives. 2015. Pdf. Retrieved from https://economics.mit.edu/files/11563.

Baldwin, Roberto. "The Robots of War: AI and the Future of Combat." *Endgadget*. Oath Tech Network. Retrieved from https://www.engadget.com/2016/08/18/robots-of-war-ai-and-the-future-of-combat/.

Bramer, Max. *Artificial Intelligence: An International Perspective*. New York: Springer, 1998.

Brundage, Miles, et al. "The Malicious Use of Artificial Intelligence: Forecasting, Prevention, and Mitigation." *Future of Humanity Institute*. University of Oxford. Feb. 2018. Web. Retrieved from https://static.rasset.ie/documents/news/2018/02/ai-report.pdf.

Dickey, Megan Rose. "Loris.ai, a Crisis Text Line Spin-Out, Raises $2 Million to Help Companies Have Hard Conversations." *Techcrunch*. Oath Tech Network. Feb 6, 2018. Web. Retrieved from https://techcrunch.com.

"Drone Warfare." *Thebureauinvestigates*. Bureau of Investigative Journalism. Web. 2018. Retrieved from https://www.thebureauinvestigates.com/projects/drone-war.

Drum, Kevin. "You Will Lose Your Job to a Robot—and Sooner Than You Think." *Mother Jones*. Mother Jones. Dec 2017. Web. Retrieved from https://www.motherjones.com/politics/2017/10/you-will-lose-your-job-to-a-robot-and-sooner-than-you-think/.

Dugan, Andrew, and Bailey Nelson. "3 Trends That Will Disrupt Your Workplace Forever." *Gallup*. Gallup Inc. Jun 8, 2017. Web. Retrieved from http://news.gallup.com/businessjournal/211799/trends-disrupt-workplace-forever.aspx.

Eidelson, Josh. "U.S. Income Inequality Hits a Disturbing New Threshold." *Bloomberg*. Bloomberg L.P. Mar 1, 2018. Web. Retrieved from https://www.bloomberg.com/news/articles/2018-05-21/supreme-court-says-employers-can-bar-worker-class-action-suits-jhgbqpz0.

Etzioni, Oren, Michele Banko, and Michael J. Cafarella. "Machine Reading." *AAAI*. American Association for Artificial Intelligence. 2006. Pdf. Retrieved from http://www.aaai.org/Papers/Symposia/Spring/2007/SS-07-06/SS07-06-001.pdf.

Ezzyat, Youssef, et al. "Closed-Loop Stimulation of Temporal Cortex Rescues Functional Networks and Improves Memory." *Natura Communications*. Vol. 9, No. 365 (Feb 6, 2018). Retrieved from https://www.nature.com/articles/s41467-017-02753-0#Sec6.

Faggella, Daniel. "AI for Social Influence and Behavior Manipulation with Dr. Charles Isbell." *Tech Emergence*. Tech Emergence. Dec 17, 2017. Web. Retrieved from https://www.techemergence.com/ai-social-influence-behavior-manipulation-dr-charles-isbell/.

Fletcher, Seth. "What Chappie Says, and Doesn't Say, About Artificial Intelligence." *Scientific American*. Nature America, Inc. Mar 6, 2015. Web. Retrieved from https://blogs.scientificamerican.com/observations/what-chappie-says-and-doesn-t-say-about-artificial-intelligence/.

"Gartner Says by 2020, Artificial Intelligence Will Create More Jobs Than It Eliminates." *Gartner*. Dec 13, 2017. Web. Retrieved from https://www.gartner.com/newsroom/id/3837763.

Gershgorn, Dave. "The US Government Seriously Wants to Weaponize Artificial Intelligence." *Quartz*. Quartz Media. Aug 26, 2016. Web. Retrieved from https://qz.com/767648/weaponized-artificial-intelligence-us-military/.

Goodwin, Bill. "Employers Face Hiring Crisis as AI Replaces Mid-Skilled Jobs." *Computer Weekly*. Tech Target. Mar 16, 2018. Web. Retrieved from https://www.computerweekly.com/news/252436997/Employers-face-hiring-crisis-as-AI-replaces-mid-skilled-jobs.

Graham-Rowe, Duncan. "Introduction: Robots." *New Scientist*. New Scientist Ltd. Sep 4, 2006. Web. Retrieved from https://www.newscientist.com/article/dn9973-introduction-robots/.

"Inductive Logic." *Plato.Stanford*. Stanford Encyclopedia of Philosophy. Mar 19, 2018. Retrieved from https://plato.stanford.edu/entries/logic-inductive/.

Kaplan, Fred. "The First Drone Strike." *Slate*. Slate Group. Sep 14, 2016. Web. Retrieved from http://www.slate.com/articles/news_and_politics/the_next_20/2016/09/a_history_of_the_armed_drone.html.

Kleinman, Zoe. "CES 2018: A Clunky Chat with Sophia the Robot." *BBC News*. BBC. Jan 9, 2018. Web. Retrieved from http://www.bbc.com/news/technology-42616687.

Lewis, Tanya. "A Brief History of Artificial Intelligence." *Life Science*. Live Science. Dec 4, 2014. Retrieved from https://www.livescience.com/49007-history-of-artificial-intelligence.html.

Lima, Marcos. "No, Artificial Intelligence Won't Steal Your Children's Jobs—It Will Make Them More Creative and Productive." *The Conversation*. The Conversation US, Inc. Feb 26, 2018. Web. Retrieved from http://theconversation.com/no-artificial-intelligence-wont-steal-your-childrens-jobs-it-will-make-them-more-creative-and-productive-91672.

Lomas, Natasha. "AI Will Create New Jobs But Skills Must Shift, Say Tech Giants." *Tech Crunch*. Oath Tech Network. Feb 28, 2018. Web. Retrieved from https://techcrunch.com/2018/02/28/ai-will-create-new-jobs-but-skills-must-shift-say-tech-giants/.

Long, Tony. "Jan. 25, 1921: Robots First Czech In." *Wired*. Condé Nast. Retrieved from https://www.wired.com/2011/01/0125robot-cometh-capek-rur-debut/.

MacDonald, Fiona. "A Robot Has Just Passed a Classic Self-Awareness Test for the First Time." *Science Alert*. Jul 17, 2015. Web. Retrieved from https://www.sciencealert.com/a-robot-has-just-passed-a-classic-self-awareness-test-for-the-first-time.

Marino, L. "Sentience," in *Encyclopedia of Animal Behavior*. Academic Press: 2010, 132–38.

Markoff, John. "Computer Wins on 'Jeopardy!': Trivial, It's Not." *The New York Times*. The New York Times Co. Feb 16, 2011. Web. Retrieved from https://www.nytimes.com/2011/02/17/science/17jeopardy-watson.html.

McGrady, Vanessa. "New Study: Artificial Intelligence Is Coming for Your Job, Millennials." *Forbes*. Forbes, Inc. Jun 9, 2017. Retrieved from https://www.forbes.com/sites/vanessamcgrady/2017/06/09/millennial-jobs/#339f902530c8.

Moon, Francis C. *The Machines of Leonardo Da Vinci and Franz Reuleaux: Kinematics of Machines*. New York: Springer Press, 2007.

Mortensen, Dennis R. "Automation May Take Our Jobs—But It'll Restore Our Humanity." *Quartz Media*. Quartz Media, LLC. Aug 16, 2017. Web. Retrieved from https://qz.com/1054034/automation-may-take-our-jobs-but-itll-restore-our-humanity/.

Orr, Christopher. "Why *Her* Is the Best Film of the Year." *The Atlantic*. Atlantic Monthly Group. Dec 20, 2013. Retrieved from https://www.theatlantic.com/entertainment/archive/2013/12/why-em-her-em-is-the-best-film-of-the-year/282544/.

Park, Edwards. "What a Difference the Difference Engine Made: From Charles Babbage's Calculator Emerged Today's Computer." *Smithsonian*. Smithsonian Institution. Feb 1996. Web. Retrieved from https://www.smithsonianmag.com/history/what-a-difference-the-difference-engine-made-from-charles-babbages-calculator-emerged-todays-computer-109389254/.

"Pioneer Short Range (SR) UAV." *FAS*. Federation of American Scientists. Mar 5, 2009. Web. Retrieved from https://fas.org/irp/program/collect/pioneer.htm.

Powell, Andrea. "AI Is Fueling Smarter Prosthetics Than Ever Before." *Wired*. Condé Nast. Dec 22, 2017. Web. Retrieved from https://www.wired.com/story/ai-is-fueling-smarter-prosthetics-than-ever-before/.

Regal, Brian. *Human Evolution: A Guide to the Debates*. Santa Barbara, CA: ABC-CLIO, 2004.

Regaldo, Anthony. "With Neuralink, Elon Musk Promises Human-to-Human Telepathy. Don't Believe It." *Technology Review*. MIT Technology Review. Apr 22, 2017. Web. Retrieved from https://www.technologyreview.com/s/604254/with-neuralink-elon-musk-promises-human-to-human-telepathy-dont-believe-it/.

Richardson, John H. "Inside the Race to Hack the Human Brain." *Wired*. Condé Nast. Nov 16, 2017. Web. Retrieved from https://www.wired.com/story/inside-the-race-to-build-a-brain-machine-interface/.

Rieland, Randy. "Artificial Intelligence Is Now Used to Predict Crime: But Is It Biased?" *Smithsonian*. Smithsonian Institution. Mar 5, 2018. Web. Retrieved from https://www.smithsonianmag.com/innovation/artificial-intelligence-is-now-used-predict-crime-is-it-biased-180968337/.

Rothman, Wilson. "Unmanned Warbots of WWI and WWII." *Gizmodo*. Gawker Media. Mar 24, 2009. Web. Retrieved from https://gizmodo.com/5181576/unmanned-warbots-of-wwi-and-wwii.

Sharre, Paul. "Why We Must Not Build Automated Weapons of War." *Time*. Time, Inc. Sep 25, 2017. Web. Retrieved from http://time.com/4948633/robots-artificial-intelligence-war/.

Simonite, Tom. "Machine Learning Opens Up New Ways to Help People with Disabilities." *Technology Review*. MIT Technology Review. Mar 23, 2017. Web. Retrieved from https://www.technologyreview.com/s/603899/machine-learning-opens-up-new-ways-to-help-disabled-people/.

Singer, Isaac Bashevis. "The Golem Is a Myth for Our Time." *The New York Times*. The New York Times, Co. 1984. Web. Retrieved from https://www.nytimes.com/1984/08/12/theater/the-golem-is-a-myth-for-our-time.html.

Singer, P.W. "Drones Don't Die—A History of Military Robotics." *History Net*. World History Group. May 5, 2011. Web. Retrieved from http://www.historynet.com/drones-dont-die-a-history-of-military-robotics.htm.

Smith, Kevin. "Artificial Intelligence Will Wipe Out Half the Banking Jobs in a Decade, Experts Say." *Chicago Tribune*. Apr 23, 2018. Web. Retrieved from http://www.chicagotribune.com/business/ct-biz-artificial-intelligence-bank-jobs-20180423-story.html.

"The Turing Test." *University of Toronto*. Psychology Department. 2017. Web. Retrieved from http://www.psych.utoronto.ca/users/reingold/courses/ai/turing.html.

Turing, Alan M. "Computing Machinery and Intelligence." *Mind*. 49 (1950): 433–60. Web. Retrieved from https://www.csee.umbc.edu/courses/471/papers/turing.pdf.

Walker, Jon. "Unmanned Aerial Vehicles (UAVs)—Comparing the USA, Israel, and China." *Tech Emergence*. Tech Emergence. Web. Retrieved from https://www.techemergence.com/unmanned-aerial-vehicles-uavs/.

Williams, Imogen Russell. "Why Golems Are Precious." *The Guardian*. The Guardian News and Media. Aug 27 2010. Web. Retrieved from https://www.theguardian.com/books/booksblog/2010/aug/27/golems-precious.

Zarka, Emily. "The Evolution of the Modern-Day Zombie." *Slate*. Slate Group. Jan 18, 2018. Web. Retrieved from https://slate.com/technology/2018/01/what-our-zombie-movies-tell-us-about-our-attitudes-toward-science.html.

# Websites

### Association for the Advancement of Artificial Intelligence
*www.aaai.org*

The Association for the Advancement of Artificial Intelligence (AAAI) is a nonprofit organization founded in 1979 that supports and funds research into artificial intelligence, machine learning, and the social, cultural impact of artificial intelligence technology. The AAAI hosts two annual symposia for professionals in the field and publishes a magazine covering recent technological and scientific advancements.

### Campaign to Stop Killer Robots
*www.stopkillerrobots.org*

The Campaign to Stop Killer Robots is a nongovernmental organization started to activists and social scientists who want to ban the use of lethal autonomous weapons. The organization is closely related to Human Rights Watch (HRW), a nonprofit that conducts international studies on human rights violations. The Captain to Stop Killer Robots published an open letter from 1,000 experts in the field calling attention to the potential threats of lethal autonomous weapons and calling to international agreements to place limits on weaponized AI development.

### Defense Advanced Research Projects Agency (DARPA)
*www.darpa.mil*

The Defense Advanced Research Projects Agency is a division of the US Department of Defense (DOD) that supports and funds research on technology as it relates to US national security. Established in 1958, DARPA has been one of the primary military research organizations funding artificial intelligence research over the last half-century and currently funds a variety of cutting edge projects in AI research.

### Institute of Electrical and Electronics Engineers (IEEE)
*www.ieee.com*

The Institute of Electrical and Electronics Engineers (IEEE) is a professional organization focused on the fields of electrical, computer, and telecommunications engineering. The IEEE has established a division, known as the Computational Intelligence Society focused specifically on organizing researchers working in machine learning and other subfields of artificial intelligence research.

### International Joint Conferences on Artificial Intelligence (IJCAI)

*www.ijcai.org*

The IJCAI is a California-based nonprofit established in 1969 to support and distribute international research on artificial intelligence. The IJCAI is the publisher of the Artificial Intelligence Journal, which is one of the most respected and oldest peer-reviewed journals covering artificial intelligence.

### Massachusetts Institute of Technology Computer Science and Artificial Intelligence Lab (CSAIL)

*www.csail.mit.edu*

MIT's Computer Science and Artificial Intelligence Lab is one of the oldest academic organizations supporting research in artificial intelligence; it was first established as "Project MAC" in 1963. Reformulated in 2003 as a combination of computer science and artificial intelligence, the organization hosts cutting edge training programs in the field and funds and supports international research programs on machine learning, computational intelligence, and the social, cultural issues surrounding artificial intelligence.

### Open AI

*www.openai.com*

Open AI is a non-profit research company promoting and funding research into artificial intelligence. The organization's stated purpose is to fund AI research in such a way as to ensure positive impact for humanity and to invite public and amateur collaboration in AI research and implementation. The organization was in part funded and supported by billionaires Elon Musk and Sam Altman and was started in 2015.

### Society for the Study of Artificial Intelligence and Simulation of Behavior (AISB)

*www.aisb.org.uk*

The AISB is the largest artificial intelligence society in the UK and was established in 1964, making it one of the oldest AI organizations in the world. The AISB has member groups from around the world and hosts an annual convention covering developments in the field. The AISB also published a quarterly newsletter containing updates on many different AI research programs around the world.

# Index